Demagogues, Power, and Friendship
in Classical Athens

Also available from Bloomsbury

Ancient Greece and American Conservatism by John Bloxham
Thucydides and the Idea of History by Neville Morley
Thucydides and the Shaping of History by Emily Greenwood

Demagogues, Power, and Friendship in Classical Athens

Leaders as Friends in Aristophanes, Euripides, and Xenophon

Robert Holschuh Simmons

BLOOMSBURY ACADEMIC

LONDON • NEW YORK • OXFORD • NEW DELHI • SYDNEY

BLOOMSBURY ACADEMIC
Bloomsbury Publishing Plc
50 Bedford Square, London, WC1B 3DP, UK
1385 Broadway, New York, NY 10018, USA
29 Earlsfort Terrace, Dublin 2, Ireland

BLOOMSBURY, BLOOMSBURY ACADEMIC and the Diana logo are trademarks
of Bloomsbury Publishing Plc

First published in Great Britain 2023

Cover design: Terry Woodley
Cover image © Fragment of the Parthenon Frieze, 445-435 BC. Musée du Louvre,
Paris. Album/Alamy Stock Photo

A catalogue record for this book is available from the British Library.

Library of Congress Cataloging-in-Publication Data
Names: Simmons, Robert Holschuh, author. Title: Demagogues, power, and friendship in
classical Athens : leaders as friends in Aristophanes, Euripides, and Xenophon / Robert
Holschuh Simmons. Other titles: Leaders as friends in Aristophanes, Euripides, and
Xenophon Description: London ; New York : Bloomsbury Academic, 2023. | Includes
bibliographical references and index. Identifiers: LCCN 2022036274 | ISBN 9781350214484
(hardback) | ISBN 9781350214491 (paperback) | ISBN 9781350214507 (epdf) | ISBN
9781350214514 (ebook) Subjects: LCSH: Leadership--Greece—Athens. | Friendship–
Greece—Athens. | Greek literature—History and criticism. | Leadership in literature. |
Friendship in literature. | Athens (Greece)—Politics and government. | Athens (Greece)—
History. Classification: LCC DF277 .S37 2023 | DDC 320.938/5–dc23/eng/20220803
LC record available at https://lccn.loc.gov/2022036274.

ISBN: HB: 978-1-3502-1448-4
         ePDF: 978-1-3502-1450-7
         eBook: 978-1- 3502-1451-4

Typeset by RefineCatch Limited, Bungay, Suffolk

To find out more about our authors and books visit www.bloomsbury.com
and sign up for our newsletters.

For Michelle, Ben, David, Alex, and Marc, who make my life so rich.

Contents

Acknowledgments

This has been a labor of two decades (with many, many separate matters intervening), since demagogues first came onto my radar in the spring of 2002 in a graduate seminar at the University of Iowa taught by John García. I had an idea about reading Euripides' *Bacchae* in terms of class dynamics, John directed me to Bob Connor's *New Politicians of Fifth-Century Athens*, and from there I wrote a term paper that I thought was implausible. John, however, thought that it could be a dissertation, for which I am enormously grateful to him, and I ended up writing it on reflections of demagogic politics in Athenian tragedy, directed by Rob Ketterer. I am grateful to Rob for his guidance and support on that project and on the offshoot of it that has become this book. I am also grateful to other faculty members at Iowa whose attention and care in classes I took, whose guidance in classes I taught, whose direction of financial support toward attendance at conferences at which I presented, whose feedback on those presentations, and whose ongoing reinforcement through the years has helped me to develop as a well-rounded professional: John Finamore, Peter Green, Carin Green, Craig Gibson, Marcia Lindgren, Glenn Storey, and Rosemary Moore.

I am grateful to my undergraduate professors at St. John's University, where I was first exposed to the field of Classics, for igniting the passion within me for this field and for the life of the mind in general. Ray Larson was an inspiringly humorous teacher and an attentive director of my senior thesis, on Dostoevsky and Plato. Rene McGraw, OSB, has been a model of an intellectually and spiritually intentional life, and he has graciously welcomed me back to campus time after time in the decades since my graduation. Diane Warne Anderson was a passionate teacher whose support and camaraderie I have appreciated many times at professional conferences through the years since graduation. Scott Richardson led me to decide to study Classics in the first place, through a vibrant style of teaching that erased the gap between the classical world and modern one. He has been my particular model as a teacher and mentor, and the friendship that he and his wife Shirley have extended to me and my family through the years has been among our groundings since college. Tim Miles, my cross country and track coach at SJU, also helped to develop in me the toughness and commitment that have been critical in continuing this project in the midst of uncountable competing obligations.

I am grateful to my colleagues at the University of North Carolina at Greensboro, with whom I worked for my first eight years out of graduate school. My two chairs, Susan Shelmerdine and Hugh Parker, were tremendous supporters of my professional aspirations, and they provided me opportunity after opportunity to expand my professional skills. My other ongoing colleagues from throughout that time—Jeff Soles, Linda Danford, Dave Wharton, Maura Heyn, Jon Zarecki, and Joanne Murphy—provided kind feedback on my ideas, offered models of structure for research and writing that have been critical to my work reaching this point, and showed unwavering kindness and support throughout my time there.

I am grateful to faculty and staff colleagues at Monmouth College, where this book has reached its final form. Classics department colleagues Tom Sienkewicz, Vicki Wine, Adrienne Hagen, and Alana Newman contributed to fostering the intellectual vibrance in the department that propelled this and many other projects forward. Political science colleague Mike Nelson has been my essential weekly goal-sharing partner for the past three years; his wise, gracious advice and guidance have gotten me past many sticking points. Political scientist Robin Johnson generously talked through ancient versus modern political coalition-building with me and provided several critical sources from his contemporary campaign work. Psychologist Sydney Greenwalt kindly shared with me some sources on ingroups and outgroups. Administrative assistants Sarah Dean and Amjad Karkout not only provided direct assistance with research for the book, searches for fellowships, processing of critical secondary sources, and assembly of the bibliography, but have been superb professionals in general, whose handling of a host of departmental matters has allowed me to direct more of my time to this book. Librarians Sarah Henderson and Anne Giffey have been critical in helping me find information in the many fields outside of Classics that I have studied for this book, and Marti Carwile has ordered hundreds of books for the library on my behalf. Monmouth College provided me a sabbatical leave in 2019–20, in which I did a tremendous amount of work toward this book; I appreciate the freedom from teaching and service duties that helped make this work come to fruition.

I am grateful to student workers Isaac Jacobs, Simone Johnson, Maddie Baker, Nate Williams, Olivia Matlock, Mikayla Moore, and Grace Passaglia, who have been invaluable to this work reaching its final form. They have not only done essential tasks like checking out library books and copying articles for me, but they have also helped structure handouts and PowerPoint presentations for steps this project has taken along the way, adjusted formatting of this book to fit Bloomsbury's expectations, and managed the painstaking work of converting my bibliography to Bloomsbury's style. Beyond specific help on the book, their willingness and ability to handle a host of departmental tasks, many of which required high levels of professional refinement, have taken a tremendous burden off of me and have, as with Sarah and Amjad, freed me to dedicate time to getting this book completed. I am particularly thankful to Mikayla, Olivia, and Grace for their dedicated assistance and encouragement during the frantic few weeks before the complete draft of this work was due.

I am grateful to audiences at the annual meetings of the Society for Classical Studies (formerly American Philological Association), the American Classical League, the Classical Association of the Middle West and South, and the Illinois Classical Conference, as well as at Monmouth College faculty colloquia, at all of which I delivered talks on topics within this book. Useful feedback that members of those audiences shared in their responses has improved the book considerably.

I am grateful to scholars who have given me individual feedback or provided other means of assistance during the course of this project. While there are many people whom I could put into this category, the ones who have been particularly generous have been Bob Connor, Willie Major, and Jeff Henderson.

I am grateful to the hundreds of students I have had the privilege to teach at the University of North Carolina at Greensboro and at Monmouth College. I have read many of the classical works cited in this book with them, and their perspectives on many of the ideas raised here have helped to shape my takes on them. Classics majors at Monmouth also did a great job of bolstering my spirits as I ground away at final revisions.

I am grateful to all of those at Bloomsbury who have worked with me with kindness and professionalism, including Georgie Leighton, Alice Wright, and Lily Mac Mahon. This book has significantly benefited also from the feedback offered by Bloomsbury's anonymous reviewers.

Most of all, though, I am grateful to my family, without whose nurturing, modeling, support, patience, and tolerance this book would not have been possible. My parents, Bill and Diane Simmons, provided me and my siblings (John, Dan, and Patty) very fine Catholic educations through college, despite the modest wages they earned as teachers and librarians that they needed to stretch to provide those opportunities for us. There were books everywhere in our house, and the public library was an extension of our home. In this vibrant learning environment, with an expectation of hard work, all of us kids were free to pursue paths that stimulated us, as reflected in the educations and careers we have intentionally and meaningfully chosen. The vibrance and purpose of my parents and siblings continues to stimulate and inspire me.

My wife Michelle and our children—Ben, David, Alex, and Marc—have been the most critical to this book coming to life. Michelle's unwavering love and kindness, and her emotional and logistical support, in all sorts of ways, of my various career aspirations, however unpromising they have seemed along the way, have provided me the emotional safety and dedicated time that have allowed me to keep plugging away at this book amidst all else that has come up. She herself has had a tremendously successful and fulfilling career, and while doing that and supporting me, she has also been a beacon of love and nurturance for our children, who have developed wonderfully, in large part because of Michelle's superhuman efforts to provide them stimulating opportunities that are giving them a chance to be the best selves possible. I can never make up to her all that she has given me and our kids, but I will continue trying to do so.

Ben, David, Alex, and Marc have inspired me with their energy and their eager embrace of our love and of the academic, athletic, and artistic chances we have tried to give them. Most importantly, they have inspired me with their consideration and thoughtfulness toward others. And I am grateful to them for their unselfishness as I have spent many, many hours on projects like this that have taken me away from one more game of ping pong, one more round of hitting pop flies, one more chapter of reading aloud, or assistance with one more electronic project. I have aimed to be the best dad I can be while pursuing other objectives as well, but I could have done more, and I appreciate these boys' forbearance tremendously.

To all of these people, and to many more whom I feel terrible for having overlooked, thank you.

Abbreviations

ARV^2 Beazley, J. D., ed. (1963), *Attic Red-Figure Vase-Painters*, 2nd ed., Oxford: Clarendon Press.

FGrH   Jacoby, F., ed. (1923–), *Fragmente der griechischen Historiker*, Leiden: Brill.

K   Kaibel, G., ed. (1899), *Comicorum Graecorum Fragmenta*, Berlin: Weidman.

KA   Kassel, R., and C. Austin, eds. (1983–2001), *Poetae Comici Graeci*, Vols. 1–8, Berlin: De Gruyter.

LSJ^9 Liddell, H. G., and R. Scott, revised and augmented by H. S. Jones (1996), *Greek–English Lexicon*, 9th ed., Oxford: Clarendon Press.

N^2 Nauck, A., ed. (1889), *Tragicorum Graecorum Fragmenta*, 2nd ed., Leipzig: Teubner.

PA   Kirchner, J. (1901–3), *Prosopographia Attica*, 2 vols., Berlin: Reimer.

PMG   Davies, M., ed. (1991), *Poetarum Melicorum Graecorum Fragmenta, Volumen I: Alcman, Stesichorus, Ibycus*, Oxford: Clarendon Press.

Introduction

A "demagogue" has, for centuries, been an intimidating caricature: a slick-talking con artist who appeals to the lowest common denominator of a given population, guiding that population to actions that are short-sighted and destructive.[1] As I write this introduction, that word is again on the ascent—right-leaning populist leaders in the US (Donald Trump), the UK (Boris Johnson), Pakistan (Imran Kahn), Brazil (Jair Bolsonaro), and Australia (Scott Morrison), among many others, have regularly had the label applied to them.[2] But even in more politically balanced times, the word never disappears; it is perpetually being assigned to leaders, across the political spectrum, whose appeal to large numbers of people that are not of the most privileged class unsettles a political or social status quo.[3]

The word originated in Athens, Greece, in the fifth century BCE, and the first leader to whom it was applied was Cleon, son of Cleaenetus.[4] That demagogue's impact through the millennia has been pronounced enough that, in *A Warning* (2019), senior Donald Trump administration official Miles Taylor (who initially released the book anonymously) spends four pages relating a cautionary tale involving Cleon, whom the author says "will sound familiar to readers" (184). In 427 BCE, Cleon convinced the Athenian people to send troops to murder or enslave all of the citizens of Mytilene (Thuc. 3.36), a previous ally of Athens who had transferred its allegiance in the Peloponnesian War to Sparta (3.2–6). Convinced by the more moderate Diodotus (3.41–9), though, the Athenians changed their minds the next day, avoiding the intended slaughter (3.49). Taylor characterizes Trump and Cleon as being equally dangerous, calling each "a foul-mouthed populist politician who uses rhetoric as a loaded gun" (186).

Not surprisingly, Cleon was more than just that characterization. And there were reasons beyond just forceful rhetoric that people supported Cleon. While some of those reasons are similar to the reasons that people support more recent public figures labeled as demagogues, others are more a function of factors particular to the classical Athenian time and place in which Cleon and the others who came to be marked as demagogues emerged. Those particularities, too, though, have parallels in the modern world. While this is not a book about demagogues in the twenty-first century, those who are interested in modern demagogues could learn quite a bit from understanding their classical antecedents.

This book is also not designed to be a comprehensive study of Athenian demagogues or of Cleon himself, but it builds on other studies of each to contribute to a fuller understanding of both, and of the implications they have had for ages to come. While many other relevant sources will be cited through the course of this work, the main book-length resources for understanding Athenian demagogues and demagoguery are Connor (1971), Mann (2007), and Hershkowitz (2018). Those focused on Cleon, including his portrayal in Aristophanes' *Knights*, our most valuable source on him, are Edmunds (1987), Lind (1990), LaFargue (2013), and Saldutti (2014).

This book does four things, though, that distinguish it from those and other scholarly efforts to understand Athenian demagogues. The first is that it aims to understand demagogues' popularity by focusing on the people who chose to support that sort of politician. Those people had reasons underlying their individual choices to support demagogues; whatever appeal demagogues had did not register instantaneously over a whole population, but rather to one person at a time, each of whom had to decide that what the demagogues offered was something with which he or she wanted to be aligned.

This ties into the second and third distinctions of this book. One of them is that it uses contemporary sociology, often undergirded by ancient Greek conceptions of aspects of the current field, to aim to understand what the demagogues' actions and self-presentations might have provoked in the people to whom they reached out. The other is an observation that what they likely provoked were feelings of friendship—thousands of Athenians appear to have attached themselves to these "new politicians" because they gave off all sorts of indications that they were inviting friendship (φιλία, *philia*), of a sort, from their followers.

The demagogues' friendship-building techniques appear to have changed the habits of Athenian leaders, demagogic and not, for decades following. The book's fourth distinction is pointing out the influence of demagogic friendship-based leadership styles in tragedies of the late fifth century BCE, and in historical biographies and histories written in the mid-fourth century. Making subordinates feel as though a leader was a friend seems to have had a lasting impact on Athenian leadership practices.

The core of the book, though, is its analysis of Cleon's style of ingratiation to political supporters; all of its other emphases emanate from there. The work on which this book most extensively draws for that purpose is Aristophanes' comic play *Knights*. More than any other extant source, it depicts Cleon (although a hyperbolic version of him) interacting with individuals, and it is the only work from Cleon's time period that discusses perceptions of what a demagogue is and how such a politician stands out from other politicians. But the foundation on which the rest of the book is built is a different interpretation of an aspect of the portrayal of Cleon in *Knights* than those of previous scholars. It focuses on what it meant to be a desirous homosexual "lover" (as *Knights* portrays him) vs. a platonic, homosocial "friend" (as this book contends was a more apt metaphor for his style of outreach), according to the norms of the time.

Significantly, this book questions the figurative accuracy of one statement—"I am your lover" (ἐραστής τ᾽ εἰμὶ σός, *Eq.* 732)—that Paphlagon, the character representing Cleon, makes to Demos, the personification of the Athenian people, in *Knights*. It instead focuses on Paphlagon's actions and words and others' descriptions of him throughout the play, which make him resemble much more closely someone acting like a friend to Demos and other common Athenians, rather than like a lover. According to comic theory, comic portrayals may stretch the truth of an audience's understanding of a familiar figure to some extent, but to be genuinely funny, they have to be true, as the audience would perceive them. It seems that the play makes sport of what Cleon does as a politician—aim to make common Athenians see him as a friend—by conflating that attempted cultivation of friendship (one kind of relationship between men) with a different, more intense form of male relationship, pederasty. But because Cleon's public persona is actually that of a *friend* to the public and the individuals that comprise it, this book's interpretation is that Aristophanes could only push the pederastic depiction so far, and needed eventually to portray him as a friend. Establishing Cleon's actions as primarily those of a friend (φίλος, *philos*) rather than of a pederastic lover (ἐραστής, *erastes*) requires a fair amount of parsing of distinctions between the two types of relationships, which brings studies of ancient friendship and sexuality into important consideration.

The book also studies Cleon's apparent influence through friendship-based styles of leadership, which were not evident in records of prior Athenian leaders. These will be revealed in extant written sources' presentations of other leaders during the Peloponnesian War era, when demagogues were most influential, and even decades after. The clearest examples of this, as that war was coming to a close, appear in the actions of leaders in two plays of Euripides: Agamemnon and Odysseus in *Iphigenia in Aulis*, and Dionysus in *Bacchae*, with the first of them echoing Odysseus and Talthybius in Euripides' *Hecuba*, written around the time of *Knights*. The long-standing impression that the demagogues made is underscored in portrayals by Xenophon, particularly in *Anabasis* and *Cyropaedia*, several decades into the fourth century, well after the demagogues' main period of influence. This all goes to paint a picture of demagogues not as "new" politicians in the sense that their contemporaries and Connor (1971: 87–198), influentially, made them out to be, but rather as politicians who developed their base of support through personal connections, as Athenian politicians had done for as long as there is record, but with some critical wrinkles that were appropriate to the population to which they were appealing, and whose methods lingered on past the point of their period of prominence.

Most of all, the book examines a previously overlooked political innovation that helped to make Athenian demagogues influential, and which has been employed through the centuries, among both politicians who might be labeled "demagogues" and many others who would not. While there is much that demagogues and other leaders can do to convince people to follow their lead, one of those things is to make potential followers feel that they are the leader's friends, or as though they *could* be friends, if circumstances were different. A key to understanding the effectiveness of this approach is to consider not just what the demagogues themselves did as leaders and how the people as a whole responded to it. Even more important is parsing the sociological impact of the demagogues' actions on the individuals who came to make up their support base. These people wanted a *friend* in a high place, and the demagogues seem to have recognized that and found a way to give them one.

1

Friendship in Athenian Politics
Prior to the Demagogues

I. Introduction: Demagogues as Friends

In the Old Oligarch's critique of Athenian democracy, written during the Peloponnesian War, he notes that the common people "like" (φιλοῦσι, *philousi*) certain politicians of low social standing (the sort that came to be called "demagogues") more than they do elite politicians (2.19).[1] The implication of *philousi* in this case could be little more than "cherish," as Marr and Rhodes translate it (2008: 51): a marker of the commons' appreciation of the demagogues' political action on their behalf. Yet the way that other sources show that demagogues interacted with their humble supporters suggests that getting the masses not just to be grateful to them, but in fact to "like" them, in the sense of φιλία (*philia*, "friendship"), was critical to their political success. Ober (1998: 21) reflects that possibility in his translation of *philousi* as "befriend."

While such a feeling from citizens to politicians is not fully consistent with most modern sentiments, it is only a development of an attitude toward citizenship and a dynamic of leadership that was in place from well before Athens' move to radical democracy. That attitude is one of the factors that seems to have brought politicians later labeled demagogues to power and to have lingered for decades thereafter. Friendship had long been privileged over dedication to the πόλις (*polis*, "city-state"); Cleon and other demagogues just seem to have taken advantage of it more effectively than others, with a different population than prior politicians had attempted to marshal.

II. Balancing *Philoi* and the *Polis*

What left an opening in leadership for demagogues to enter was a negotiation over time of the balance of prominent political figures' expressed commitment to φίλοι (*philoi*, "friends and family members"), on the one hand, and to the *polis*, on the other.[2] Athenians (and other Greeks) throughout the archaic and earlier classical periods tended to prioritize allegiance to *philoi*, and corresponding enmity toward ἐχθροί (*ekhthroi*, "personal enemies"), over allegiance to the *polis* as a whole, except in situations of direct civic peril.[3] The outward emphasis of a few politicians on the well-being of the *polis*, and away from the specific benefit of their *philoi*, however, established precedents that demagogues later exploited for their own purposes.

A. Helping Friends and Harming Enemies

The *locus classicus* of the traditional ideology comes from Solon, an Athenian lawgiver who lived in the late seventh and early sixth centuries; his dearest wish, despite his clear attention to the well-being of Athens as a whole, was "to be sweet to [his] friends and bitter to [his] enemies" (εἶναι δὲ γλυκὺν ὧδε φίλοις, ἐχθροῖσι δὲ πικρόν, fr. 13.5 *PMG*).[4] His sentiments are reflected repeatedly in the fifth and early fourth centuries. In Euripides' *Heracles*, dated to *c.* 415 BCE, Amphitryon approvingly tells his son Heracles, "It is characteristic of you, child, to be a friend to your friends and to hate your enemies" (πρὸς σοῦ μέν, ὦ παῖ, τοῖς φίλοις <τ'> εἶναι φίλον / τά τ' ἐχθρὰ μισεῖν, 585–6).[5] In Plato's *Republic*, dated to the first third of the fourth century BCE, Cephalus similarly approves of the validity of such an attitude in his agreement with Socrates' paraphrase of the poet Simonides (from Ceos in the sixth and fifth centuries): "He is saying that justice is doing well to one's friends and badly to one's enemies?" (τὸ τοὺς φίλους ἄρα εὖ ποιεῖν καὶ τοὺς ἐχθροὺς κακῶς δικαιοσύνην λέγει; 332d7–8).[6] Other expressions of the sort come up in numerous other texts from the period.[7]

On a few occasions, individuals are portrayed as explicitly favoring personal or family interests (sometimes overlapping with religious duties, too) over not just personal enemies, but over the city's laws as well. In Sophocles' *Antigone* (produced between 442 and 438 BCE), Antigone declares that it is her divine obligation to perform burial rites for a *philos* even when such action goes in the face of civic law, calling it "committing holy crimes" (ὅσια πανουργήσασ, 74), i.e., public offenses that are divinely justified, to bury her brother, whose interment is "forbidden in the city" (ἀπόρρητον πόλει, 44).[8] Crito, too, in Plato's *Crito*, expresses his belief that it would be seen as only "through some baseness and cowardice on our part" (κακίᾳ τινὶ καὶ ἀνανδρίᾳ τῇ ἡμετέρᾳ, 45e6) that Socrates' friends not rescue the philosopher from prison when they have the chance (after his death sentence that has been mandated through legal processes), and he warns Socrates that his not cooperating with the breakout would be perceived as "base and disgraceful" (τῷ κακῷ καὶ αἰσχρά, 46a).[9] The general sense among Athenians, as Adkins puts it (1960: 231), was that "where the city's interests are not threatened, or seem irrelevant to the case in hand, there is nothing ... to prevent the *agathos polites* ["good citizen"] from attempting to thwart the laws of the city on behalf of his family and friends, with whom he has closer ties."[10]

The requirements of political office did not seem to diminish Athenians' sense of *philia* as their central motivation. Themistocles, in the early fifth century BCE, supposedly claimed that, when he was archon, those who were his friends would always have more from him than those who were not ('μηδέποτ'' εἶπεν 'εἰς τοιοῦτον ἐγὼ καθίσαιμι θρόνον, ἐν ᾧ πλέον οὐχ ἕξουσιν οἱ φίλοι παρ'ἐμοῦ τῶν μὴ φίλων,' Plut. *Mor.* 807b1–2).[11] Plato's Meno, too, likely in the early fourth century, claims that, while it is a mark of a man's excellence (ἀρετή, *arete*) to tend to the affairs of the city (τὰ τῆς πόλεως πράττειν, *Men.* 71e3), the purpose in doing so is to benefit his friends and harm his enemies (πράττοντα τοὺς μὲν φίλους εὖ ποιεῖν, τοὺς δ' ἐχθροὺς κακῶς, 71e3–4).[12] Consistent with this attitude that a politician's responsibilities to his *philoi* are at least on a par with those to his *polis* is Pericles' belief that his guest-friend (ξένος, *xenos*), the Spartan king Archidamus, might have considered sparing Pericles' farm during the Spartans' devastation of the Attic countryside, wishing to do him a private favor (ἰδίᾳ βουλόμενος χαρίζεσθαι, Thuc. 2.13.1).[13]

B. The Power of Aristocratic Friends in Athenian Politics

While all Athenians' loyalties were principally to their *philoi*, the fact that politics, for generations prior to the Peloponnesian War, was driven largely by aristocrats gave that group an extraordinary edge over the rest of the population in benefiting from public action. Their primary loyalty was to other aristocratic allies, and they appear at least on occasion to have been able to guide the whole political process to pass measures favorable to themselves.[14] Alliances were grounded not just on *philia*, but also on groups of comrades sometimes labeled ἑταιρεῖαι (*hetaireiai*) or συνωμοσίαι (*sunomosiai*) ("clubs, associations"), whom I will address more shortly.[15]

In turn, politics influenced in large part by *philia* connections was not favorable to common Athenians. Relationships between *philoi*, and between members of *hetaireiai* and *sunomosiai*, were based in part on personal compatibility and mutual fondness, but also to a large extent on reciprocal usefulness, in politics and other practical aspects of life.[16] And while people at all socioeconomic levels could have been useful to, and thus valued by, others at a similar level to themselves, people at low socioeconomic levels would have had a hard time establishing and maintaining friendships with people who were wealthier, and thus whose more significant influence on others would tangibly benefit them. As Aristotle makes clear, if unequal friendships existed, they did so, in most cases, between people who were considered by nature to be unequal, yet who were connected by unavoidable circumstances: fathers and sons, husbands and wives, and rulers and subjects (*Eth. Nic.* 1158b11–22). Mismatches in ability, resources, or quality between other sorts of people generally would not lead to friendship in the first place, unless each party contributed something that the other did not have (1158b1–3); Aristotle does not think that such relationships were likely to last, though (1158b3–4), and friendships in which there was no reasonable hope of reciprocity of some kind would almost inevitably dissolve (1159a1–6). Moreover, records of people being sought out as *philoi* for the high-level benefits they could provide those who sought them, and corresponding references to the extent to which the poor were avoided as *philoi*, make it seem as though being labeled someone's *philos* at all (or being a part of a *hetaireia* or *sunomosia*) implied, in most cases, a degree of obvious capability, to which was attached prestige.[17] And this prestige brought with it exclusivity, leaving out large numbers whose personal or material resources were too limited to hold up their end of a reciprocal *philia*.[18]

Hetaireiai or *sunomosiai* often went beyond mere disregard for civic well-being in their support of their members, sometimes to the point of treason, which does more damage to those of limited resources than to those of greater.[19] Chroust (1954) documents instance after instance of *hetaireiai* actively working against Athens for their own political and personal advantage, from Cylon's conspiracy to seize Athens in 632 (Thuc. 1.126) to the invitation of Lysander to Athens by radical oligarchic *hetaireiai* to help them establish the tyrannical Thirty.[20] Among these are many further occasions, during the Peloponnesian War, of individuals putting the advancement of their *hetaireiai* ahead of state interests. Andocides' *hetaireia*, for example, mutilated the Herms in 415 (Andoc. 1.61–4, cf. 49, 54), a gesture that was taken by the city to communicate an imminent revolution against the democracy (Thuc. 6.27.3).[21] Andocides depicts his comrade (ἑταῖρος, *hetairos*) Euphiletus as telling him that his status as either a personal enemy (*ekhthros*) or friend (*philos*) depends on whether or not he kept the group's culpability a secret (1.63).

How limited the consequences could be for prominent Athenians who acted with their *hetaireiai*, and against the *polis*, is exemplified by Alcibiades. Even in the midst of his six-year service as general (στρατηγός, *strategos*), he is alleged to have taken part in the mutilation of the Herms, and also in the desecration of the Eleusinian Mysteries.[22] He then fled to Sparta to assist in its efforts against his homeland when he was to face a reckoning for his role in the actions of his *hetaireia*.[23] That this man was recalled to Athens to reassume his role as *strategos* not long thereafter (Thuc. 8.97.3) underscores the fact that Athenians did not put a premium on patriotism in the modern sense, particularly for the wealthy and powerful. They recognized the multiple allegiances an individual person felt (including to *philoi* and *hetaireiai*) and did not demand single-minded dedication to the *polis*, but rather just enough dedication when the situation especially called for it.[24]

C. Challenges to *Philia*-Focused Politics, Setting the Stage for Demagogues' Innovations

From the origins of democracy, though, certain prominent politicians took actions of different sorts to devote their political energies to the *polis*, or at least *not* to their own *philoi*, laying foundations for the innovations that Cleon and other demagogues made during the Peloponnesian War. Among the most poignant examples is that of Cleisthenes, as part of the move that brought

Athens from the rule of tyrants to radical democratic governance late in the sixth century. Herodotus claims that Cleisthenes "made the people (δῆμος, *demos*) his comrade (*hetairos*)" (τὸν δῆμον προσαιρίζεται, 5.66, cf. 5.69.1) as part of his moves to reshape Athenian politics.[25] Pseudo-Aristotle ([*Ath. Pol.*] 20.1) is yet more explicit in his description of Cleisthenes' break from his *hetaireiai*, but as a pragmatic maneuver: "being inferior in the matter of *hetaireiai*, he enlisted the common people (*demos*), giving the power of government to the mob (πλῆθος, *plethos*)" (ἡττώμενος δὲ ταῖς ἑταιρείαις ὁ Κλεισθένης, προσηγάγετο τὸν δῆμον, ἀποδιδοὺς τῷ πλήθει τὴν πολιτείαν).[26] The lack of records of Cleisthenes' specific actions leaves scholars only to guess at what these portrayed actions mean in practice—perhaps they refer only to his reforms, in all of their democratic breadth—but they certainly suggest, in political actions, attention to and faith in those who are not his close associates.[27]

Others, in the first few decades of Athens' settled democracy, took less radical but still noteworthy steps not to be unduly influenced by those close to them. Early in the fifth century, Aristides supposedly avoided his *hetairoi* when in office in order to avoid being drawn into the unjust actions *hetaireiai* were prone to take, or feeling compelled to reciprocate a favor they did for him (Plut. *Arist.* 2.5–9). In the mid-fifth century Ephialtes also is supposed to have turned down a payment of ten talents from his *hetairoi*, despite his poverty, because he did not want to be pressured to repay them through unjust actions (ὑμᾶς καταχαρίσασθαί τι τῶν δικαίων), nor to do his *hetairoi* no favor at all in return for their payment, and thus to seem ungrateful (Ael. *VH* 11.9).[28]

Closer to the Peloponnesian War are examples of attempts to reconcile personal alliances and prosperity with dedication to the *polis*, rather than holding the two commitments as incompatible. In *Antigone*, Creon counters Antigone's unwavering devotion to the proper burial of Polynices, her brother and thus one of her closest *philoi*, with his own attitude that he could never have a *philos* who was hostile to the land (οὔτ᾽ ἂν φίλον ποτ᾽ ἄνδρα δυσμενῆ χθονὸς / θείμην ἐμαυτῷ, 187–8). Creon's approach initially seems to fit tidily in line with the *polis*-centered one of Aristides and Ephialtes.[29] But Creon justifies his patriotism in terms of *philia*, claiming that the development of *philoi* is dependent on the security that comes with a stable and safe *polis* (188–90).[30] Later, however, he backs off from the patriotic concern of even that stance, lamenting the miserable outcomes (ἄνολβα, 1265) of his strategies (βουλευμάτων, 1265) because the dead were all his family members (ἐμφυλίους, 1264).[31]

Leading into the Peloponnesian War, Nicias, who has certain things in common with demagogues and is included among their number in a few sources, similarly tried to govern patriotically but had difficulty breaking from the benefits of his *philoi*.[32] Plutarch has him working long hours on public affairs and avoiding friendly interactions (*Nic.* 5.1), yet it was his *philoi* who engaged with visitors lingering at his doors (οἱ δὲ φίλοι τοῖς ἐπὶ ταῖς θύραις φοιτῶσιν ἐνετύγχανον) and shooed them away so that he could get work done (5.2). Titchener (1988: 128–9 *ad* 5.1) suggests that his reluctance to strike up new friendships was to avoid "the rancor of those friends' enemies," placing his actions squarely in the realm of *philia* and ἔχθρα (*ekhthra*, "personal hatred"). Plutarch also portrays Nicias adjourning the Athenian assembly, over which he was presiding on that day, to dine with *xenoi* (ἑστιᾶν μέλλων ξένους, *Nic.* 7.5), the act of someone who openly values his personal interests even when they are in direct conflict with the business of the *polis*.

III. Pericles and the Bridge to the Demagogues

The last link between the traditional *philia*-based, aristocratically benefiting style of government and that which particularly distinguishes the demagogic style is Pericles. Not only was his family among the most prominent in Athens over many generations, but he was also exceedingly well-regarded on his own merits, being elected general of his tribe each year from 443 to 429.[33] It is his death in 429 BCE that leaves the power vacuum that Cleon, then other demagogues, fill. As much as, or even more than, other politicians noted above, though, he seems to have distanced himself from his personal *philoi* and dedicated himself to the well-being of the *polis*. But Pericles' approach and profile are not as radical as those of the succeeding generation of politicians, as both his actions and the appraisals of near-contemporaneous analysts show.

Certain of Pericles' actions certainly fall in line with those of prior politicians whose interests appear to focus on the *polis* as a whole. Like Aristides, Pericles supposedly avoided distractions and extralegal influences by avoiding casual contact with nearly everyone during his period of power. One way of doing this was to use only the road that led him to the ἀγορά (*agora*, "marketplace") and βουλευτήριον (*bouleuterion*, "council building," Plut. *Per.* 7.4).[34] He also avoided dinner invitations and casually friendly interaction of any sort (κλήσεις τε δείπνων καὶ τὴν τοιαύτην ἅπασαν φιλοφροσύνην καὶ συνήθειαν ἐξέλιπεν, 7.4).[35] L. G. Mitchell (1997: 44–5) contends that Pericles' actions were a way to "mak[e] all the citizens his friends" (much as he refers to himself as φιλόπολις (*philopolis*), "friendly to the *polis*," Thuc. 2.60.5) and in doing so to introduce systems of reciprocity between himself and them on an impersonal scale, an approach that Connor (1971: 91–108) attributes to the demagogue Cleon.[36] That would certainly fall in line with Socrates' claim (Xen. *Mem.* 2.6.13) that Pericles had a magical way of making the *polis* like him (ἐποίει αὐτὴν φιλεῖν αὐτόν).[37] That interpretation, though, is challenged by the fact that *philia* and its benefits were not transacted impersonally in Athens, as will be discussed at length in chapters to come; a *polis* cannot actually like anyone— and, as Tamiolaki (2016: 31) notes, "the image of love of the Athenians for ... Pericles ... is not corroborated by ancient sources." But Pericles' actions were certainly a step toward the *polis*-centrism of the demagogues that employs *philia* in an innovative way.

Like Creon in *Antigone*, Pericles also tried not just to separate himself from the influence of his *philoi*, but also to justify patriotism as not just noble, but as part of a good life. In his funeral oration at the end of the first year of the Peloponnesian War, Thucydides has him announcing his belief that individuals are better off when the *polis* is strong than when they are individually prosperous in a faltering *polis* (2.60.2–4).[38] Showing his commitment to this principle, he tied the city's well-being to his own, offering (as mentioned above) to donate his farm to Athens during Sparta's march on the city, not wanting to seem to profit from his friendship with the Spartan king Archidamus if his farm were spared when many others were not (2.13.1).

Other records of Pericles' public actions and stances, however, have led several analysts, both ancient and modern, to contend that he was little different from those labeled "demagogues" who succeeded him. Hornblower (1991: 346–7 *ad* Thuc. 2.65.10), for instance, notes that, early in Pericles' political career, he was similarly forceful in speech and similarly likely to concede to dissenting voices as the demagogues who will be introduced in the next chapter, though later in his career he aimed to make himself less conspicuous, so that the appearances he did make were more noteworthy (Plut. *Per.* 7.5). Pseudo-Aristotle also attributes demagogic tactics to Pericles, and in fact uses the terms δημαγωγεῖν (*demagogein*, 27.1) and ἀντιδημαγωγῶν (*antidemagogon*, 27.2) to refer to some of his actions, citing in particular several of Pericles' initiatives that emboldened οἱ πολλοί (*hoi polloi*, "the many," a term for the Athenian masses) to become more involved in city governance (27.1–2).[39] Azoulay (2014: 130–1) notes that supposed demagogues' financial measures to help common Athenians and direct attention to common people's interests were little different from certain measures of Pericles', such as the introduction of jury pay in the 450s. And Davies (1975: 376–7) argues that the evidence for the period prior to the Peloponnesian War is insufficient to make claims about things changing between Pericles and demagogues at the beginning of the war.[40]

Despite these arguments, the vehemence of the main sources concerning the politicians that followed Pericles suggests that the new politicians were indeed of a different sort, or at least were widely perceived that way. Even as pseudo-Aristotle attributes demagogic actions to Pericles, he also places him as just one in a long line of "heads of the people" (προστάται τοῦ δήμου, *[Ath. Pol.]* 28.2–4), along with other revered aristocrats including Solon, Peisistratus, and Cleisthenes, none of whom would be confused with Cleon in their backgrounds or methods. Furthermore, he distinguishes between the positive affairs of state during Pericles' leadership of the *demos* and the steep downturn when Cleon and the other demagogues took over (28.1, cf. 3–4):[41]

> ἕως μὲν οὖν Περικλῆς προειστήκει τοῦ δήμου, βελτίω τὰ κατὰ τὴν πολιτείαν ἦν, τελευτήσαντος δὲ Περικλέους πολὺ χείρω. πρῶτον γὰρ τότε προστάτην ἔλαβεν ὁ δῆμος οὐκ εὐδοκιμοῦντα παρὰ τοῖς ἐπιεικέσιν· ἐν δὲ τοῖς πρότερον χρόνοις ἀεὶ διετέλουν οἱ ἐπιεικεῖς δημαγωγοῦντες.

> As long, then, as Pericles stood as head of the people, the affairs of the state went better, but when Pericles was dead they were much worse. For the people now for the first time adopted a head who was not well-regarded by the elite, whereas in former periods people in that class always continued to lead the people.

Isocrates (8.126–7), echoed by the scholiast to *Peace* (Σ Ar. *Pax* 681b) also discusses an abrupt change in approaches to leadership after Pericles' death, with consequent negative repercussions for Athens. For Isocrates, it was largely a matter of disingenuousness on the demagogues' part that led to suffering for the people to whom they claimed to be dedicated (127): "the mass of us, for whom they say they care, are in such a state that none of the citizens lives with pleasure or ease, but instead the city is full of lamentations" (τὸ δὲ πλῆθος ἡμῶν, οὗ κήδεσθαί φασιν, οὕτω διακείμενον ὥστε μηδένα τῶν πολιτῶν ἡδέως ζῆν μηδὲ ῥᾳθύμως, ἀλλ᾽ ὀδυρμῶν μεστὴν εἶναι τὴν πόλιν).

Aristophanes, too, writing just a few years in the wake of Pericles' death and during the height of Cleon's power, has the Second Slave claim in *Knights* (191–2) that leading the people (δημαγωγία, *demagogia*) is no longer (οὐ … ἔτ᾽) a task for an educated man or one who is "refined" (χρηστός, *chrestos*) in his habits, implying that it was before, such as, apparently, when Pericles was recognized as a προστάτης τοῦ δήμου (*prostates tou demou*, "head of the people") (ps.-Arist. [*Ath. Pol.*] 28.1).[42] Thucydides is also clear that, while Pericles had a good rapport with the populace, like the demagogues that followed him, he was unquestionably in command of it, unlike his successors (2.65.8–10).[43] Thucycides frames the demagogues' sort of politics as "being led" by the people, as opposed to what Pericles supposedly did, which was to "direct them freely" and to "lead" them (κατεῖχε τὸ πλῆθος ἐλευθέρως, καὶ οὐκ ἤγετο μᾶλλον ὑπ᾽ αὐτοῦ ἢ αὐτὸς ἦγε, 2.65.8).[44]

It thus might be best to look at Pericles, as Connor (1971: 119–28), followed by Ober (1989: 90) and Rhodes (2016: 244), does, as a "transitional figure" between the old aristocracy and the demagogues, employing some tactics of the latter, but maintaining the authority and connections of the former. Even if the difference between Pericles and the demagogues is not as stark as Thucydides makes it appear, manners of self-presentation and interaction with common Athenians seem a clear and significant distinction that affected the way each led, as succeeding chapters should show.

IV. Conclusion

The so-called "demagogues" who came into power following Pericles' death in 429 did so in the context of a decades-long tradition of Athenian politicians weighing their commitment to the Athenian *polis* against that to one's own *philoi.* Throughout the fifth century in Athens, as certain statesmen's outwardly expressed and demonstrated loyalties to the *polis* outbalanced those to *philoi*, the idea of *philia* in the political realm itself may have begun to evolve. The direct evidence of this evolution does not appear during Pericles' period of power, though his *polis*-centered actions and policies are the most pronounced on record since the introduction of democracy. The steps that Pericles took opened up prospects for his successors, who were of a more modest social profile from him, to transact politics in a way that was both radically different from and distinctly similar to how it had been for decades prior.

2

Cleon and the Rise of Friendship-Based Athenian Demagogy

I. Introduction: Enter the Demagogue

Variants of the word δημαγωγός (*demagogos*, "demagogue") do not appear in extant Athenian literature until 424 BCE, when they show up twice in Aristophanes' *Knights*: ἡ <u>δημαγωγία</u> γὰρ οὐ πρὸς μουσικοῦ / ἔτ᾽ ἐστὶν ἀνδρὸς οὐδὲ χρηστοῦ, "For <u>leading the people</u> is no longer for an educated or upper-class man" (191–2); and τὰ δ᾽ ἄλλα σοι πρόσεστι <u>δημαγωγικά</u>, "In other ways, <u>leading the people</u> is just for you" (217).[1] *Demagogos* itself does not appear until Thucydides' use of the term, later in the century or early in the next, to characterize Cleon as ἀνὴρ δημαγωγός, "a demagogic man" (4.21.3.2).[2] When this term, in its various forms, does appear, its connotation is rather diverse for nearly a century, on a continuum from a neutral expression used to describe a politician who showed sympathy to the interests of the non-elite, to one with pejorative connotations of an underqualified politician manipulating the non-elite to vault himself into wealth and prominence.[3]

Hershkowitz (2018: 33–4) emphasizes the ambiguity in different sources as to whether the *demos* in *demagogos* refers to the populace as a whole or to the lower classes, the word's two main meanings, and he contends that *demagogos* primarily refers to a "guide to the *polis*" (34).[4] Yet a widely accepted point of view, articulated by Connor (1971: 109–10 n. 34), is that *demagogoi* in the fifth and fourth centuries were seen as at least significantly reaching out to the non-elite classes, who comprised a significant majority of Athenian citizens.[5]

The issue in this book, though, is not the behavior of people only when they were specifically referred to as *demagogoi*, nor how broad the focus of their leadership might have been seen to be. The issues, instead, are as follows: the process through which people who were most consistently given that label in classical Athens cultivated supporters (mainly those of lower classes); the ways they led groups over whom they won influence; the ways their styles of ingratiation and leadership seem to have caught on; and the staying power of those styles. This chapter's particular focus will be on critical first steps in that progression: prominent demagogues' apparent adjustment of focus from *philia* with their own established friends to an outward focus on the *polis*, while leaving openings for different sorts of *philia* connections that their backgrounds and circumstances allowed.

While *demagogos* and its variants were applied to dozens of fifth- and fourth-century Athenians (Hershkowitz 2018: 37–49 and 85–91), focus will be on three in particular, all from the fifth century, and all of whom particularly stood out as demagogues at their time, as has been noted or will be: Cleon, Hyperbolus, and Cleophon. Others will be cited along the way as well to provide context. The time when these demagogues operated is one in which source material documenting their actions, or at least others' reactions to them, is comparatively abundant, and through which their influence on subsequent leaders can plausibly be traced back to them.

II. *Philia* and the *Polis* in the Demagogues' Rise

After Pericles' death in 429 BCE, a number of Athenian politicians took even further steps toward stressing the centrality of the *polis* in their platforms, while integrating a different sort of *philia* into their approaches to leadership. Along with de-emphasizing their previous loyalties to their own *philoi*, these distinctive politicians—primarily Cleon, Hyperbolus, and later Cleophon, although Alcibiades, Nicias, and several others of less renown shared much in common with them—shifted the idea of loyalty to the *polis* during their period of influence away from the *polis* as an abstraction and toward it as a concrete embodiment of the large majority of Athenian citizens, with whom they aimed to cultivate more personally felt relationships.[6] The public personae of these politicians—whose fathers were typically the first in their families to attain significant wealth—and the civic policies for which they fought seem to suggest, in many cases, a distinct sympathy not just for the *polis* in general, but for the wishes and needs of common Athenians, that borders on *philia*. For their policies and approaches, as well as their backgrounds that are portrayed as non-elite, they were widely ridiculed in comedy, oratory, and historiography. Yet they and other demagogues managed to maintain significant influence in Athens over more than two decades despite considerable upper-class discontent—or, quite possibly, at least in part, *because* of that discontent—and even a bloodless oligarchic revolt.

A. Demagogues' Transition to Power through a Different Sort of *Philia*

The prime exemplar of this shift in Athenian politicians' profiles and loyalties to the *polis* through attention to the masses is Cleon, whom those Athenian masses found to be the most persuasive politician at the time of Pericles' death (τῷ τε δήμῳ ... ἐν τῷ τότε πιθανώτατος, Thuc. 3.36.6).[7] According to Plutarch (*Mor.* 806f9–13), he renounced all of his *philoi* upon entering into public life, ostensibly so that he would not be distracted by them from making the soundest possible policy.[8] This symbolic gesture is much like those of Aristides and Pericles, except that it did not make him stand out from his political peers, but rather just helped him to fit in.[9] Thucydides says Pericles' successors, more equal to one another than Pericles was to the top politicians of his generation, aimed for prominence via popularity, gained by organizing public affairs according to "the fancy of the commoners" (ἡδονὰς τῷ δήμῳ, 2.65.10).[10] Isocrates, too (8.127), specifies that post-Periclean politicians of lower social standing sacrificed their private matters (ἰδίοις) in favor of irrepressible dedication to common affairs (κοινῶν) and to the masses (*plethos*).[11] Even Alcibiades, who was certainly not of low social standing, consciously chose not to use his *philoi* to advance his political fortunes with *hoi polloi*, but rather to focus on his considerable rhetorical skills to win them over (Plut. *Alc.* 10.2).[12]

These successors of Pericles did not merely play down their personal friendships and individual matters to focus on governing the *polis* prudently, but rather directed their energies specifically toward appealing to the common people, the *demos*. Connor influentially contends that Cleon and other demagogues sought to make common Athenians, as a group, feel as though they had moved into the role of friendly insiders that was previously reserved for the economic and social elite.[13] And Cleon at least claimed, in his rhetoric, that the relationship was not a one-way street, but rather that, for the political support and guidance that *philoi* had traditionally given politicians, he was turning intentionally to the common people of Athens. Thucydides records Cleon declaring that the humbler people (φαυλότεροι, *phauloteroi*) of Athens are better civic administrators than those who are more knowledgeable (Thuc. 3.37.3–4), and encouraging them to be active, critical participants in decisions of the state (3.38.7).

Along with this expression of respect for common Athenians, terminology for friendly fondness toward the Athenian *demos* comes into regular use in the last quarter of the fifth century, initially attributed to figures closely connected to Cleon, if not expressed by the demagogue himself. In *Knights*, produced in 424, as Paphlagon (Cleon's proxy) and the Sausage-Seller are competing to win over the character Demos, Demos calls the Sausage-Seller φιλόδημος (*philodemos*, "friendly to the people," 786) when the latter gives Demos a cushion.[14] This term plays, obviously, on the character Demos' name, but also on care and fondness for common Athenians.[15] A character named *Philodemos* itself appears the next year in *Clouds* (1187), used by Phidippides to compliment Solon for one of his laws that would favor his indebted father, Strepsiades.[16] The year following, the same idea is put periphrastically in *Wasps*, with Bdelucleon (who, as his named indicates, loathes Cleon) praised for "cherishing the people" (τὸν δῆμον … φιλοῦντος, *ton demon … philountos*) more than others do (888–9).[17]

Similar terms in *Knights* and other sources underscore the extent to which at least outwardly friendly feelings toward the masses had become valorized at this time, quite possibly by Cleon, and in decades following. The antonym of *philodemos*, μισόδημος (*misodemos*, "hating the people"), appears as a criticism in *Wasps* (474) and in several later sources.[18] Politicians who *appear* as though they are "pandering to the people" (δημιζόντων, *demizonton*, *Vesp.* 699), while actually showing little regard for common Athenians, are also ridiculed.[19] Another expression that seems to have had lingering populist resonance, εὔνους τῷ δήμῳ (*eunous toi demoi*, "well-disposed to the people"), comes up in oblique form in *Knights*: Paphlagon, addressing Demos, says that a central criterion on which Demos chooses between Paphlagon and the Sausage-Seller should be who is "more well-disposed to [him]" (εὐνούστερος σοι, *eunesteros soi*, 748).[20] The Old Oligarch as well ([*Ath. pol.*] 3.10) distinguishes the attitude of "the best sort" (τὸ βέλτιστον) from that of "the worst" (τὸ κάκιστον) in that the latter is *eunous toi demoi*, while the former is not.[21]

The impact of the political emphasis on the *demos* of Cleon and those following his lead was twofold. First, in giving greater attention to the *demos* in shaping Athenian policy, Pericles' heirs obviously shifted the balance of political discourse and power in the *polis* toward the commons and away from the elite. As these demagogues, like almost all of their predecessors who attained political influence, were notably wealthy, so too, most likely, were their *philoi*.[22] Thus the demagogues' reported distancing of themselves from their own *philoi*, the consequent reduction of access to power of those *philoi*, and the connected marginalization of other *philoi*-centered elite politicians moved many members of the elite out of the direct influence that they previously would have had.

On a second level, demagogic politicians' emphasis on distancing themselves from their personal *philoi* and focusing on the *demos* as the core of the *polis* would not necessarily imply to the citizenry that *philia* as a political binding principle was diminishing. It seems to have meant, instead, that there was now an opening for a broader part of the population to move into the role of influential *philoi* with demagogic politicians that was not available with more traditional politicians. Individual members of the masses, then, had opportunities for greater influence.

Why it occurred to Cleon and other demagogues to go this far in their outreach to the *demos* has some fairly straightforward possible answers, but why those efforts succeeded is a bit more complicated.

B. *Philia* between Demagogues and the *Demos* through Feeling of Personal Connection? Demagogues' Modest Backgrounds

It is possible that Pericles' successors' dedication to the masses resulted at least in part from genuine feeling of personal connection with that group, which common Athenians may have reciprocated in turn.[23] While these new politicians were far from poor, they were (with the exception of Alcibiades) descended from non-elite families that benefited from the industrial labor of enslaved people to make their fortunes (Davies 1981: 41).[24] Cleon inherited a tannery from his father Cleaenetus; Hyperbolus' family owned a lamp-making factory; Cleophon very likely inherited the lyre-making factory he ran from his father Cleippides; and Nicias (included by some as a demagogue, as noted earlier) owned a thousand enslaved people, whom he leased for silver mining, likely inherited from his father Niceratus.[25] The families of these demagogues were not completely undistinguished: Cleon's father, Cleanetus, performed a liturgy at the Dionysia of 460/459; Cleophon's father, Cleipiddes, was a στρατηγός (*strategos*, "general") in 428 and candidate for ostracism in the 440s; and Cleon, Hyperbolus, and Cleophon are held, at least by some, as being on a high social level.[26] However, being just two generations removed from common social status likely provided different outlooks than those who were from long-term elite families, and certainly affected their public reception.

This is a distinct change in demographics from politicians of the two centuries before. As Rhodes (1981: 344–5 *ad* [*Ath. Pol.*] 28.1) notes, all eleven of the προστάται τοῦ δήμου (*prostatai tou demou*, "heads of the people") from Solon to Pericles that pseudo-Aristotle includes at [*Ath. Pol.*] 28.1–2 were "of the great families of the archaic period or were capable of forming alliances with those families." Exceptions were Themistocles, who was a lesser aristocrat, and Ephialtes, whose background is unknown. Starting with Cleon's generation, though, none of the five *prostatai* listed from the rest of the fifth century is elite, and Rhodes (ibid.) adds that the only two prominent politicians at all from that period who were of the old aristocracy are Alcibiades and Critias. Davies (1981: 114–27) contrasts this evolution of politicians' class status with the consistency of the class status of *strategoi,* who maintain roughly the same predominant percentage of aristocrats from the beginning of the fifth century to the end of the fourth (156–66), but who also rarely ventured into domestic political debate after 429.[27]

Public efforts to malign demagogues' family backgrounds (real or rumored) and the businesses they ran may actually have increased the common majority's sense of attachment to them. Common tactics by comic poets and orators were to portray the demagogues' parents not just as non-elite, but as either foreigners or slaves; to bring attention to the lines of work in which the demagogues earned their fortunes; and to conflate the demagogues with the foreign enslaved people who were the main means of production.[28] Cleon, whose (and whose father's) tannery made a fortune off of the labor of enslaved people, appears in the *Knights* as a Paphlagonian slave—either implying Paphlagonian ancestry through his mother, or making it seem as though he is interchangeable with the enslaved people who did his work—and is repeatedly referred to as a tanner himself.[29] Hyperbolus, whose family's slave-labored lamp factory propelled them from poverty to considerable wealth, is regularly associated with lamps, and is portrayed in various sources as a common laborer and a foreigner; his father as well is alleged to be a public slave, and his mother is portrayed as an alien, a drunk, a prostitute, a breadseller, and a moneylender.[30] Cleophon, whose father used enslaved people to man the lyre factory that made the family rich, is repeatedly labeled a Thracian and a person of low birth, and both of his parents are called Thracians as well.[31] Nearly all such criticisms mocked them for being, in many ways (other than their likely exaggerated foreignness), like the large majority of the Athenian people, which likely increased sympathy between common Athenians and the demagogues, on which I will elaborate below.[32]

C. *Philia* through Gratitude or Persuasion? Previous Views and Complications of Reasons for Demagogues' Success

How this change of demographics among the *prostatai* might have come about so abruptly, and how these non-aristocratic politicians managed to maintain their influence throughout the Peloponnesian War, are subjects of some dispute. There are certain skills and methods of demagogues that the historical record either highlights or suggests which prior scholars have argued explain their success. While those factors are likely consequential to an extent, they also have limits, but in several cases tie into this book's thesis about the value of *philia* to the demagogues' efforts.

1. Philia *through Gratitude for Practical Skills and Populist Approaches*

Part of the demagogues' appeal has been attributed to their utilitarian skills and foci. First, Andrewes (1962: 83–4) argues that the new politicians' business acumen, learned from their own and their fathers' commercial endeavors, prepared them to manage Athens' expanding empire.[33] Kallet-Marx (1994: 237) underscores that they were at least *perceived* this way. He argues that the fact that they regularly spoke in the *ekklesia*, sometimes about finances, likely led people to attribute expertise on the topic to Cleon and others like him, whether or not they actually had it. Hershkowitz (2018: 118–63), however, points out that our primary sources highlight neither particular financial savvy in these demagogues nor public recognition of this quality in them. The function of whatever skill they might have had to offer in this area might have been limited, in any case. Thompson (1981) asserts that Athenian economics and income sources, on a macro scale, were quite simple (156); there do not appear to have been precise budgets requiring careful forethought (157–8); and cost projections were likely to be vastly imprecise (158). Whether or not their business experiences genuinely gave them an edge as financial guides for the city, those experiences may have contributed to their perception by at least some citizens as pragmatic leaders, whose skills and initiative managed to vault them into wealth. In this way, they may have been perceived as relatable to the majority of Athenians: their success could be seen as a function of traits that they developed, which others, in turn, might see themselves as able to develop.

Along those same pragmatic lines, demagogic politicians are credited with bringing to pass tangible politically negotiated benefits for their main supporters, with personal components tied to those initiatives. The Old Oligarch says the masses' attachment to demagogues was based on demagogues being "useful" (ἐπιτηδείους) and "profitable" (συμφόρους) to them (2.19). Indeed, records of the political actions of two of the most notorious demagogues strongly suggest their financial dedication to the poor, at the expense of the rich. Cleon raised jury pay from two to three obols per day, making jury service a more appealing option for the poor.[34] He helped fund initiatives of this sort with an assault on the resources of the wealthy. He worked to levy a property tax against the rich to help pay for the war, the first time such a domestic tax was put in place.[35] And he rejected public support for the cavalry, which was composed of citizens wealthy enough to own their own horses.[36] While there are no records of Hyperbolus' specific policies, Plutarch's disparaging comment (*Alc.* 13.5) that "the masses often used him when they were intent on besmirching or extorting respectable people" (ἐχρῆτο δ' αὐτῷ πολλάκις ὁ δῆμος ἐπιθυμῶν προπηλακίζειν τοὺς ἐν ἀξιώματι καὶ συκοφαντεῖν) indicates that the commons felt they could count on him to work on their behalf against the wealthy.[37] Finally, Cleophon, considered the greatest demagogue of his time (Diod. Sic. 13.53.2), introduced the διωβελία (*diobelia*), a two-obol daily payment to all Athenians that was the equivalent of a day's meal money for four, which the poor could use far more than the rich.[38] Aristophanes parodies such appeals to common people's material self-interest in his portrayal in *Knights* of the very tangible offers that Paphlagon (who represents Cleon) and the Sausage-Seller (who likely represents one of a few other demagogues) make to try to win over Demos, who personifies the non-elite Athenian majority (*Eq.* 1100–6, 1164–99; cf. *Vesp.* 716–18).[39] That depiction, sarcastic as it is, characterizes this successful direction of public funds to common Athenians as reflecting a personal dimension of the relationship between demagogues and the masses.

2. Philia *through Persuasion: Oratory as a Means of Personal Connection*

This personal element is further apparent in the demagogues' approach to oratory, to which their success, particularly with common Athenians, is also widely attributed. Aristotle (*Pol.* 1305a12–13), for example, claims that demagogues' rhetorical abilities were at the core of their leadership of the *demos*.[40] And the fact that the term ῥήτωρ (*rhetor,*"orator") became synonymous with "politician" during the last third of the fifth century, the time when demagogues made their mark on Athenian politics, implies that speech in the *ekklesia* and *boule* must at least have been an important component of their rise to power.[41]

While they were obviously not the first or only effective speakers in Athens, the manner on the speaker's platform of both Cleon and Cleophon was marked by dramatics that appeared designed to draw attention to themselves as individuals, rather than merely as speakers on behalf of particular issues or groups.[42] Cleon made his mark through a flamboyant, gesticulating speaking style and memorably confident turns of phrase, such as his dismissal of the assembly, possibly after he had taken significant part in the capture and imprisonment of 292 Spartans at the battle of Sphacteria, with the claim that he "needed to entertain some foreign guests" (ξένους ἑστιᾶν μέλλοντα, Theopomp. *FGrH* 115 F 92.6), a line that the gathered Athenians apparently found enormously clever (Plut. *Nic.* 7.7, *Mor.* 799d).[43] Cleophon is renowned for a similarly grand gesture, appearing in full armor to argue against peace negotiations with Sparta.[44] Other politicians of the time as well, some of whom were referred to as demagogues, also earned nicknames that indicate that audiences were noticing them as individuals with personalities, not just as deliverers of political points of view.[45]

Beyond the histrionics, magnetism, and eloquence of individual speakers, though, rhetoric *always* has a highly personal, emotional component to it, and demagogues seem to have thrived in part through mastering that aspect of the art. As Aristotle claims in his *Rhetoric*, two of the three components in effective rhetoric have nothing to do with the merits of the argument, but rather how the speaker's presentation makes the audience *feel* about supporting it: the speaker's portrayed character (ἦθος, *ethos*: 1356a4–13, 1378a6–19), and the emotions the speaker stirs in the audience (πάθη, *pathe*: 1356a14–16, 1378a19–1388b30).[46]

This emotional component is apparent in the regular use of the term πιθανός (*pithanos*) to capture common Athenians' impression of demagogues.[47] Meaning "persuasive" or "credible," it most often refers, prior to the Peloponnesian War, to the believability of stories for which there is no independent verification. Herodotus, for example, uses the term on several occasions to refer to stories as believable.[48] Euripides, as well, uses *pithanos* in *Thyestes* to refer to falsehoods that appear credible and in *Antiope* to refer to arguments that are persuasive.[49]

But when it applies to people or their actions, as it does in works produced during the Peloponnesian War, it is always to individuals whose personal standings do not give them immediate credibility, and who rely on the plausibility of their arguments and presentations of themselves to win over audiences.[50] On all but a few occasions, those individuals are either politicians widely identified as demagogues or thin dramatic glosses of demagogues. Notably, Thucydides twice describes Cleon as being πιθανώτατος (*pithanotatos*, "supremely credible"), in both cases to common Athenians. At 3.36.6, Thucydides calls him τῷ τε δήμῳ ... ἐν τῷ τότε <u>πιθανώτατος</u>, "the <u>most persuasive</u> to the people at the time," and at 4.21.3, he is ἀνὴρ δημαγωγὸς κατ' ἐκεῖνον τὸν χρόνον ὢν καὶ τῷ πλήθει <u>πιθανώτατος</u> ("a demagogic man of that time, and <u>most persuasive</u> to the masses," 4.21.3).[51] Thucydides employs the same term to describe Athenagoras, a Syracusan whom Thucydides labels *demou . . . prostates* ("a head of the people"): ἦν ... ἐν τῷ παρόντι <u>πιθανώτατος</u> τοῖς πολλοῖς ("he was, in that time, <u>most persuasive</u> to the many," 6.35.2).[52] The Sausage-Seller in *Knights* uses *pithanotat'* to describe the things Paphlagon (representing Cleon) was saying to the *boule* (628–9).[53] And Euripides uses *pithanos* in *Orestes* to describe the orator Tyndareus hires, who since antiquity has been thought to reflect Cleophon or other contemporaneous demagogues.[54] As summed up by Hershkowitz (2018: 21), the term may be "suggestive of partisan connotations"—in this case, partisanship of elite authors against the masses and their demagogic leaders.

Persuasiveness, in itself, is not a quality that is often attributed to non-demagogic speakers during this time frame. Persuasion (Πείθω, *Peitho*), as a concept, appears frequently in literature of the time and prior, and people persuade (πείθω, *peitho*) others extensively throughout extant Greek literature, but people *being* persuasive (*pithanos*) is not seen prior to the rise of the demagogues. When a well-established orator such as Pericles is praised for his persuasiveness, it is in terms of ability to speak; characters in Eupolis' *Demoi* (fr. 102 KA) say that he was "best in speaking" (κράτιστος . . . λέγειν) and that he "defeated the orators in speaking" (ᾖρει λέγων τοὺς ῥητόρας).[55]

Someone's act of persuading, though, seems to be predicated on being seen as credible. People from well-established families appear to have received that distinction automatically. While other politicians of more prestigious provenance were certainly persuasive in speeches they delivered, the reputations of their families provided them instantly with the recognition and credibility that a less-known figure would not have. Moreover, concentrated blocs in the audience of both the personal friends and enemies of elite speakers often did much to affect the full audiences' senses of the effectiveness of speeches and the credibility of speakers; biased audience members' conspicuous reactions impacted how unbiased ones received speakers and speeches.[56]

When others, who did not have distinguished family backgrounds to lend them that credibility, came to take a bigger part in public discourse, though, it seems that they needed a precise adjective to validate them. While *pithanos* implies false persuasion in many cases, it appears also to suggest the ability to facilitate persuasion by striking an audience as being worthy of personal trust.[57]

For the demagogues, credibility, and the success that depended on it, were determined in large part through their performances in front of audiences; for them, success was built on being *pithanos*. As people who made a name for themselves to a great extent because of their ability as speakers, the demagogues needed to possess the sort of dexterity in that arena not just to persuade the majority of the population to follow their lead, but to do so because their self-presentation made them seem deserving of the audience's trust, despite not deriving from families that had earned such trust over generations, as will be discussed in Chapter 3.

A sense of such trust is implicit in even hostile accounts of the interchange between demagogues and lower-class Athenians. While, in passages noted earlier, Thucydides derisively claims that demagogues "even offered the conduct of affairs to the whim of the people" (2.65.10), and Plutarch disparagingly says of Hyperbolus (*Alc.* 13.5), "the masses often used him when they were intent on besmirching or extorting respectable people," the model they imply is symbiotic: demagogues had their supporters in mind, and because they used their skills to advance those supporters' interests, they earned the loyalty of those people on future issues.[58] Thucydides, as cited in Chapter 1, Section III, frames this sort of politics as "being led" by the people, as opposed to what Pericles supposedly did, which was to "direct" and "lead" them (κατεῖχε τὸ πλῆθος ἐλευθέρως, καὶ οὐκ ἤγετο μᾶλλον ὑπ' αὐτοῦ ἢ αὐτὸς ἦγε, 2.65.8). In the model Thucydides presents, politics is a zero-sum game, with leader and led each vying for a finite quantity of influence. For the demagogues, though, there appears to have been no such divisive outlook, but rather an effort to make their constituents feel as though they, along with the demagogues themselves, were all *part* of a common political process built on understanding of and trust in one another, rather than competitors for a limited amount of power within the process. This is one of the ways through which the *demos* assumed the role of *polis* for the demagogues, while also, as will be explained later, acting as these demagogues' *philoi*.

III. *Philia* through Common Membership in a Maligned Ingroup: Aristocratic Ridicule Binding Demagogues and the *Demos*

Whatever the reasons that these demagogues moved into and maintained power, their public influence clearly touched a nerve among the Athenian elite. Comic and tragic playwrights, historiographers, pamphleteers, philosophers, and other intellectuals, producing work both contemporaneous to and after the periods of influence of individual demagogues, harshly condemned demagogues in general, demagogues they specifically named, and the masses to whom those demagogues appealed, for their impact on the Athenians' well-being. All of that abuse that the champions of the underclasses absorbed—and that the members of the underclasses themselves did as well, either directly or indirectly—quite possibly had the reverse of its intended effect. Rather than undermining the demagogues' popular support, it may have led many common Athenians to see themselves as part of an ingroup with demagogues—all of them victims of the disdain of an elite outgroup—and to underscore loyalty between them.[59]

A. Building an Ingroup through Ridicule of Demagogues and the Masses Together

One of the ways in which beneficial ingroup connections between demagogues and the masses could have been built is through the disparagement that the groups received together in popular media. In written work and dramatic performances from the mid-420s until close to the end of the fifth century, a message communicated about both contemporaneous and prior demagogues was that their impact, as a group, was wholly deleterious, that the shift of influence to the *demos* and away from the elite was largely to blame for this impact, and that the commonness of the demagogues themselves was largely what made the demagogues' efforts so destructive. This sort of ingroup development through unifying criticism may also have solidified the bond that common Athenians felt with demagogues not just when they were being disparaged together, but when the demagogues were being maligned individually, because of their implied representation of their supporters.

The most elaborate of the extant joint criticisms is in the demagogic Paphlagon and Sausage-Seller's courtship of the personified Demos in *Knights*, to which I will give more attention in Chapter 3. Leadership of Demos is described as "no longer for an educated or refined man" (οὐ πρὸς μουσικοῦ / ἔτ' ἐστὶν ἀνδρὸς οὐδὲ χρηστοῦ, 191–2), which insults common Athenians' ability to find well-qualified leaders.[60] It is a further insult that the qualities that *are* seen as positive in Demos' eyes are those that make the leader typical of common Athenians: humble birth, an unpleasant voice, and a manner suiting the marketplace (217–18).⁶¹ At the end of a play full of little other than disparagement of Cleon's proxy, Demos' supposed triumph is his disavowal of what is portrayed as his previous foolishness (1339–55) after Sausage-Seller has boiled him down and transformed him "from ugly to handsome" (καλὸν ἐξ αἰσχροῦ, 1321). Generally, people tend not to be swayed away from their allegiance to leaders by being told that they are foolish for supporting such leaders, and particularly when the foolishness is based on their favored leaders' supposedly deficient qualities being like their own; they are more likely to redouble their feelings of connection to those leaders, which may help to explain Cleon's election as general of his tribe not long after this play was first performed.⁶²

Around the same time, the Old Oligarch's *Athenian Constitution* also linked together criticism for both demagogues and their common followers. He claims that the *demos* favors politicians who are useful (ἐπιτηδείους) and profitable (συμφόρους) to them, as noted in Chapter 1, even though such politicians are πονηροί (*poneroi*, which can be read as "worthless" or as code for "lower-class"), unlike the better-qualified χρηστοί (*khrestoi*, "valuable" or "elite") ones that they disdain (2.19).⁶³ As in *Knights*, there is the disparaging contention that common Athenians support politicians not who are best for the city, but who are like them and tend to them—those with whom they perceive that they share an ingroup.⁶⁴ Isocrates (8.122–3), several decades into the fourth century, underlines the perceived effectiveness of *khrestoi* relative to *poneroi* when he claims that it was the former, who were far better suited for leadership in the first place, who guided Athens out of both of its oligarchic revolutions, not the latter, who originally brought Athens to civic upheaval.⁶⁵

Thucydides attributes Athens' military mistakes during the Peloponnesian War after Pericles' death to governmental dynamics between the *demos* and those who aimed to gain leadership over it (2.65.10–11).⁶⁶ He specifically links the failure of the Sicilian Expedition to both groups: while he blames demagogic leaders' attacks against one another in an effort to gain leadership over the common people (κατὰ τὰς ἰδίας διαβολὰς περὶ τῆς τοῦ δήμου προστασίας) as the cause of the failure, members of the *demos* had to be willing participants in the demagogues' competition and its consequences. While, when word of the Sicilian Expedition's disastrous outcome reached Athens, the citizenry tried to blame "the orators" (τῶν ῥητόρων) for misleading them (8.1.4–5), Thucydides notes the voters' culpability (8.1.5–6), tying the majority of citizens to the mistakes that he earlier attributed to demagogues.[67]

Aristophanes' *Frogs* (produced in 405 BCE) similarly overlaps disparagement of demagogues and the masses in a manner that likely underscored ingroup feelings between them.[68] At *Frogs* 718–37, the leader states that the city deals with the καλοί κἀγαθοί (*kaloi k'agathoi*, "the beautiful and good," a term for elites) as it does with its silver and gold unalloyed coinage, putting them both aside in favor of inferior products. In political terms, as the chorus leader elaborates in that same speech, this means granting political power to aliens, redheads, and lowlifes from lowlife families (ξένοις καὶ πυρρίαις/καὶ πονηροῖς κἀκ πονηρῶν, 730–1), while the people with good pedigrees and traditional educations are neglected (οὓς μὲν ἴσμεν εὐγενεῖς καὶ σώφρονας / ἄνδρας ὄντας . . . καὶ τραφέντας ἐν παλαίστραις καὶ χοροῖς καὶ μουσικῇ,/προυσελοῦμεν, 727–30).[69] The chorus leader thinks it is not too late to turn things around, though: with a concerted effort toward giving political responsibility to wellborn individuals (εὐγενεῖς, 727), either Athenians' fortunes would turn, or at least they would know they had given their best (734– 7).[70]

B. Extension of Ridicule of Individual Demagogues to the Common Ingroup

Once ingroup identity has been established, attacks on individuals within the group—particularly highest-status ones—tend to cultivate a further sense of protective attachment and bond from the rest of the group.[71] Thus the extent to which a range of politicians commonly identified as demagogues, including Cleon and Hyperbolus, were maligned in public media, often in ways that implicated common Athenians as well, likely furthered the feeling of unity of their common supporters with them. Much of the extant maligning that demagogic figures endured has already been covered or will be in chapters to come, and much more appears in a host of plays known as "demagogue comedies," of which little remains other than some of Aristophanes' plays.[72] As examples of the sorts of criticism of named demagogues that was circulating— either performed as the targeted individuals looked on, or published some years after their deaths, but reflecting judgments circulating as the demagogues were operating—I will make use of comedy and Thucydides. The focus in this examination of these two prominent demagogues' portrayals will be on ways in which their supporters, or supporters of later politicians who operated like these two, would have had reason to feel that the attacks against the demagogues were also attacks against their ingroup. For rhetorical fluidity, I will handle Hyperbolus first, since there is less extant material on him.

A main line of attack that Thucydides and others leveled against Hyperbolus is that he was undeserving of the prestige of the ostracism he faced, which, in turn, is a diminution of the judgment of the Athenian majority.[73] Thucydides (8.73.3) downplays Hyperbolus' ostracism as a function not of any greatness he shared with other victims of ostracism such as Aristides, Cimon, and Thucydides son of Melesias, but "because of his base stature and disgracefulness to the city" (διὰ πονηρίαν καὶ αἰσχύνην τῆς πόλεως).[74] Plato Comicus (fr. 203 KA=187 K, cited in Plut. *Nic.* 11.6 and *Alc.* 13.5) also asserts that Hyperbolus was not of the proper sort to be ostracized.

Yet Hyperbolus is mentioned repeatedly in comedies, oratory, and inscriptions from before 426 and even after his ostracism in 416 or 415, suggesting that he made a big impact on the Athenian civic scene.[75] The fact that Alcibiades and Nicias had to assemble a broad aristocratic coalition to rid themselves of Hyperbolus by this most prestigious of punishments (*Nic.* 11.4, *Alc.* 13.4) further shows that, whatever Hyperbolus' reputation among historical authors, he obviously wielded considerable political power.[76] The portrayed attenuation of Hyperbolus' lofty status in Athens as a whole, and particularly among common Athenians, as laid out in the previous paragraph, likely led to a greater sense of attachment to him of the common Athenians whose interests he was noted as having served.

While Cleon was a lightning rod for a range of different factors, two of them were also particular assaults on the judgment of his ingroup: his ability to lead an army, and his suitability to guide Athenian civic decisions.[77] *Knights* repeatedly disparages his military leadership at Sphacteria, including attributions to Demosthenes of credit for the victory there (54–7, 74–6, 355, 392–4, 1005, 1054–60, 1067–72, 1200–5).[78] These cuts against him as a military leader implicitly attempt to sway the judgment of his tribesmen, who would soon be voting for him for *strategos*, and they also attempt to alter the perception of reality of his many supporters, for whom his surprising victory at Sphacteria was a mark of pride.[79]

Thucydides' communication of a similar sense of Cleon's military incompetence, along with his deficiency as a political leader, could have further rallied ingroup support, not necessarily around him (since he was dead by the time Thucydides' work was widely circulated), but around those following in the demagogues' populist tradition. The historian repeatedly (and probably unfairly) portrays him not just as belligerent, self-interested, deceitful, and defamatory as a politician, but also inadequate and cowardly as a general, often in contrast to those he was leading in battle, or those whom he should have been defeating there.[80]

The introduction Thucydides gives Cleon (which is also mentioned earlier) before the demagogue delivers his only direct speech of the *History* sets the tone for Thucydides' portrayal of him in the rest of the work, and it does not flatter the many who supported him: "Cleon, the son of Cleaenetus, who carried the motion the previous day to execute the Mytileneans, [was] the most violent (βιαιότατος) of the citizens in respect to other things as well, and by far the most persuasive (πιθανώτατος) to the common people" (3.36.6).[81] This introduction is generally regarded as the most hostile of those of all the major characters.[82] First, Cleon's characterization as superlatively persuasive to the *demos* is not a compliment either to him or the *demos*, considering Thucydides' sense of the problems that resulted when the masses began to play a bigger role in determining civic policy (cf. 2.65.10–11), as discussed above, in Section III.A.[83] The historian's attention to Cleon's violent tendencies also underlines the draconian attitude he has Cleon expressing on the previous day and in the speech to come, that all Mytilenean men should be killed, and all women and children enslaved (3.36.1–3, 3.37–40).[84] Furthermore, the fact that Thucydides defines him, in this context, by these two traits suggests that whatever authority Cleon has is misplaced. He is both violent and persuasive, but apparently too much of one and not enough of the other. The fact that his harsh stance against the Mytileneans is overturned on the day after it passed indicates that he is not persuasive enough to outweigh the assembled citizens' sense, in retrospect, that his was an excessively cruel solution (3.36.4). This introduction, then, highlights the demagogue's first significant political loss and the fact that the common people whom he aims to persuade outstrip him in their moral judgment.

In his portrayals of Cleon's unexpected first military victory at Pylos, Thucydides is careful to make him first look foolish and cowardly, an amateur who only once exceeded potential expectations in battle due to assistance from a more competent colleague, which is, again, an insult to the many who supported him. Thucydides initially shows Cleon drawing an unreasonably hard line with Spartan envoys, who have come calling for a treaty to release more than four hundred of their soldiers from a blockade at Sphacteria (4.20–2).[85] Even though Thucydides again notes that he was "the most persuasive (πιθανώτατος) to the mob at that time" (κατ᾽ ἐκεῖνον τὸν χρόνον ὢν καὶ τῷ πλήθει πιθανώτατος, 4.21.3; cf. 3.36.6), the historian specifies that Cleon's belligerent stance to keep pressure on the besieged Spartans became increasingly unpopular in Athens as the siege grew more difficult to maintain (27.1–2). Cleon challenged the Athenians to attack Pylos with full vigor, a proposal that Thucydides makes clear was not strategic, but rather designed to overshadow the demagogue's mistake (27.3–5).[86] He led the force that eventually took the stronghold at Sphacteria, but again Thucydides is careful to undercut Cleon, emphasizing in advance of the victory that, though Cleon had boasted of his ability to resolve the problem in Pylos (4.27.5), he was afraid to follow through on his boast when the Athenians called him to account for it (4.28.1–3).[87] Thucydides further notes that the sensible (σώφρονες) Athenians were pleased when Cleon was awarded the generalship: it meant that Cleon would either come back victorious or dead, both appealing prospects to them (4.28.5).

Additionally, Thucydides uses the battle of Amphipolis in 422 to contrast Cleon's inadequacy for a role of leadership with that of his Spartan opponent. Having given little notice to several victories Cleon earned on the way to Amphipolis, and perhaps having ignored others, Thucydides provides abundant detail of Cleon's supposed failings in his last, mortal battle.[88] He has Cleon moving his army from Eion to Amphipolis in full view of Brasidas, a foolishly overconfident action that the more seasoned Spartan general expected from him (5.6.3). The historian focuses next on the Athenian soldiers' disdain for their general, having them compare the daring and skill of Brasidas with Cleon's ignorance and effeminacy (ἀνεπιστημοσύνης καὶ μαλακίας, 5.7.2). The following section (5.7.3–8.4) contrasts Brasidas' strategic caution (mainly due to his fear of the top-notch Athenian troops, not—it is implied—Cleon's skill as a general, 5.8.2) with Cleon's naive self-assurance. Soon thereafter, Cleon's supposedly sloppy retreat strategy gives Brasidas an opening for attack that he cannot resist, catching the Athenians in disarray (5.10.4–8).

While Thucydides separates Cleon's performance from that of his soldiers, the demagogue's portrayed failures are still a function of the majority vote that got him his position. The historian frames his depiction of Cleon's death to contrast the general's cowardice and disorganization with the courage and composure of both the Athenians under his command and of Brasidas. Cleon's death is noted in only one short clause embedded in a long antithetical sentence (5.10.9): "Cleon, on the one hand, since from the start he had no intention of holding his ground, began to run but was overtaken and killed by a Myrcinian peltast" (ὁ μὲν Κλέων, ὡς τὸ πρῶτον οὐ διενοεῖτο μένειν, εὐθὺς φεύγων καὶ καταληφθεὶς ὑπὸ Μυρκινίου πελταστοῦ ἀποθνῄσκει).[89] Framing this clause about his death in flight are two others highlighting the contrasting poise and fortitude of his subordinates. First, an introductory statement sets the general scene: "While the right flank of the Athenians made a better stand ..." (τὸ δὲ δεξιὸν τῶν Ἀθηναίων ἔμενέ τε μᾶλλον ...). Then, a second δέ clause provides the antithesis to Cleon's actions:

> οἱ δὲ αὐτοῦ ξυστραφέντες ὁπλῖται ἐπὶ τὸν λόφον τόν τε Κλεαρίδαν ἠμύνοντο καὶ δὶς ἢ τρὶς προσβαλόντα, καὶ οὐ πρότερον ἐνέδοσαν πρὶν ἥ τε Μυρκινία καὶ ἡ Χαλκιδικὴ ἵππος καὶ οἱ πελτασταὶ περιστάντες καὶ ἐσακοντίζοντες αὐτοὺς ἔτρεψαν.

> [H]is hoplites, on the other hand, having formed in close order, repelled Clearidas' attacks two or three times, and did not finally give in until the Myrcinian and Chalcidian cavalry surrounded them and the peltasts routed them by pelting them with javelins.

The impression once again is that Cleon was a step below his subordinates in his actions in battle, and inconsequential to the battle's outcome: Thucydides does not even dignify Cleon's death with its own sentence, and his troops do not seem to notice his absence.[90] In contrast, Thucydides gives Brasidas' death and the honors showered upon him roughly a half-page of coverage (5.10.11–11.1). Once again, the impression is that Cleon was out of his element as a general, that he was a lesser commander than his own troops were, and that he was far inferior to the real general on the Spartan side.[91] Lafargue (2013: 71–81), however, points out a variety of circumstantial factors that made this a difficult battle to win, and the fact that a skilled enemy commander was killed implies a much more successful battle strategy and execution than Thucydides lets on.

Moreover, these harsh portrayals of Cleon contrast with other indications of the Athenian majority's attachment to Cleon and their recognition of the value of his skills. Some months after his victory at Sphacteria that Thucydides sought to undermine, Cleon was elected general of his tribe, and thus was entrusted by people who knew him best to head future military engagements. And for all of his portrayed incompetence at Amphipolis, he was leading troops at that battle because his tribe had elected him general a second time.[92] There was clearly loyalty that Cleon had inspired in people closest to him, and it was not diminished, and may well have been increased, by the public ridicule he faced from elites like Aristophanes and Thucydides.[93]

IV. Conclusion: Leadership by Winning over the *Demos* as *Philoi*

The main innovation in leadership style that the political successors of Pericles—i.e., Cleon and others later labeled "demagogues"—made was to operate toward the mass of common Athenians as though they were the demagogues' particular focus, in the way that elite personal *philoi* were to traditionally oriented politicians, and that the *polis* as a whole previously was to more democratically leaning statesmen. There were certain gestures in speeches made and public actions taken by Cleon, in particular, that communicated that his interests and allegiances lay not just with the well-being of the *polis* as a whole, but with the humble *demos* more specifically. The business acumen and rhetorical skill of demagogues may have helped them win the confidence of people who were unaware of them previously because of their undistinguished families. And the comparatively modest family backgrounds of most of those labeled demagogues, which were raised repeatedly in comedy and oratory, may have been both the spur to the demagogues' expressed allegiance with the *demos* and a critical factor that made it seem likely to members of the *demos* that demagogues' expressed affinity for them was legitimate, that they should conceive of themselves as members of an "ingroup" in common. Once that connection was established, public criticism of both demagogues and the *demos* likely only reinforced the protective quality that friend-like connection.

These factors lay the groundwork for an additional one that seems even more to set the demagogues apart from prior politicians in their styles of ingratiation, and that establish them as early precursors of modern democratic politicians. Chapter 3 will discuss demagogues' development of more intentional and individualized personal connections as a critical means of winning over and retaining supporters, and modern political science validates the efficacy of such feelings when a politician is being maligned by adversaries. As Johnson (2022) puts it, "once voters know a candidate, they are less likely to believe the worst of them," such as in hyperbolic modern attack ads, or in the case of classical Athens, against hyperbolic presentations in comedy or historiography. And such "knowing" cannot be felt from a distance; developing relationships based, as much as possible, on face-to-face contact, provide, as Michigan State Representative Darrin Camilleri puts it in the same article, "a shield" against political attack.

3

The Sociology of Making Individual
Philoi among the Masses

I. Introduction

There is a considerable difference between feelings of *philia* that arise from members of a group for an individual, and feelings of *philia* between one individual and another. That latter sort of *philia* is one in which scholars commonly claim that demagogues did not participate, since they are often seen as essentially self-interested manipulators who "purchased loyalty with food and wages and stole from the demos."[1] Yet application of a few relevant sociological principles to Aristophanes' *Knights*, Euripides' *Hecuba*, and several other classical sources seems to suggest that Cleon and other demagogic types of politicians were aiming to win over not just the *demos* as a whole as a *philos*, but the individuals comprising that group as particular *philoi*.

If, as I propose, the public persona that Cleon put forward was that of a *philos* not just to the *demos* as a whole, but to individual members of that group, a relevant question is why any of these people would feasibly conceive of themselves as his *actual* friends, and not just beneficiaries of his friend-like services. The prior chapter follows the model of Connor (1971) in taking Cleon and other demagogues as *philoi* of the *demos*, focusing almost entirely on the traits, behaviors, and circumstances that would make them positively received and relatable enough to common Athenians as a group that they could seem to be playing friendly roles relative to those Athenians. However, such a model leaves out the reciprocal personal connection that is critical to *philia*, even at its most pragmatic. While Cleon (or other demagogues who followed him) might conceivably have envisioned the mass as a single, collective *philos*, if individuals in the group to which he was appealing did not feel a sense of personal connection to him, but rather supported him only out of a sense of self-interest, then the model would more accurately be *kolakeia* ("flattery"), rather than *philia*, which will be explained more in Section III of this chapter.

Yet evidence suggests that the *philia* model, implying a reciprocal sense of personal connection that goes well beyond mere rhetoric and imagery, is accurate. *Knights*, primarily, along with *Hecuba* and other extant Peloponnesian War-era sources, implies that Cleon, and likely others following his lead, took deliberate, conspicuous steps to cultivate a sense of friendship between himself and *individual* common Athenians, and application of contemporary approaches to friendship development suggests that those steps would have been effective. Furthermore, certain personal commonalities, such as those documented in Chapter 2, which he and the other demagogues of the time shared with the mass of Athenians, made the prospect of a sense of friendship between demagogues and individuals feasible, despite their considerable differences in wealth and status. Individual ties developed by a demagogue to even a portion of the *demos* likely led others to feel similar links, whether they actually had a direct relationship with the demagogue or not. In this way, it was possible for Cleon and other demagogues to cultivate a sense of *philia* with lower-class Athenians not as indistinguishable members of a political bloc, but rather as individuals who chose to support the demagogues based on a feeling of personal friendship, which they happened to share with thousands of others like them. This, then, could lead acts taken on the level of civic politics to come to resonate with individual common Athenians as reflections of actions of individual friendship.

II. The Propinquity Effect in Friendship Development and Athenian Politics

One of the techniques that Cleon seems to have employed to win friends among common Athenians was simply to be physically close to a considerable number of individuals in that group, as will be detailed more below. While intentional proximity is an ages-old practice for anyone to build a sense of attachment with anyone else, Cleon appears to be the first to use it in a deliberate fashion to build a political bloc among the masses.

The physical proximity between people is one of the markers of the extent of the relationship they feel they have with one another: those whom people let closest to themselves are individuals who, at root, they feel will not physically harm them, the most critical distinction between a *philos* and an *ekhthros* (enemy). When Alcibiades, for example, returned to Athens from exile in 407 BCE, concerned that he would face resistance, he physically surrounded himself with family members (οἰκείους) and friends (φίλους), who were prepared to repel anyone who tried to touch (ἅπτοιτο) him when he disembarked from his ship (Xen. *Hell.* 1.4.18–19).[2] Outside of a wish for safety, people tend to have physically closest to them those with whom they feel most personally comfortable, whether because of common backgrounds, common interests, or personal chemistry on some level.

Proximity not only reflects friendship, but can also generate it. Numerous studies of friendship development in contemporary sociology show that physical closeness between people, by chance or design, is a critical component of their likelihood of developing feelings of friendship. The first major work on the subject of what its authors call the "propinquity effect" found that repeated exposure in daily life is a better predictor of a sense of friendship between people than other commonalities between them (Festinger, Schachter, and Back 1950). Even limited contact can greatly promote such feelings. Homans' (1950) study on group building reached a similar conclusion: "the more frequent the interaction between people, the stronger in general their sentiments of liking or affection for one another" (444). Smith and Zipp (1983: 73) confirmed previous authors' findings in their own study: "[P]airs are likelier to develop acquaintanceships or friendships through neighborly experiences rather than on the basis of shared backgrounds and related common interests."[3] Current political science backs up the political value of propinquity; politicians who speak face to face with individual voters, such as in door-to-door outreach and through making themselves available in public places for anyone to access them, see that practice as building loyal relationships that serve them well for years, even decades.[4]

Two anecdotes of actions from the fifth century (recorded by authors in the fourth) indicate that proximity in Athenian culture, too, was seen as a way of building feelings of personal connection between people who would otherwise not have been friends. First, when the wealthy Crito wished to have the benefit of the impoverished Archedemus' skill as an orator on Crito's behalf, he did not stop with just giving Archedemus gifts of produce from his farm (Xen. *Mem.* 2.9.4); he also invited Archedemus to join him for sacrifices, then encouraged Archedemus' use of Crito's home as a refuge (2.9.4–5).[5] Using this technique of allowing Archedemus near him, even into his home, Crito made Archedemus feel like a *philos*, and thus Crito's calling Archedemus as much (2.9.8) felt sincere. Crito was thus able to benefit from Archedemus' advocacy on his behalf, while making Archedemus feel the prestige of being more than just a hired hand. Archedemus, in turn, agreed to help others of Crito's friends who needed a skilled speaker (2.9.7).[6]

Cimon, several decades before Cleon, appears to have employed this sort of approach in the political realm as well, though in a somewhat different manner, and not on the apparent scale of Cleon's effort. He is famed for his generosity to those less fortunate than he (following the example of Pisistratus), doing things such as leaving open his fields for anyone to harvest, and giving food, clothing, and money to those who needed it.[7] Pseudo-Aristotle treats this behavior as no different from Pericles' use of public funds for the benefit of the poor, both of which actions, he thinks, were done for their political benefit ([*Ath. Pol.*] 27.4). Connor (1971) includes this sort of behavior as fitting in with what he calls "the politics of largess," practiced also by Nicias and Alcibiades during the Peloponnesian War, in which "generosity to city and to citizen wins the gratitude of its beneficiaries and is converted into political support" (21–2).[8]

Yet Cimon seems to have realized a particular benefit in combining personal contact with that material liberality. First of all, while Pisistratus apparently stopped at leaving his fields open to anyone who needed food from them, Theopompus specifies that Cimon opened the private space of his home to all people (τὴν οἰκίαν παρεῖχε κοινὴν ἅπασι, *FGrH* 115 F 89.6–7), and the poor accepted the offer (7–9), in the same way that Archedemus did Crito's invitations to his home.[9] Cimon also added an element of personal contact to other displays of generosity. Theopompus notes that when he went out in public, he brought with him two or three boys to give money to whoever would *approach* him (προσέλθοι, 13). It was through all these actions (ἐκ δὴ τούτων ἁπάντων, 17–18) that he became first of the citizens; letting people close to him, with whatever feelings of connection such encounters engendered, certainly did not diminish, and likely contributed to, his success.[10]

As Aristotle specifies, *philia* is based not on protestations of friendship, but rather on acting like a friend (Arist. *Eth. Nic.* 1155b33–56a5, *Eth. Eud.* 1236a14–15), and Athenians seemed to recognize that allowing someone near is a good way to act like a friend, and thus to cultivate feelings of friendship.[11] Crito wanted Archedemus to grant him the ongoing benefits of reciprocal aid that come with friendship, so he made Archedemus feel like a friend by letting Archedemus close to him, rather than just paying him for his services. Cimon similarly seems to have seen a political advantage not just in giving things to those in need, but also in letting those people close to him, so that there was more of a sense that he was not merely a disinterested benefactor, but a friend who was doing them a service that they might reciprocate, in this case politically.

Proximity also indicated political alliances in Athens, which further underscores the political benefit to Cleon of spending time in the midst of his most populous constituency. As Calhoun first pointed out, one of the ways to designate a group of associates with common political interests was with expressions meaning "those around" or "those with" someone: οἱ περί τινα (*hoi peri tina*), οἱ μετά τινα (*hoi meta tina*), or οἱ ἀμφί τινα (*hoi amphi tina*), with *tina* replaced in each phrase by the name of the figure at the head of the group's effort.[12] Such allies of a given politician were also noted in less distinctive terms as being conspicuously in the politician's presence (Thuc. 6.13.1; Ps.-Arist. [*Ath. Pol.*] 34.3; Dem. 18.143; cf. Ar. *Eccles.* 296–9), and sometimes were simply labeled as his *philoi* (e.g., Plut. *Per.* 10.1–2).[13] These people were not necessarily *philoi* in the sense of mutually choosing to spend great amounts of social time with one another, but they were political *philoi*, who could at least tolerate being in one another's presence, and whose interests were best served by remaining loyal to one another.[14] Their proximity to one another cemented their sense of themselves as a mutually beneficial unit, and it also communicated to others that the individuals in the group were to be identified with one another, and with the politician at the center of their group.

III. Demagogues' Manipulation of the Propinquity Effect

Very few of the sparse records that are available of the actions and movements of demagogues portray their interactions with individuals; the large majority of sources depict them engaging with the city as a whole via speech or policy, leading armies, or particularly attending to the mass of common Athenians.[15] Yet a few of the depictions in comedy of Cleon, the demagogue of whom we have by far the most extant records, backed up by a contemporaneous portrayal in tragedy of a figure who appears to reflect his habits, suggest not only that he did not abandon individual *philia* as a means of cementing and expanding his political influence, as discussed in Chapter 2, Section II.A, but in fact that he *relied* upon it to help him develop his base of power. And one of the ways that he developed and cultivated an underserved *philoi* base was by taking advantage of the propinquity effect.

Noteworthy for purposes of this study is the portrayed proximity of Cleon/ Paphlagon to a host of individuals who appear to be representative of the masses of Athenians, and what that proximity suggests about the relationship of demagogues, as leaders, to common Athenians, as their main constituency. In *Knights*, for instance, Aristophanes has the Sausage-Seller mention a mass of young vendors of leather, honey, and cheese surrounding Paphlagon (852–4):

ὁρᾷς γὰρ αὐτῷ στῖφος οἷόν ἐστι βυρσοπωλῶν
νεανιῶν· τούτους δὲ περιοικοῦσι μελιτοπῶλαι
καὶ τυροπῶλαι·

You see there really is an array of young tanners pressed close to him, and sellers of honey and cheese dwell around them.[16]

All of these people are portrayed as being willing to support Cleon in an ostracism bid (854–7), the sort of behavior one would associate with *philoi*.[17] Yet these are not particularly prestigious friends to have, at least as they are depicted here; not even worth identifying beyond their humble jobs, they are generally assumed to play a role as nothing more than pawns whom Cleon bribed, politically or financially, to vote for his political measures.[18] There are similar depictions of Cleon in *Knights* and *Wasps* interacting closely with people who are named, but who are not held in high repute.[19] In *Knights*, Demos claims that a certain Thuphanes is Cleon's partner in cheating Demos (*Eq.* 1102–3). And in *Wasps*, Aristophanes portrays Cleon enjoying a symposium with Theorus, Aeschines, Phanus, and Acestor (*Vesp.* 1220–1; cf. 42–51, 418–19). Additionally, in *Wasps* and *Peace*, the chorus neither names nor even identifies the occupations of a crowd of people surrounding Cleon, but rather refers to them only as "a hundred heads of flatterers" (*Vesp.* 1033–4=*Pax* 756–7):

ἑκατὸν δὲ κύκλῳ κεφαλαὶ κολάκων οἰμωξομένων ἐλιχμῶντο
περὶ τὴν κεφαλήν.

A hundred heads of groaning flatterers hold their tongues out, snake-like, around his head.[20]

In all of these cases, proximity between Cleon and these supposedly disreputable or undistinguished people is highlighted. Whatever their status, they have close access to one of the most powerful people in the *polis*.[21]

Euripides' *Hecuba*, too, produced within a few years of *Knights* and *Wasps*, provides another example of an authority figure choosing close contact with subordinates when communicating a message of importance.[22] As will be discussed later in this chapter, *Hecuba* gives many indications of engaging with the demagogic politics of the time. One way in which it does is to portray leadership by propinquity. When Neoptolemus motions for the prominent herald Talthybius to quiet the army, Talthybius describes his steps before doing so as follows (531): κἀγὼ καταστὰς εἶπον ἐν μέσοις τάδε ("and I stood down in their midst and said these things"). This deviates from the standard model of a leader addressing a group from the front of it, as in the Athenian *ekklesia*; the assumption that a leader would address subordinates from before them is reflected in such matters as the designation of the leader of the common people as προστάτης τοῦ δήμου (literally, "the before-stander of the people").[23] Talthybius' action provides further implication that, at the time of Cleon's peak power and the performance of *Knights*, it was recognized that leaders being surrounded by subordinates, with all of its implications of friendship with them, was one useful way to win allegiance and get one's point across.

While, in *Wasps*, those subordinates surrounding Cleon are the ones referred to as "flatterers," Cleon and other demagogues are more commonly the ones depicted as the flatterers, insincerely trying to ingratiate themselves to others for their own benefit.[24] One of the demagogues' practices that led them to be accused of flattery was their efforts to push through political measures seen as particularly serving non-elites.[25] As the examples above show, however, personal contact, too, could be interpreted as flattery, because friendships, with all of their benefits, can be built through such interactions, and the line between friendship and flattery is difficult to deduce.

Maligning either the demagogues or those surrounding them as "flatterers" is likely a great oversimplification of the relationship that they felt that they had with one another. *Kolakeia* ("flattery, fawning") is a charge often leveled against people aiming to establish connections that, to some extent, are seen as identifiably serving their interests, however much more complex those connections might be.[26] What distinguishes *kolakeia* from *philia*—from the perspectives of not just the performer of it, but also observers of it—is not the type of behavior, but rather the intensity of it and the sincerity underlying it.[27] Aristotle himself highlights the potential ambiguity of such behavior by putting *kolakeia* at the far end of a continuum of relations between people, with *ekhthra* ("hostility") at the other end and *philia* in the middle (*Eth. Eud.* 3.7, 1233b30–34a32). Whether a relationship is properly characterized as one or the other is difficult for an outsider to determine. For one notable example, Archedemus specifies that, despite their ostensible inequality, his relationship with Crito is not a situation of flattery (κολακεύοι): both Crito and Archedemus consider the other a *philos*, and they considered their exchange reciprocal (Xen. *Mem.* 2.9.8). Similarly, the depictions of Cleon and other demagogues flattering, or being flattered by, humble Athenians could simply reflect that those demagogues were commonly out in public, interacting in close proximity with the full range of Athenians.[28]

Thus it is quite likely that many such Athenians, who shared space with Cleon, would have conceived of him as their *philos*, and of themselves as his *philoi*, particularly considering a factor that will be discussed in the next section. Scholars often reduce the supporters of Cleon referred to above as "allies and associates" (Connor 1971: 131) or "'toadies' or 'hangers-on'" (Stockton 1990: 132), focusing on their role relative to Cleon's political purposes.[29] However, since *philia* had played a critical role in Athenian politics for centuries, and since proximity was a clear indicator of personal and political connection to a prominent figure, it is more probable that the ones who were allowed closest to Cleon would have felt that the long-standing rules of *philia* and its relation to politics had remained intact, and that they were being included in Cleon's circle.[30] While Fisher (2008: 200) is alone in specifying that Cleon himself would have *called* those surrounding him his *philoi*, Cleon's actions likely communicated the implicit feeling, whether his words did or not.

The feelings of friendship would certainly have been particularly strong from the followers of Cleon toward Cleon himself, with Cleon's own *genuine* feelings toward these people not particularly relevant to their feelings toward him. Aristotle notes a particular impulse to friendship with people of high status or renown if such people *seem* to want to be friends with the lower-status individuals as well.[31] Several contemporary studies have confirmed that feelings of friendship tend to be stronger from the lower-status individual to the higher-status one in a pairing.[32] As Boissevain (1974: 85) puts it, "a person may consider that he has a relationship with a powerful person, though the latter may not recognize this." Thus Cleon's power and influence in Athens at this time would unquestionably have enhanced the positive feelings directed toward him from the low-status people whom he let close to him, regardless of how he truly felt toward the various vendors linked to him in *Knights*, the "hundred heads of flatterers" surrounding him in *Wasps* and *Peace*, or the others with whom he is portrayed engaging socially or for business.[33] That same phenomenon is likely why it was also so easy for Crito to win over Archedemus as a friend; though Archedemus attained prominence as a public figure himself, Crito's wealth and higher social status made him a desirable friend to have, expediting the success of his efforts to win over Archedemus.[34]

IV. The Homophily Effect in Friendship Development and Athenian Politics

It was more than just shared space with Cleon, though, that would have made lower-class Athenians feel a sense of friendship with him. There were some barriers to overcome in common Athenians' development of such feelings. That sources suggest they did cross those barriers, however, was a function of the unusual class and status positions that Cleon and other prominent demagogues occupied.

As elaborated on in Chapter 1, relationships between friends (*philoi*) in ancient Greece were based not just on personal compatibility and mutual fondness, but also on reciprocal usefulness.[35] While people at different wealth and status levels could be fond of one another, mismatches in ability, resources, or quality between people generally would preclude friendship, unless each party was able to contribute something that the other did not have (Arist. *Eth. Nic.* 1158b1–3, 11–22). Then, as now, disparities in wealth and status tend to interfere with conceptions of genuine friendship between people on opposite sides of a class divide (Arist. *Eth. Nic.* 1158b31–1159a2). Thus some might consider the anonymous lower-class people associated with Cleon to be so far beneath him in status that they would not have harbored delusions of actually being friends with him. Indeed, in the realm of the *philia* between a married couple, Athens was class-stratified enough that it was not at all out of place for Electra's husband to claim that he was too far beneath his regal wife to have sexual relations with her (Eur. *El.* 45–6).[36]

In a similarly class-stratified society, Q. Tullius Cicero advised a potential politician (quite possibly his brother) that he should reach out to equestrians— the aspiring politician's peers in wealth and status—because they are attracted to friendship (*amicitia*, *Att.* 8.33). Yet when Q. Cicero moves to addressing how to court the masses, he begins: "Since enough has been said about establishing friendships . . ." (*quoniam de amicitiis constituendis satis dictum est . . .*, 11.41). He then specifies that one of the advisable qualities to show toward common Romans is constant presence (*adsiduitas*), which is a desirable quality in a friend (e.g., Cic. *Att.* 12, 33), yet he does not bring up the idea of friendship itself, or even the impression of it, with members of the *plebs*. Instead, Q. Cicero recommends just remembering names (*nomenclatio*) while practicing flattery (*blanditia*) and kindness (*benignitas*) and maintaining a good reputation (*rumor*) and public prominence (*spes in re publica*). The implicit reason for a wealthy Roman politician not to try to treat members of the masses as friends is that there was no way that such interaction could possibly be taken as a friendship; the propinquity effect was useful only for ameliorating the plebeians' feelings for the aspiring politician, not erasing the chasm between them that would separate them in other circumstances.

This ties into another general rule in friendship development, recognized by Aristotle and underscored by numerous contemporary studies: people tend to become friends with others whom they perceive as being like them. This concept is called "homophily."[37] The requisite similarity can be recognized on any number of levels, with differences between friends often glossed over in favor of what the friends perceive to be overriding commonalities. One main such commonality is wealth; it was such an obvious tie between people that the main proofs for it as such come not from people's friendship being explained in part by their wealth similarities, but rather when disparities in wealth are noted as dividing people (Eur. *Med.* 561; *El.* 605–9, 1131).

Yet wealth is not the only thing that makes people consider themselves similar enough that they could reasonably be friends; note, again, the case of Archedemus and Crito, and of the avowedly poor Socrates and all of his wealthy followers.[38] In both situations, the common gentility or perceived excellence of the partners seemed to override their wealth disparity. In the same way, a sense of commonality in background or social status, independent of wealth, also can make people feel as though friendship is feasible between them.

Although demagogues were considerably wealthier and more powerful than common Athenians, perceptions of *philia*, and not just casual acquaintance, between the groups were conceivable based on the similar status of their families over generations. According to the concept of "essentialism," people perceive certain qualities of others as a part of their *essence*, independent of other personal factors, and can thus envision friendly connections that would not be predictable based on external or demographic features.[39] For demagogues, whose somewhat ambiguous social status allowed them potentially to be identified with any number of other groups, the "essential" homophily that common Athenians could perceive with them would allow the demagogues' efforts at propinquity to take root in realistic senses of *philia*.

As noted in Chapter 2, Section II.B, none of the most prominent of the fifth-century demagogues (Cleon, Hyperbolus, and Cleophon) was from a traditionally elite family; each one's family attained considerable wealth only in the generation before them, in each case through ownership of factories that owed their success to the manual labor of enslaved workers.[40] The fact that both their connections to lower-class occupations and distance from the elite in a range of ways (albeit often with considerable exaggeration) were regular topics for comic poets and historiographers suggest that the Athenian commons would have been well aware of this link that they shared with the demagogues. The common conflation, in such discourse, of the demagogues with the manual work of their families' businesses likely highlighted their similarities to the working people of Athens. For example, as noted previously in Chapter 2, Section II.B, Cleon is regularly called, or implied to be, a tanner (βυρσοδέψης) or other sort of leather worker or merchant; Hyperbolus is similarly likened to a lampseller or lampmaker; and Cleophon is portrayed as a lyremaker.[41] The same sort of distortion to common occupations could not be done, and was not, to other prominent politicians like Pericles and Alcibiades, whose public standings came from generations-old family wealth.

Beyond those periodic reminders of demagogues' connections to backgrounds and occupations in common with the majority of Athenians, the repeated links in *Knights* between demagogues' political success and their connections to the ἀγορά (*agora*, marketplace) strongly suggest that Cleon, at least, had a personal manner that would have made him fit in with the broad range of Athenians that assembled in that common civic gathering place. Some comments, such as the Sausage-Seller's exclamation to Paphlagon, "I *too* was brought up in the *agora*" (ἐν ἀγορᾷ κἀγὼ τέθραμμαι, 293), while perhaps intended as jabs at Cleon's somewhat humble family background, underscore that he *fits* in that milieu, in the midst of the working people who congregated there.[42] A use of an adjectival form of *agora* further suggests that connections to the *agora* were significant not just in the demagogue's past, but in how he operated in his political life. Demosthenes tells the Sausage-Seller (217–18) that it is not just that he was born low (γέγονας κακῶς, *gegonas kakos*) and has a screeching voice (φωνὴ μιαρά, *phone miara*) that make him a good candidate for demagoguery (δημαγωγικά, *demagogika*), but also that he is ἀγοραῖος (*agoraios*).[43] While this term can connote baseness and the ability to speak persuasively, at root the word simply means "in, of, or belonging to the *agora*."[44] The specific reference to the Sausage-Seller's birth in the same sentence, with *gegonas kakos*, would seem to make an implication of an undistinguished family in this use of *agoraios* redundant. And a citation of his voice (*phone miara*) as one of his qualifications seems to cover the value of attention-getting speech that is a part of any politician's success.

In this context, then, *agoraios* appears to connote the broad meaning of "belonging" to the *agora*—a comfort with that milieu, and a manner that is characteristic of the many unrefined people transacting their business there—as Imperio translates it, "a man of the square."[45] The fact that such a descriptor of the Sausage-Seller marks him for success as a demagogue implies that it applied to Cleon as well, or at least was close enough to applying to him to make the joke work. The fact that the Sausage-Seller likens himself to Paphlagon in their each being πονηρός (*poneros*, "working-class; base," *Eq.* 336) underscores that perception. Common Athenians, then, likely supported Cleon, and potentially conceived of him as a potential friend, in no small part because they saw him as being *like* them. He is someone with whom they not only shared a similar class background (going back two generations in a culture that had a *long* memory), but who continued to reflect that class background in his personal manner. He is someone whom they might feel comfortable approaching. Furthermore, if we believe the sources noted above, he is someone whom at least a notable number of them *did* approach. For that matter, it is quite possible that Aristophanes chose to base *Knights* on face-to-face interactions between an alter ego of Cleon and an unvarnished representative of the *demos* because it was not uncommon for Cleon to be witnessed having interactions of that very sort.[46] And those interactions were very likely provoking feelings of friendship in the lower-status people interacting with this approachable political star.

V. Transitivity, and the Influence of Demagogues on Xenophon

However, regardless of perceptions of similarity between themselves and demagogues, and regardless of demagogues' apparent practice of interacting with, or at least putting themselves in proximity to, common Athenians, not every single member of the political and social underclass would have had the chance to linger in the presence of Cleon or other demagogues, and to feel the sense of direct personal *philia* that many of their peers apparently did. Yet studies in contemporary sociology have shown that there does not have to be direct contact between two individuals, but merely a friend in common, for at least one of those individuals to feel a sense of nascent friendship with the other. Contemporary political science, too, affirms the value of a personal connection between two people, one of whom is at least an acquaintance of a politician, and another who is not, in the second person feeling connected to the politician as well. This sense of friendship at one remove, and benefits between the not-quite-friends that simulate those of actual friends, are evidenced in classical sources.[47] For one example, in Euripides' *Electra*, Electra's husband offers hospitality to Orestes and Pylades (who have not revealed their true identities) because they have passed themselves off as "friends of a friend" (παρὰ φίλου φίλοι, 361).

The concept identified by contemporary sociologists is called "transitivity"; through it, people who are not themselves friends, but who are aware of one another through a friend in common, tend to feel drawn to friendship with one another as well, and the friend in common tends to encourage friendship between the non-friends to whom she or he is linked.[48] The contemporary research along these lines focuses on conventional balanced friendships, while the situation here extends the idea of friendship to include unbalanced relations such as those under study, in which lower-status people tend to feel a stronger bond with higher-status ones than the latter feel with subordinates. This book treats the transitive impulse to friendship as something that occurs not just toward friends of friends, but even toward a friend of acquaintances or peers, if that "friend" is of high status (such as a political or military leader), yet is perceived as accessible enough that friendship is conceivable.[49] Recent political science studies back up this model; people are considerably more likely to vote for a candidate if others who make appeals on behalf of that candidate are, ideally, their friends, or, short of that, someone from their community, especially those who have earned trust as part of their everyday operations.[50]

An explicit illustration of this model appears in Xenophon's *Cyropaedia*, produced a few decades following the height of the demagogues, but by an author raised, and deeply involved in civic affairs, during that period.[51] The work highlights a Persian king, and portions of the *Cyropaedia* may have been fictional, but Xenophon almost certainly wrote with at least an Athenian (and perhaps also a Spartan) audience in mind, and his portrayal had to resonate with that audience to be received well.[52] The source portrays Cyrus—hardly a demagogue, but using similar techniques on a similarly large population of subordinates—skillfully manipulating friend-like connections with some who are far below him in status to derive a benefit from others who are also far below him in status, based on transitive feelings of friendship.[53] Like Cleon, Cyrus uses propinquity and homophily initially to win soldiers' loyalty through friendship. But what the *Cyropaedia* further highlights is how a leader can benefit from feelings of friendship even from subordinates who have not had direct contact with him. The friendly loyalty of those with whom he directly interacts serves his purposes, and his apparent friendship with these subordinates establishes his legitimacy and desirability as a *potential* friend to the many other lower-status people who can know him only from a distance but are likely to identify with those whom he has "befriended."

Xenophon depicts Cyrus showing keen attention to what connotes authentic *philia* to others through his attention to what others would perceive as friendly behavior and his judicious use of the term *philoi*. Cyrus clearly expresses his sense of what it takes to make subordinates feel that overtures of friendship are sincere, so that they will return the friendship: being "evident in doing good" for them (εὖ . . . ποιοῦντα φανερὸν, *Cyr.* 1.6.24) through "good words and good deeds" (ἀγαθοῖς . . . λόγοις καὶ ἔργοις, 2.4.10).[54] He also shows sensitivity to the value of intermediaries in winning over people to whom he cannot make a direct connection. Instead of speaking directly to the troops of newly acquired allies to explain his plans, he asks the troops' established leaders to do so, since, as he says (showing an implicit sense of the power of propinquity), "You are near to them" (πλησιάζετε αὐτοῖς, 3.3.39).[55]

Moreover, he uses *philoi* to refer only to people toward whom he has behaved in a way that would make them feel as though his use of the term was sincere. A key expression that Cyrus uses to address those who would reasonably think of themselves as personal friends of his is ἄνδρες φίλοι (*andres philoi*, "men, friends," as Ambler 2001 consistently translates it).[56] While he sees an enormous benefit to his military and political cause in acquiring friends, the situations in which he does, and does not, use that expression communicate a sense of when he thinks it is reasonable that the audience to which he addresses it would think of it as genuinely meaningful, and not just insincerely flattering.[57]

When a sense of friendship, whether direct or transitive, between himself and certain others would not realistically derive from the connections they have made or similarities they share, he makes no attempt to gloss over a lack of friendship. In Xenophon's account of Cyrus' adult life, Cyrus normally addresses people as *andres philoi* only if they are personal friends—long-time comrades, high-ranking officers, or leaders of other nations with whom he has interacted enough to make friendship seem likely[58]—and the two exceptions to this rule, which I will address shortly, are noteworthy. If he addresses a group that, in addition to friends, includes people from other nations with whom he does not have close personal connections, he always adds καὶ σύμμαχοι (*kai summakhoi*, "and allies") to *andres philoi* (4.5.37, 6.4.13, 7.5.42). And he distinguishes both friends and prominent allies from those who are not of the elite, unless they clearly serve his purposes, as I will specify below. To make it abundantly clear that common subjects of his empire in Babylon are not entitled to the same favors as his friends, despite their expectations to the contrary (7.5.45), he deploys a group of lancers to encircle him and his close companions so that the masses cannot get close to them (7.5.41).

Yet when Cyrus needs great numbers of people of that same class to fight for him, he begins acting much more like a friend toward them, and his language follows suit.[59] When he first encourages common Persians to join Persian Peers as hand-to-hand fighters and acknowledges that he does not know them personally, despite their common nationality, he calls them ἄνδρες Πέρσαι (*andres Persai*, "Persian men," 2.1.15).[60] But as the campaign goes on, he adopts a friendlier approach to non-elite Persians. At 2.1.30, Xenophon notes that, in addition to the officers whom Cyrus had made a habit of inviting to dine with him, he begins to invite rank-and-file soldiers, sometimes squads of five or ten, sometimes a whole platoon or company.[61] Here, again, he is showing his sense of the power of propinquity, in inviting these people to be close to him in his private space.

These invitations are based on performance, not status or connections, and the idea that he wants these guests to see themselves as equals rather than subordinates is underscored by Cyrus' insistence that all diners, regardless of status, be fed as he is (2.1.30). These emphases invoke homophily: he encourages the soldiers to see themselves as being like him, all working successfully toward the same project, of fighting effectively for their mutual benefit. Having people dine with him, as opposed to meeting him in some other way, is also significant. Xenophon's narrator elsewhere (7.1.30) distinguishes friends (φίλων) from other allies (συμμάχων) in that the former are "companions and tablemates" (ἑταῖροί τε ... καὶ ὁμοτράπεζοι), and the others are not.[62]

Shortly after the anecdote about the wide range of countrymen whom Cyrus has join him for dinner, his term of address to the full army takes on a specifically friendly tone, which is one of the exceptions noted above: he no longer calls the group *andres Persai* ("Persian men"), but switches to *andres philoi* ("men, friends," 2.3.2).[63] Though the soldiers would clearly not *all* fall under that heading, even defined loosely, transitive understandings of friendship make this new referent for the individuals who made up the full army one that many of the soldiers might see as valid. *Some* of them spent time with Cyrus in the way that friends spend time together, and those who did, did so because of behavior of which *any* of them was capable. All soldiers could then see themselves as part of an appealing "ingroup," on the same level as those who hobnob with the top ranks of the military, with each one's individual status raised as a result of their connection to those close to the top.[64]

A soldier named Pheraulas justifies this feeling of transitive connection to Cyrus from a soldier's perspective. Described as a "Persian of the commoners" (Πέρσης τῶν δημοτῶν), he has become "acquainted with and pleasing to Cyrus" (Κύρῳ ... συνήθης καὶ ἀρεστός). This connection to the king, and approval by him, disposes Pheraulas so positively to Cyrus that he speaks up before the fully assembled army on behalf of the general's plan to base soldiers' compensation on achievement, with Cyrus the determiner of each soldier's wages, rather than on equal distribution of resources (2.3.7). Pheraulas emphasizes the common expectations to which every Persian is held, which he claims put each of them "on equal footing" (ἐκ τοῦ ἴσου) in pursuing virtue (2.3.8). And more significantly, he states that "whoever is clear in doing this without hesitation, I see him obtaining honor from Cyrus" (ὃς ἂν φανῇ τοῦτο ἀπροφασίστως ποιῶν, τοῦτον ὁρῶ παρὰ Κύρου τιμῆς τυγχάνοντα).[65] This is obviously an exaggeration; Cyrus could not possibly take personal notice of every soldier in his army. But the logic individual soldiers might use in believing such a statement is the same as the logic of believing that it is valid for Cyrus to call people *philoi* when he has never met them. Cyrus honors, or acts as a friend toward, people like them; he does things to make himself seem an equal of people like them; and their equality with those who are honored or treated as friends means that they, too, can see themselves as worthy of honor or friendship. For Cyrus, earning feelings of friendship leads to political advantage: the Persian soldiers vote to put the determination of their wages in the hands of Cyrus (2.3.16), whom most have at least observed being amicable and accessible to people like them.

The same logic could have led to feelings of friendship from numerous common Athenians to Cleon for his similar strategic behaviors. As in the case of Cyrus, Cleon's employment of propinquity and homophily appears to have won him the direct friendship of many lower-status individuals. Through transitivity, as well, both Cyrus and Cleon likely dramatically increased the number of those outside of immediate contact with them who would feel personally connected enough to conceive of themselves as *philoi* to these high-status figures as well.

VI. The Exchange of Favors in Friendship Development in *Knights* and *Hecuba*

While Chapter 5 will include more on Xenophon's reflection of demagogic, friendship-based leadership techniques well into the fourth century BCE, a move back to drama produced during Cleon's life will provide one more example of demagogic leadership as having friend-like components, of a sort clearly recognizable at the time. *Knights* and *Hecuba* seem to connect Cleon (and likely other contemporaneous demagogues) to the providing of benefits to those close to him, which propriety then requires the recipients to reciprocate. The main term linked to this practice, often in cognate forms, is χάρις (*kharis*), which, in one of its common senses, means a favor done for someone, typically a friend (LSJ⁹ s.v. III).[66] While the character of Paphlagon in *Knights* explicitly represents Cleon, Odysseus' character in *Hecuba*, too, is commonly recognized as reflective of Cleon and other demagogic leaders of the time.[67] The appearance of χάρις attached to these Cleon-like characters further underscores a pattern of behavior that seems to have been associated with demagogic sorts of leaders.

While Paphlagon uses a cognate of *kharis* in *Knights* just once to capture a technique he uses to ingratiate himself to the representative of common Athenians, the term is applied to Odysseus several times in *Hecuba* to express a similar purpose. In *Knights*, while making a case that his affection for Demos is greater than the Sausage-Seller's, Paphlagon claims that he took any number of liberties against other Athenian citizens so long as he could "do a favor" (χαριοίμην) for Demos (776).[68] Likewise, early in *Hecuba*, the chorus leader, angered that Odysseus convinced the Danaans to sacrifice Polyxena at Achilles' grave, calls him a δημοχαριστής (*demokharistes*), a "mob-indulger" (132).[69] *Hecuba* thus uses nearly the same terms as in *Knights* to express a demagogic figure's habit of doing services for the *demos* that friends do for another, with an implicit requirement of reciprocation.

Hecuba later plays on the typical association of *kharis* with friends, but colored by Odysseus' treatment of the masses, in her speech berating Odysseus for not standing up for Polyxena. She is particularly outraged by Odysseus' failure to spare her daughter, because doing so would have been fitting repayment for the favor that she did for him during the height of the war: "I lay hold of these same parts of you in turn and demand a return of the <u>favor</u> from then" (ἀνθάπτομαί σου τῶνδε τῶν αὐτῶν ἐγὼ / χάριν τ᾽ ἀπαιτῶ τὴν τόθ᾽, 275–6); she had earlier spared his life when she became aware of his true identity as he was on a spying mission within Troy (239–53). She links this lack of reciprocity to his demagogic tendencies in the play, labeling as ἀχάριστον (*akhariston*, "ungrateful, ungracious") the breed of those who seek honors as δημηγόροι (*demegoroi*, "popular orators," 254–5).[70] Hecuba then makes a direct connection between *kharis*, friendship, and demagogic appeals for the favor of the masses, belittling Odysseus for abandoning his *philoi* while instead speaking to *hoi polloi* ("the people") in a way that serves πρὸς χάριν (*pros kharin*, "as a favor") to them (255–7).[71]

While *pros kharin* (257) could be taken much more neutrally, such as "pleasing," two uses of *kharis* or a derivative within four lines, both in the context of the reciprocal duties that friends are supposed to do for one another, seem to suggest a link, in the context of friendship, between the two appearances of the word.[72] One more use of *kharis*, shortly thereafter (276), solidifies its use in this context as a reciprocal favor that friends do for one another. When Hecuba states that Odysseus owes her *kharis* (276) for saving his life when he was a suppliant, as she is now (273–6), Odysseus replies that his obligation would be to save her life (301–2); since that is not in danger, his duty is to a friend (φίλῳ, 311), in this case the deceased Achilles, who has served his interests (304–12).[73]

No single appearance of *kharis* in *Knights* or *Hecuba* decisively indicates that friendly favor-trading is among the main leadership techniques of Cleon or other demagogues. However, these several appearances of *kharis* and its cognates relating to these demagogic characters may suggest that this aspect of friendship-building, as with the practices explained earlier in the chapter, is something that was observed as part of the repertoire of Cleon and perhaps his peers, in a fashion similar to their portrayals building friendships with humble figures in other ways. As suggested earlier regarding the portrayal in *Knights* of Paphlagon's personal interactions with Demos, it may be that Cleon so commonly engaged with individual common Athenians as a friend that *kharis* was a natural concept to connect to figures portraying or reflecting him in drama, whether he regularly used the term of not in his standard civic interactions.

VII. Conclusion: Cleon as a "Personal" Friend to Lower-Class Athenians

Connor (1971) was correct about *Knights* as evidence for Cleon's use of *philia* as a method of outreach to the Athenian masses. The effectiveness of that outreach seems to be more sociologically explicable and individually based than Connor noted, though. Cleon's apparent willingness to come into close personal contact with all manner of people (propinquity), and the perception that he shared traits in common with the bulk of Athenians (homophily), despite his powerful status (essentialism), likely sent the message to many lower-status Athenians that, however improbably, they shared a friendship of sorts with him, perhaps underscored by his use of familiar friendship terminology with them. This, then, would have made them his political *philoi*, who helped him, in their own ways, and he in turn helped them politically through the reciprocity of *philia*. Through "transitivity," many more people of that status who did not have the opportunity to come into close contact with Cleon could still feel friendship with him at one remove. Any citizen, no matter how humble, could then see himself as part of an appealing "ingroup," part of the machinery of Cleon's power.

As noted in the example from Xenophon's *Cyropaedia*, the value of techniques that Cleon used seems to have been recognized even decades after he and his most notorious demagogic successors were long dead. Chapter 5 will lay out more of the progression that traces that influence back to Cleon. Chapter 4, though, will first take a step back to consider one obstacle to the perception of Cleon as a *philos* to members of the Athenian *demos*.

4

Distinguishing Desire from Friendship in Leadership Models in Aristophanes' *Knights*

I. Introduction: "Demos, I am *Not* Your Lover"

There is a notable impediment to conceiving of Cleon as having convinced great numbers of the Athenian *demos* that he was their *philos*. In Aristophanes' *Knights*, the play in which he (or, rather, his stand-in, Paphlagon) is featured most prominently, Paphlagon professes to Demos, "I am your lover" (ἐραστής ... εἰμὶ σός, *Eq.* 732); the Sausage-Seller later claims that this is the sort of language that speakers (apparently including Paphlagon/Cleon) often used in the Athenian assembly (1340–4).[1] Rogers (1910: 188 ad *Eq.* 1341) characterizes utterances in this play such as this one as "flowers from Cleon's rhetorical garden"; several scholars follow Rogers in taking the Sausage-Seller's claims as accurate, treating the parody of Cleon (as represented by Paphlagon) as based on the politician's genuine figurative use of the language of παιδεραστία (*paederastia*, "pederasty," romantic relations between adult men and boys), which Cleon employed to dramatize his attentive commitment to the Athenian people.[2]

Connor (1971), too, had difficulty with this characterization in his proposal of the *philia* model as Cleon's political strategy for winning over the *demos* as a whole (esp. 91–119). He uses *Knights* as a source to support his interpretation only hesitantly (96–8), largely because of this sticking point. While he reconciles those two forms of personal connection by portraying pederasty as "the most intense *philia*" (98), this justification gives insufficient weight to two important factors. One of them is that *philia* and pederasty are two markedly different sorts of relationships; it would tell a very different story about Cleon if he were widely perceived as an ἐραστής (*erastes*), a desirous lover in a pederastic relationship, rather than a *philos*. Another is that pederasty as a political image was so common in classical Athens that to treat Cleon as a political *erastes* is to see him as a much more conventional politician than both Connor and I contend that he was.

This chapter will thus go into some depth in arguing against the figurative accuracy of Paphlagon's claim to be the *erastes* to the personified Demos. First, Paphlagon's portrayal throughout the play is not consistently that of an *erastes*, as is particularly apparent when weighed against the much more directly pederastic behavior of his supposed rival for Demos' affections, the Sausage-Seller. Most notably, Aristophanes largely excises the ἔρως (*eros*, "sexual passion, desire") from Paphlagon's role as an *erastes*. Paphlagon's language and behavior, though, make him appear to be engaged in a different relationship with Demos: that of a *philos*. Paphlagon, the Sausage-Seller, and Demos are not particularly likely participants in a pederastic relationship to begin with: as Yates (2005: 42) points out, Demos' age makes him an unlikely ἐρώμενος (*eromenos*, younger "beloved" figure in a pederastic relationship), and the modest social statuses of Paphlagon and the Sausage-Seller, his rival for Demos' affections, make them non-traditional models of *erastai*.[3] However, the Sausage-Seller does not let these peculiarities deter him from speaking and behaving as a standard *erastes*, suggesting that Aristophanes was attentive in *Knights* to what defined an *erastes* to most Athenians, and Paphlagon was not it. While Scholtz (2007: 44) calls the dynamics of the threesome "a dystopian vision of political friendship," the "friendship" part of that vision seems only to be coming from one party.

To make this point, this chapter will cover a fair number of nuances of what it was to be an *erastes* in classical Athens, as the Sausage-Seller is clearly portrayed to be, versus what it was to be a *philos* at the time, which is what this book argues Paphlagon/Cleon was portrayed to be, reflecting the political persona that I contend he aimed to project. Second, it will contend that the "*erastes* of the *demos*" language was likely not something that Cleon used. A range of scholars contends that so many others used the language and imagery of political pederasty that Cleon could have had similar use of such language projected onto him.[4]

Even if Cleon himself did not use that specific language or imagery, though, the metaphor clearly fit him to some extent in order to justify Aristophanes' use of it. In any parody, while certain qualities of the object of mockery have to be embellished to create humor, others need clearly to be familiar to the audience; otherwise the critique of the targeted figure rings false.[5] Aristophanes acknowledges his own recognition of the need for a certain degree of accuracy in parodic portrayal when he has one of Paphlagon's enslaved attendants announce to the audience that, despite Paphlagon's mask not resembling Cleon, the audience would recognize the demagogue in Paphlagon's depiction and actions in the play (*Eq.* 231–3).[6] What made the *erastes* model not inapplicable to Cleon will be addressed later in the chapter, but my contention is that the connection was, at best, tangential.

In limiting the erotic component of Paphlagon's performance of the role of *erastes* as he does, despite the parodist's freedom to distort familiar figures for humorous effect, and in portraying other aspects of his relationship with Demos that do not fit the pederastic model, Aristophanes seems to be illuminating the public figure that Cleon genuinely did cut. If Cleon had actually presented himself rhetorically as an *erastes* of the *demos*, as Aristophanes has Paphlagon do in the play, and acted the part in his dealings with the Athenian people, it would have been perfectly natural to invest that image in the play with the kind of lustful associations and stereotypical patterns of behavior seen regularly with other uses of erotic imagery in political contexts, including the behavior of the Sausage-Seller in this play. Yet in *Knights*, Aristophanes stops short of portraying Paphlagon, the supposed *erastes*, as anything more than a caring and helpful (if also self-interested) mentor, even in situations when sexualizing the role would have been perfectly consistent with the plot.

In stopping short of depicting literal pederasty, yet in presuming to portray Cleon's alter ego as possessing certain traits of an *erastes*, Aristophanes appears to reveal the genuine political persona that the Athenians associated with Cleon—as a *philos* to the *demos*—to which Aristophanes seems to have felt bound in his caricature. This chapter lays out the intricacy with which Aristophanes uses pederasty, a type of relationship that Cleon likely never applied to himself in his political rhetoric, in a peculiarly mild form to jab Cleon, while still paying respect to the more reciprocal *philia* imagery that Cleon almost certainly *did* use as a large part of his outreach to the *demos*. This reading of *Knights* reinforces the validity of Connor's ideas while refining them, and underscores the value of *Knights* as a critical source on Cleon and his role in Athenian political life early in the period of the demagogues.

II. The Language of Pederasty and *Philia* in *Knights*

One of the ways in which Aristophanes' careful choice to limit the association of Cleon with pederasty, and to tie him more clearly to friendship, is apparent is in Paphlagon's avoidance of explicitly sexualized language. While, as noted above, Paphlagon refers to himself as Demos' *erastes* (ἐραστής … εἰμὶ σός, 732), and the Sausage-Seller quotes that line as one that speakers (such as Paphlagon) were wont to say in the assembly (1341), in both cases the expression is either immediately preceded or followed by a much milder φιλῶ σε (*philo se*, "I love you," or "I like you").[7] When φιλέω (*phileo*) is understood in terms of "love," it is generally in the sense of the stable love that spouses, family members, and friends have for one another (LSJ[9] s.v. I.1–3).[8]

Of the few other times that the expression *philo se* (whether in that order or some other) appears in literature of the classical period or times prior to it, in all cases but one it is clearly used to express only friendly fondness, and the exception is used by a woman to a man (Myrrhine to Cinesias: σ᾽ οὐκ ἐρῶ γ᾽ ὡς οὐ φιλῶ, "I won't say that I don't love you," Ar. *Lys.* 905).[9] Subordinate partners in romantic relationships (as women and *eromenoi* were seen to be) by convention expressed their affection more mutedly than dominant partners (such as *erastai*) did, with erotic passion (expressed with ἐράω, *erao*), as will be explained more below, something that women did not initiate, but rather only reciprocated (with ἀντεράω, *anterao*), and with *phileo* being a common way for women, and the only acceptable way for *eromenoi*, to express their feelings for their lovers.[10] Thus it is not as though *philo se* is simply the conventional way for one lover (regardless of whether it is the active or passive partner) to express his or her passionate attraction to another.[11]

Yet it is forms of *phileo* that Paphlagon consistently uses to express his fondness for Demos (732, 773, 791, 821), and Demos, as well, characterizes Paphlagon's expressed feelings for him with that term (946).[12] Moreover, on five of the seven occasions when the Sausage-Seller uses *phileo* (or the equally benign στέργω, *stergo*) in regard to Demos, he is just passing on what he claims Paphlagon says to the object of his affection, or what Paphlagon's true feelings supposedly are (779, 792, 848, 870, 1341).[13] Henderson (1998) translates φιλῶ σ᾽ at 732 as the ambiguous "I adore you," and generally otherwise expresses forms of *phileo* in *Knights* as "cherish" (773, 791, 792, 848, 870, 1341). But he expresses the Sausage-Seller's criticism of Paphlagon to Demos, οὐχὶ φιλεῖ σ' (779), as "he is not your friend," a rendering that clearly distinguishes that verb from desire, an *erastes*' main feeling; Bartlett (2020) goes even further along those lines, using the word "friend" for each of his translations of *phileo*, including expressing φιλῶ σ' at both 732 and 1341 as "I am your friend" to balance "I am your lover."[14]

The Sausage-Seller, when expressing his own attitude toward Demos, on the other hand, uses the more explicit terminology that was typically associated with the feelings of *erastai*. Immediately after Paphlagon says φιλῶ σ', ὦ Δῆμ', ἐραστής τ' εἰμὶ σός ("I care for you, Demos, and I am your lover," 732), the Sausage-Seller identifies himself as ἀντεραστὴς τουτουί ("his [Paphlagon's] competitor as an *erastes*," 733), but is more typical of *erastai* in his specification of his feelings, after his initial identification of himself: ἐρῶν πάλαι σου βουλόμενός τέ σ' εὖ ποιεῖν ("desiring you always, and wanting to do well for you," 734).[15] He wishes well for Demos, as Paphlagon does, but he also feels sexual passion for him, as is appropriate for an *erastes*. The difference in connotation between *phileo*, the word attributed repeatedly to Paphlagon, and *erao*, the Sausage-Seller's choice to express his feelings, is considerable.

A. Parsing the Terminology and Ideals of Pederasty and *Philia*

A form of *phileo* can be used to express some aspect of the feelings of an *erastes* for his *eromenos*, but in courtship, in which Paphlagon and the Sausage-Seller are engaged, other verbs are standard. Verbs used to express an *erastes*' genuine erotic passion, which is what is at issue in courtship, and which distinguishes an *erastes* from any other *philos*, are *erao*, which appears in this play only in the Sausage-Seller's use of it, and, to a lesser extent, ἐπιθυμέω (*epithumeo*), which does not appear in *Knights*.[16] At Xenophon, *Hiero* 11.11, Simonides, in laying out for Hiero the benefits coming to him if he should surpass other heads of state in the prosperity of his nation, documents the distinction between *phileo* and *erao* as one between fondness (*phileo*) and sexual passion (*erao*), with the latter accompanied by efforts at seduction:

ὥστε οὐ μόνον <u>φιλοῖο</u> ἄν, ἀλλὰ καὶ <u>ἐρῷο</u> ὑπ' ἀνθρώπων, καὶ τοὺς καλοὺς οὐ πειρᾶν, ἀλλὰ πειρώμενον ὑπ' αὐτῶν ἀνέχεσθαι ἄν σε δέοι.

> Thus you would not only be <u>liked</u>, but also <u>desired</u> by people, and you wouldn't need to make passes at attractive people, but instead to endure the passes they would make at you.

Furthermore, in discussions in Plato's *Symposium* and *Phaedrus* of pederasty (though it is only called *eros* in those works; the pederastic component of such passion is implicit throughout both dialogues), forms of *erao* appear 111 times, and *epithumeo* 20 times, to capture the feelings characteristic of an *erastes* for an *eromenos*.[17] In contrast, most of the few uses of forms of *phileo* in those dialogues to capture feelings or behavior of *erastai* toward *eromenoi* (all of them appearing in *Phaedrus*) either refer to kissing (255e3), or they express skepticism about the true intentions of *erastai*: Socrates, apparently quoting an aphorism, sarcastically cautions potential *eromenoi* that *erastai* care for (φιλοῦσιν) boys just as wolves cherish (ἀγαπῶσιν) lambs (*Phaedr.* 241d1), and Phaedrus relates (231c1–7) Lysias' supposed dubiousness about *erastai*'s professions to care for (φασιν φιλεῖν) the *eromenoi* they desire (ἐρῶσιν).[18]

Even the one time that a form of *phileo* appears to express part of the genuine feelings of an *erastes* for an *eromenos*, it is clearly subordinate to *eros*. At *Phaedrus* 253c2–6, Socrates communicates Stesichorus' supposed idea that the desire and initiation of true lovers (i.e., *erastai*) (προθυμία ... τῶν ὡς ἀληθῶς ἐρώντων καὶ τελετή) bring happiness to a cherished one (φιληθέντι) (i.e., an *eromenos*) through a friend who has been inspired by passion (ὑπὸ τοῦ δι' ἔρωτα μανέντος φίλου). In this case, while it is noteworthy that the *eromenos* is described as "having been cherished" (φιληθέντι), the happiness only comes about because of the *eros* of the *erastes* for the *eromenos*, even though the *erastes* is referred to as a "friend" (φίλου).[19]

The same is true of uses of *phileo*, and of uses of the nominal form *philia*, to refer to *erastai*'s feelings for *eromenoi* elsewhere in Plato and in Aristotle: *philia* is invariably either subordinate or subsequent to *eros* or ἐπιθυμία (*epithumia*). At Plato, *Lysis* 221b, Menexenus agrees with Socrates that a person cannot help but like (φιλεῖν) someone whom he desires (ἐπιθυμεῖ), and for whom he yearns (ἐρᾷ).[20] A similar sentiment comes up at *Phaedrus* 233a1–7, in which Socrates notes that people who were previously friends (φίλοι, *philoi*) can continue their friendship (τὴν φιλίαν) even if passion enters the relationship. In both cases, it is clear that to like someone, in the sense of *phileo*, can certainly be part of pederasty; it is just not the identifying part of it.[21]

Moreover, while passion can produce *philia*, that passion needs to be present to define the relationship as pederasty. A few lines later in *Lysis* than the passage cited above, Socrates gets Menexenus to agree that desire is the source of friendship (ἡ ἐπιθυμία τῆς φιλίας αἰτία, 221d), and *philia* is mentioned repeatedly in *Symposium* and *Phaedrus* as one of the goals of a pederastic relationship.[22] Yet, correspondingly, *philia* is portrayed as something achieved in a higher form through an initial relationship based on a lover's *eros* (e.g., *Symp.* 179c1–3, 182c3–4, 209c5–7; *Phaedr.* 253c4–6). As these passages highlight, *philia* comes *through* passion; the passion, expressed as *eros* and/or *epithumia*, is what precipitates the friendship in pederasty, and is what marks a relationship as pederasty, particularly in its early stages.[23]

Aristotle (*Pol.* 1262b11–13) communicates a similar impression in his interpretation of Aristophanes' allegory of *eros* in the *Symposium*, but with an important twist. He paraphrases Aristophanes (*Symp.* 192c1–e10) as claiming that "it is from the extreme fondness of those who are in love" (τῶν ἐρώντων διὰ τὸ σφόδρα φιλεῖν) that the desire of those lovers to unite as a single being derives. In doing so, Aristotle seems to treat *philia* as something that is integral to a relationship of *eros*.[24]

Yet the sort of relationship Aristotle has in mind is one that is highly developed and refined; not every single individual who feels *eros* for another wishes to be united in body and spirit with that other for eternity. The *philia* that is a part of *eros* as Aristotle portrays it, then, is just like the ideal *philia*—which develops over time through a philosophical approach to *eros*—that is apparent in the previous examples.[25]

The pederasty in *Knights*, however, is far from meeting anyone's philosophical ideal. In short, while *philia* is certainly often a part of pederasty, *eros* is what *makes* it pederasty, and *eros* is not something that Paphlagon expresses or demonstrates.

III. The Performance of Pederasty and Friendship in *Knights*

Not only do Paphlagon's words in *Knights* mark him as far more *philos* than *erastes* in his methods of aiming to win over Demos, but so, too, do his actions, particularly when compared with those of the Sausage-Seller. As Monoson

(2000:67) puts it, "'lovers' (*erastai*) has very clear erotic and sexual connotations," whatever the context in which the word appears.[26] Yet Paphlagon's actions in *Knights* are not those of a lustful *erastes*, to a conspicuous degree, just as his words are not. He is portrayed as sexual, certainly, but within the norms that Athenian comedy applies to a broad swath of men in public life, and very little in ways that fit someone in an actively pederastic relationship. The Sausage-Seller, however, does fit common norms of a desirous *erastes*. Primarily, Paphlagon's portrayal as a sexual being stands out only for how much more muted it is than the rampant sexuality attributed to the Sausage-Seller.[27]

While Henderson claims that Paphlagon "is presented as both a pathic and a *paedicator*, the aggressor in homosexual contact" (1991: 68), such a characterization, where it appears in the play, either fits conventional portrayals of Athenian men in Old Comedy, or serves a rhetorical purpose that falls outside of sexuality. What it does *not* do is tie him to pederastic behavior with Demos. There is no question that Paphlagon is linked to passive homosexual behavior (*Eq.* 78, 379–81, 878–80), but so is the Sausage-Seller: the latter is treated as not just pathic (423–8, 483–4, 639–40, 721), but a prostitute (1242). And while Paphlagon is accused of performing cunnilingus (352), the Sausage-Seller is encouraged to perform fellatio (167); while the former operation can be objectionable only if performed immoderately, the latter is behavior that generally is restricted to paid sex.[28] But neither one's characterization as such is particularly unusual; comedy is rife with sexual humor, and Aristophanes attributes pathic behavior not just to almost everyone who is prominent in Athens, but also to almost *everyone* in Athens.[29]

More important to this argument, though, is Paphlagon's lack of active pederastic behavior or interest, made particularly apparent when compared with the Sausage-Seller.[30] While Hubbard (1991: 68) refers to Paphlagon's supposed "sodomy and rape of the people," and Henderson (1991: 69) calls him "the violator of the people," the text shows no such sexual interest from Paphlagon to Demos, whether violent, exploitative, or otherwise. The one time that Paphlagon speaks of himself playing an active homosexual role (κασαλβάσω τοὺς ἐν Πύλῳ στρατηγούς, "I'll nail the generals at Pylos like prostitutes," 355), the expression is unquestionably figurative, and it has nothing to do with Demos.[31] Metaphors of sexual violence, like this one, are common, in classical Athens and elsewhere, to express domination over adversaries.[32] Just in Aristophanes, the Sausage-Seller threatens the same fate to Paphlagon at *Knights* 364; the chorus in *Wasps* puts the rough treatment to which Cleon has subjected the poet outside of the play in terms of sexual violence as well (1284–9); and Euripides' kinsman threatens similar violence against an enslaved employee of Agathon's at *Thesmaphoriazusae* 59–62.[33] Several scholars contend that Paphlagon may be hinting at sexual violence at *Knights* 261–3 also;[34] but the possibility of such implication in Paphlagon's supposed shakedowns of vulnerable magistrates or wide-eyed, wealthy expatriates does not imply an *erastes'* desire either.[35] In short, "nailing generals" says nothing at all about Paphlagon's *eros* for an *eromenos* like Demos.

There is only one occasion when there could be even an implication of sexual interest from Paphlagon to Demos, and even there it more likely underscores his *lack* of pederastic *eros*. At 962–3, Paphlagon says that, if Demos trusts the Sausage-Seller, he (Demos) will become a μολγός (*molgos*, a wineskin), to which the Sausage-Seller replies (963–4) that, if Demos trusts Paphlagon, he will become a ψωλός (*psolos*, someone circumcised, or with foreskin retracted). While most commentators treat this exchange as referring to matters that have nothing to do with either character's sexuality, there is certainly room for more lascivious interpretation.[36] First, *molgos* is commonly used to refer to the leathery anuses of people who have been penetrated many times.[37] Henderson (1991: 68) treats Paphlagon's utterance as implying that Demos will become like the Sausage-Seller in sexual passivity, without the Sausage-Seller playing any direct role in that transition.[38] Yet it seems reasonable that the Sausage-Seller would be the one turning Demos' anus to leather by repeated penetration, given that a desire to penetrate an *eromenos* is a typical (if not universally accepted) impulse of an *erastes* who feels genuine *eros* for his *eromenos*, as the Sausage-Seller claims he does (734).[39]

As for the Sausage-Seller's reply (963–4) that Demos will become a *psolos* if Demos trusts Paphlagon, Dover (2016: 204) explains the image of Demos' retracted foreskin as implying that Paphlagon would be pulling back the foreskin as he grasped Demos' penis while penetrating him from behind. Henderson's (1991: 68) interpretation of the image as implying that Paphlagon would teach Demos deep sexual penetration, up to the pubic hair (μέχρι τοῦ μυρρίνου), with the foreskin retracted, though, seems to serve as a more appropriate companion to the implicit sexuality of *molgos*.[40] When a common expression for a well-worn anus (*molgos*) is followed by one for a sexually ready penis (*psolos*), the differing role of each body part in male homosexual congress would seem to be a logical connection between them. Thus the implicit contrast seems to be between being penetrated (*molgos*, which the Sausage-Seller would teach to Demos) and doing the penetrating (*psolos*, which Paphlagon would teach to Demos).

The *psolos* image, if taken that way, could then be understood in one of two ways, neither of which would implicate Paphlagon as a lustful *erastes* of Demos, and which might suggest that Paphlagon does not actually *want* to be an *erastes*. One possibility is that Paphlagon would make Demos *like* himself, "all hard-on" (Henderson 1991: 68): Paphlagon would encourage Demos to become an active partner to someone else, either male or female. Another possibility, unlikely in the context, is that Demos would be turning the tables on Paphlagon, making him into the *eromenos* in their relationship. In both cases, Paphlagon's status as the active partner in a pederastic relationship with Demos is undermined, in contrast to the portrayal of the Sausage-Seller's status relative to Demos: in the latter case, Paphlagon says that Demos is sure to learn his role as passive partner, whether by being treated as such by the Sausage-Seller, or by seeking out others who are the sort of energetic penetrator that the Sausage-Seller is.

Unlike Paphlagon, the Sausage-Seller is tied to active pederastic behavior on several other occasions as well. First of all, there is the obvious phallic symbolism of the wares the Sausage-Seller vends; if anyone is "all hard-on," it is he.[41] In addition to his threat, referenced above, to "stuff [Paphlagon's] anus like a sausage-skin" (ἐγὼ δὲ βυνήσω γέ σοι τὸν πρωκτὸν ἀντὶ φύσκης, 364), he suggests his broader appreciation of penetrating young men by encouraging Demos to bend over an enslaved youth who has been assigned to carry a folding chair for him (1384–6).[42] Further, after he has defeated Paphlagon in their competition to be Demos' *erastes*, he may imply an intention to dominate Demos sexually, when he says that no one is better than he for "the city of Gapenians" (τῇ Κεχηναίων πόλει, 1263; cf. 78, 261, 380, 755, 804). Κεχηναίων ("Gapenians") blends "Athenians" with a form of χάσκω, the main meaning of which is "yawn" or "gape" (LSJ[9] s.v.).[43] It is used commonly, though, to refer to anuses that have become more open due to repeated penetration of them.[44] The Sausage-Seller's expressed suitability to this city full of men ready to be anally penetrated could, of course, reflect his own experience in this regard (cf. 167, 423–8, 721, 1242).[45] On the other hand, as the victorious *erastes*, he could well be implying a wish to take advantage of the sexual opportunities these wide-anused "Gapenians" would allow him.

IV. Gifts and Favors in Pederasty and *Philia* in *Knights*

However, despite Paphlagon's language and actions being notably less erotic than the Sausage-Seller's, the *erastes–eromenos* model is still in place in this play, and the portrayed relationship of Paphlagon with Demos is an unequal one.[46] As is typical of Athenian pederasty, Paphlagon and the Sausage-Seller are the dominant figures, and Demos is a willing subordinate, a passive object of affection and gifts, with no apparent expectation of like-for-like reciprocity for them.[47] This model implies that all of the favors that Paphlagon claims that he has done for Demos are merely a lover's tokens; by extension, so would be Cleon's legislative efforts that benefited common Athenians (or soaked the wealthy) to which the play refers.[48]

Yet, while wooing and offering gifts are part of the courtship practices of *erastai*, what Paphlagon specifically does along these lines to try to win over Demos is far more consistent with a relationship of *philia* rather than of pederastic *eros*, just as what Cleon did for the Athenian *demos* was.[49] In the same way that propriety seems to have restricted how *erastai* were to satisfy their sexual urges for *eromenoi*, so, too, were there limitations on the offerings that *erastai* could make to express their fondness in their efforts to win over the objects of their desires.[50] For one, while there are some notable exceptions in extreme circumstances, *erastai* typically did not present themselves as physical defenders of their *eromenoi*, most likely because it would imply that these young men moving into adulthood were unable to defend themselves.[51] And there were limits on how much material sustenance an *eromenos* could accept, for fear of looking like a πόρνος (*pornos*, prostitute).[52] For the most part, the gifts offered by *erastai* were small, and *erastai*'s main personal role lay in nurturing their *eromenoi* toward adulthood.[53]

What Paphlagon offers Demos, though, goes considerably outside of those boundaries. First, he plays much more of a role of protector and provider than is standard for Athenian *erastai*. His supposed profession to Demos, "I alone care and look out for you" (κήδομαί σου καὶ προβουλεύω μόνος, 1342), could be taken as an expression of an *erastes'* appropriate concern for his *eromenos*, but the details of what he provides reveal his oversteps.[54] First of all, while κήδομαι is a term used by contemporaries and near-contemporaries of Aristophanes to express concern and consideration for fellow citizens (Thuc. 6.14.1, Pl. *Apol.* 24c, Isoc. *De pace* 51), προβουλεύω has a strong connotation of operating in the βουλή on behalf of someone else (LSJ[9] s.v. III), implying the inability of the assisted party to represent himself.[55] Supporting this implication of Demos' passivity and helplessness are Paphlagon's claims to feed Demos (799), protect him (790–1), and fight on his behalf (764–8, 1037–9).[56] Further along these lines, Paphlagon refers to himself as a watchdog (κύων) who barks in protection of Demos (1017–19, 1023–4), an image that the Sausage-Seller accepts but twists (1025–7, 1030–4).[57] The protection that Paphlagon the watchdog offers, though, is not physical, but worse, if the relationship were pederastic: material. He specifies to Demos that he, as watchdog, "provides you pay" (σοὶ μισθὸν ποριεῖ, 1019), and the currency of that pay appears throughout the play: wage increases for jury service (51, 255, 797–800), barley and other daily necessities (1100–14), a stool (1164), and assorted foodstuffs (52, 1166–7, 1171–2, 1177, 1181–2, 1190, 1192).[58] It is this sort of generosity dedicated to basic sustenance (despite Demos' disappointment that Paphlagon did not give him more, 1217–25), out of step with expectations of pederasty, that has led some scholars to see in the relationship, both in the play and between Cleon and the Athenian *demos* outside the play, implications of prostitution.[59]

Such assistance from Paphlagon to Demos (and from Cleon to the Athenian *demos*) *could* be perfectly acceptable, however, if each side conceived of their relationship as *philia* rather than pederasty. As long as there was an understanding that reciprocal benefit would be returned in some way, not necessarily in kind, it was part of the job of a *philos* to help his *philoi*, both materially and otherwise.[60] Crito's friends also refer to Archedemus as a good dog (ἀγαθὸν κύνα), but in the sense of a protector (φύλακα), welcome to shepherds (Xen. *Mem.* 2.9.7). A shepherd and a watchdog offer different benefits, but theirs is a partnership, as is the unbalanced relationship of Archedemus and Crito.[61]

So, too, in *Knights*, while Paphlagon's relationship with Demos is presented as one of an *erastes* pursuing an *eromenos*, with notes of the flattery (*kolakeia*) often associated with unbalanced relationships, the relationship on which it was based may be more properly understood as one of *philoi*. As such, each party is less bound by the societal restrictions on acceptable assistance to, and care for, one another than are *erastai* and *eromenoi*, and they need only have an understanding of the reciprocity of their relationship that satisfies each party.[62] Demos' assurance to the chorus that, despite appearances, he is in fact in control of his relationships with politicians (*Eq.* 1111–50), underscores that relationships, particularly those with the open parameters of Athenian *philia*, tend to be more complex than others may perceive them to be.[63]

V. Why Pederasty Imagery Might Have Been Tied to Cleon

A likely reason that the relationship of Paphlagon and Demos, based on that of Cleon and the Athenian *demos*, is billed as pederasty, but looks and sounds in most ways like *philia*, is that Aristophanes wanted to give the audience a good laugh, but was aware that those in attendance would recognize *philia* as the model that Cleon used as he cultivated his political base.[64] One of a comic's tools is hyperbole, and Aristophanes may well have thought that it would be funnier to make a politician who built much of his success based on personal connections into an *erastes* rather than into some sort of "super-friend," of which there was no similarly established institution. There is nothing outside of this play to suggest that Cleon himself would have portrayed his feelings for the *demos* in terms of *eros*; it is quite possible that Aristophanes projected the "*erastes* of the *demos*" metaphor onto Cleon without the demagogue ever using such an expression.

However, there is no shortage of tangential material on which to base such a distorted image. Perhaps Cleon enforced restrictions on the civic involvement of convicted male prostitutes (if *Eq.* 875–9 implies as much), and thus Aristophanes ironically projected onto him the sort of sexual activity he was discouraging.[65] Or his second speech against the Mytilenians (Thuc. 3.37–40) could have started Aristophanes' thought process. There, Cleon denounces the approach of many of the Athenian people merely to take pleasure (ἡδονή) in public speeches (Thuc. 3.38.7, 3.40.2), and maligns those who view political oratory as an entertainment rather than an active civic duty (3.38.4–5).[66] Cleon admonishes the assembly of Athenians that, instead of being passive in public affairs (a role that, in a pederastic relationship, would be played by the *eromenos*), leaving the active role (that of the *erastes*) to be played by orators, its members should be active, critical participants in decisions of the state (3.38.7).[67] In sum, this speech, along with the circumstances noted above, indicate that Cleon was linked closely enough to sexual angles on political matters that distorting his actual exploitation of such angles for humorous use could have been a rather organic process.

Furthermore, Aristophanes could simply have labeled Cleon an *erastes* because imagery of pederasty in political contexts, in all genres, is common in classical Athens. Unlike with Paphlagon's portrayal, though, it is typically conceived of as an extended metaphor, with genuine desire being part of the supposed pederastic mindset.[68] For example, in Pericles' exhortation of Athenians to be *erastai* of their city (τοὺς δὲ λοιποὺς χρὴ … ἐραστὰς γιγνομένους αὐτῆς, "You that remain ought … to be [Athens'] lovers," Thuc. 2.43.1), he elaborates on the image by asking them to gaze, as a lover does, upon the power of Athens (τὴν τῆς πόλεως δύναμιν καθ' ἡμέραν ἔργῳ θεωμένους).[69] Plato's works, too, reveal a sense that pederastic imagery in politics is not a purely platonic metaphor. While his Socrates does not expand on such imagery in *First Alcibiades* when he expresses concern that Alcibiades is a *demos*-lover (δημεραστής, 132a), Socrates specifically equates that sort of political passion with erotic yearning for a beloved in *Gorgias* 481d. There, he tells Callicles that the two of them are alike in desiring (ἐρῶντε) two things: each one his *eromenos* (Alcibiades plays that role for Socrates, as Pyrilampos does for Callicles), plus another pursuit for each that would not outwardly seem erotic: philosophy, for Socrates, and, for Callicles, the *demos* of Athenians (Ἀθηναίων δήμου).[70] The same distinctly erotic feelings tied to figures portrayed as political *erastai* appear as well in Aristophanes' plays other than *Knights*. In *Acharnians*, performed in 425, the year before *Knights*, the Athenophile Thracian king Sitalces underscores that he is "a true lover" of Athenians (ὑμῶν τ' ἐραστὴς ἦν ἀληθής, Ar. *Ach.* 143) by writing Ἀθηναῖοι καλοί ("Athenians are beautiful," 144) on walls; he treats a citizen body as something to which someone can be visually attracted, as Pericles treated the city's power.[71] And a decade after *Knights*, Aristophanes has a herald in *Birds* (414 BCE) announce not just that many people are lovers (ἐραστάς) of Cloudcuckooland (Ar. *Av.* 1279; cf. 324), but that they feel passion (ἔρωτες) for it (1316).[72] In short, when imagery of pederasty is used in political contexts in this period, it is not treated as a metaphor that applies only on the level of "really liking" the city or *demos*, or altruistically wishing it well, as several scholars have suggested that Paphlagon's pederasty might be interpreted.[73] While not every appearance of *erastes* as a political metaphor is reinforced with other sexually explicit terminology or imagery, the frequency with which such terminology or imagery does accompany the term, particularly in Aristophanes, suggests that such ideas were implicit when it was used.[74]

VI. Conclusion

While Paphlagon/Cleon explicitly calls himself an *erastes* to Demos in *Knights*, his portrayal throughout the play is much more consistent with the language and behavior of a *philos*. This is made clear in large part through comparison with the language and behavior of the Sausage-Seller, which does not deviate from what would be expected of a typical Athenian *erastes*. It is likely that Aristophanes' choice to portray Cleon's stand-in as an *erastes* is based on the commonness of pederastic imagery in Athenian politics of the time. The poet seems to realize, though, that he needs to portray Paphlagon/Cleon as a *philos* in order not to deviate from what it appears audience expectations of him were. It is that model, of leader as *philos*, that seems to have had a lasting impact on Athenian politics, as the next chapter will show.

5

Later Developments of the "Leader as *Philos*" Model

I. Introduction

Our extant sources on the specific actions of politicians identified as demagogues are far sparser in the decades after Cleon's death than they were during his life, so it is difficult conclusively to substantiate a claim that others following him sought to cultivate friendships with individual members of the masses in the way that Cleon seems to have done. But there are plenty of continuities between Cleon and subsequent politicians that suggest his influence, starting with the types of people who rose to power and the way that they used the power that they acquired. Notably, Hyperbolus, who succeeded Cleon in demagogy until his ostracism in 416 or 415 BCE, and Cleophon, the most prominent demagogue of the last stretch of the Peloponnesian War (Diod. Sic. 13.53.2) and who lived until 406, were very similar to Cleon in their *demos*-favoring legislation, their family backgrounds, the ways in which they were ridiculed by comic poets and orators, and, in the case of Cleophon, his ostentatious style of speaking.[1] The expressed irritation of Aristophanes' chorus in *Frogs* (produced in 405) over the influence on Athens of politicians who—as the stereotype went with Cleon, Hyperbolus, Cleophon, and others labeled "demagogues" by one source or another—were outsiders from the traditional elite (730–3) further suggests continuity with Cleon nearly two decades after his death in 422.[2]

A broader ethic of being well-disposed to the mass of Athenians also clearly continued to be valued in public discourse well past Cleon's death. When enemies of Alcibiades tried to tie him to the mutilation of the Herms in 415, they thought it a potentially stinging criticism to classify his behavior as reflecting a criminal pattern that was not "concerned for the people" (δημοτικὴν, *demotiken*, Thuc. 6.28.2).[3] Andocides, hoping to be recalled to Athens after being exiled for his own role in the mutilation, used that same word (δημοτικῷ, *demotikoi*, 2.26) to characterize the mindset he would hope to maintain if he were allowed back. And when Alcibiades the Younger tried to rehabilitate his father's image after the latter's death, he characterized the elder Alcibiades as having shown "friendship toward the people" (Τὴν ... φιλίαν τὴν πρὸς τὸν δῆμον, Isoc. 16.28) through public service as a valiant soldier and general (16.29–30).[4] Expressions and characterizations of this sort, either valorizing dedication to the mass of Athenians or maligning a shortage of attention to that group, show up repeatedly throughout the rest of the classical period.[5]

What is not extant, however, are precise records that politicians who followed Cleon's lead in many respects also did so in striving to win over constituents by making them feel a sense of friendship with the politician. Yet the way that leadership is portrayed by individuals in charge either of armies, or of other groups of dedicated followers, in two tragedies at the end of the Peloponnesian War (Euripides' *Iphigenia in Aulis* and *Bacchae*), and in biographically focused works of history written perhaps forty years after it (Xenophon's works, particularly the *Anabasis* and, as noted above, *Cyropaedia*), suggest that developing a sense of personal *philia* with a significant number of the commons was still associated, to an extent, with types of leaders who fit the demagogic model, but also simply came to be associated with effective leadership.

II. Odysseus in *Iphigenia in Aulis*

It is made clear from early in *Iphigenia in Aulis* (*IA*) (on which Euripides was working until his death in 406 BCE, and which was first performed in 405) that power in the Panhellenic army is not attained and held through one's status relative to other kings.[6] It is due, instead, to one's status in the eyes of the army, and its members demand a personal touch, sometimes literally.[7] Menelaus recounts to Agamemnon how critical one-on-one interactions with "commoners" (δημοτῶν, *demoton*, 340) were to Agamemnon's successful campaign to be leader of the Trojan expedition (337–42):[8]

οἶσθ᾽, ὅτ᾽ ἐσπούδαζες ἄρχειν Δαναΐδαις πρὸς Ἴλιον,
τῶι δοκεῖν μὲν οὐχὶ χρήιζων, τῶι δὲ βούλεσθαι θέλων,
ὡς ταπεινὸς ἦσθα, πάσης δεξιᾶς προσθιγγάνων
καὶ θύρας ἔχων ἀκλήιστους τῶι θέλοντι δημοτῶν
καὶ διδοὺς πρόσρησιν ἑξῆς πᾶσι, κεἰ μή τις θέλοι,
τοῖς τρόποις ζητῶν πρίασθαι τὸ φιλότιμον ἐκ μέσου;[9]

Do you remember, when you were endeavoring to lead the Greeks to Troy—
seeming as though you had no interest in leading, but clearly wanting badly
to do so—how humble you were, shaking every hand, leaving your door
open to any of the commoners who wished to see you, and accosting even
those who didn't, seeking by these methods to buy your exalted position
from the multitude?[10]

Agamemnon's practice of letting people near to him, as reflected in
handshaking, allowing people through the door into his private space, and
reaching out to others who did not approach him, was essential to gaining
their support. And as Menelaus makes clear in laying out why Agamemnon
later lost the soldiers' support, the fact of their shared proximity and comfortable
interactions, as documented in the passage above, clearly communicated to
Menelaus that there was an implicit friendship between the soldiers and
Agamemnon (344–5): "you were no longer a friend, as before, to those who
were previously your friends, being hard to approach and keeping yourself
scarce within doors" (τοῖς φίλοισιν οὐκέτ᾽ ἦσθα τοῖς πρὶν ὡς πρόσθεν φίλος /
Δυσπρόσιτος ἔσω τε κλήιθρων σπάνιος).[11] Because Agamemnon was acting
like a friend when he was pushing to gain popular support, despite the
differences in status between himself and the soldiers, he was perceived to be
the soldiers' friend, not a flatterer, though Agamemnon had no genuine interest
in them other than the role that they could play in his rise to power. This is
another illustration of the impact of propinquity between a leader and
subordinates, as between Cleon/Paphlagon and common Athenians in *Knights*
and *Wasps*, and between Cyrus and his soldiers in *Cyropaedia*.

The figure who steps into the power vacuum is Odysseus, who practices the
sort of inclusive leadership that Agamemnon's behavior prior to his choice as
leader suggested that he himself would. Odysseus is a peculiar figure to cast
the shadow he does over the play, considering he never appears onstage, and is
only mentioned three times.[12] But the last two of those passages either assert

or imply his power to compel the masses to overwhelm any resistance, and the first of them hints at the potential threat he poses because of privileged information about Agamemnon that he possesses. At 106–7, Agamemnon notes him as one of three others who know about Calchas' prophecy and Agamemnon's ruse to draw Iphigenia to Aulis.[13] At 524–37, Agamemnon claims that Odysseus would kill Iphigenia as well as Agamemnon and Menelaus, and potentially destroy Argos, if Agamemnon were to try to keep Iphigenia from being sacrificed; it can be assumed that Odysseus would not attempt such violence on the most powerful family in Greece without the popular support of the military.[14] And at 1362–8, Achilles claims that Odysseus will lead the countless soldiers who will come to take Iphigenia for sacrifice, despite Achilles' and Clytemnestra's efforts to protect her.[15] Odysseus gains this power over the army by breaking down the barrier of distinction between himself and those he would lead, much as Cleon did, consistently treating the masses as a partner in operations of mutual benefit. When Agamemnon says that Odysseus' natural manner aligns him with the rabble (ποικίλος ἀεὶ πέφυκε τοῦ τ' ὄχλου μέτα, 526), he seems to indicate that Odysseus possesses a facility and identification with that group that leads its members to receive him comfortably; that is homophily.[16] Using the term ὄχλος (*okhlos*, "throng, mob") there (and at 450, 517, 735, 1030, and 1338) to designate the army may reflect a connection—conscious or not—of the play to contemporaneous Athenian affairs; that term, along with οἱ πολλοί (*hoi polloi*, "the many," forms of which appear at 1357 and 1358), πλῆθος (*plethos*, "mass, mob"), and *demos*, as noted in Chapter 1 (nn. 25, 26, and 39), were commonly used terms during the Peloponnesian War to refer to the mass of lower-class Athenian citizens, often as a political force, and sometimes with a demagogue guiding them.[17]

What it takes to be such a leader of this group (in the play) seems to be lost on Agamemnon, despite his earlier, successful efforts to appeal to them through propinquity. When Agamemnon describes Odysseus' leadership, he makes it sound as though Odysseus leads in the way that Homeric heroes do: he will "grab" (ξυναρπάσας) the Greek army and "order" (κελεύσει) it to kill Menelaus, slaughter Iphigenia, and destroy Mycenae (531–5) if Agamemnon tries to keep Iphigenia from the sacrifice to which he has previously agreed.[18] But Odysseus' actual style is likely better captured by one detail that Agamemnon includes in this same speech. Agamemnon envisions Odysseus not standing in front of the soldiers when making these commands, but standing in their midst (ἐν Ἀργείοις μέσοις, 528–9) as he does so; in this way, he is like figures in drama from Cleon's time whose portrayals appear to reflect a common practice of Cleon's: Cleon/Paphlagon surrounded by vendors (Ar. *Eq.* 852–4) and supposed flatterers (*Vesp.* 1033–4=*Pax* 756–7), and Talthybius surrounded by soldiers whom Neoptolemus had asked him to silence (Eur. *Hec.* 531), as discussed in Chapter 3, Section III. Small gestures of this sort that break down boundaries between the leader and those he leads appear to explain at least part of Odysseus' success, just as, I contend, they did Cleon's.[19]

Comparison with the leadership style of Odysseus in the *Iliad* (well before the period of the demagogues, obviously, and non-Athenian) further highlights Odysseus' approach in *IA*, and adds further details to the friendship-based leadership style identified in Chapter 3.[20] In the *Iliad*, as in *IA*, Odysseus is much more of a hands-on leader than Agamemnon is, but the epic portrays him as considerably more authoritarian in his approach. When Agamemnon's motivational speech to the troops in *Iliad* 2 backfires, Odysseus goes among the troops to turn them back to the assembly, but without question as their superior, not their peer. He first grabs Agamemnon's scepter, the symbol of the king's divinely ordained power (2.185–7), and uses it to strike any fleeing "man of the people" (δήμου ἄνδρα) he sees shouting (2.198–9), demanding that they "listen to [their] betters" (ἄκουε / οἳ σέο φέρτεροί εἰσι, 2.200–1) and maligning them as "completely insignificant both in battle and in council" (οὔτε ποτ᾽ ἐν πόλεμωι ἐναρίθμιος οὔτ᾽ ἐνὶ βουλῆι, 2.202). He also recognizes and follows a clear chain of command. He tells the soldiers that there is room for only one king, Agamemnon (2.202–6). And when he comes across a minor leader who has fled, he encourages that leader to play a role in getting the troops back to the assembly (2.191).

In short, in roughly parallel situations (in the *Iliad* and in *IA*) in which Odysseus takes over leadership of a substantial group of subordinates from Agamemnon, effective executive communication in *IA* includes Odysseus implying, through his propinquity, a sense of implicit friendship that he strove to cultivate with those subordinates, much like the characters in tragedy and comedy from Cleon's period of prominence. This stands out markedly from Odysseus' portrayal as a leader in a similar situation in Homer, and also from the more unilateral way that Thucydides (2.65.8) approvingly portrays Pericles as having led the Athenian masses (as discussed in Chapter 1, Section III). The consistency in these portrayals of demagogic leadership, with Odysseus spotlighted, both during Cleon's time and well after it, suggests that aspects of Cleon's style of leadership continued to be employed, even well after his death.

III. Dionysus in the *Bacchae*

Dionysus and his maenads in Euripides' *Bacchae*, written for the same tetralogy as *IA*, provide another portrayal of effective leadership of masses of sub-elite subordinates late in the period of the demagogues that, again, is predicated on friend-like relationships between a leader and his subordinates.[21] A god whose main followers are Lydian women might not initially seem like a leadership analogue to a general (like Odysseus or Agamemnon in *IA*) earning the allegiance of Greek soldiers, nor to Athenian demagogues winning the loyalty of the local masses. Yet common interpersonal structures and language choices between the *Bacchae* and *IA* suggest that, as in *IA*, this play's depiction of Dionysus and his main followers reflects leadership and social models that were in common circulation during this time. In line with that interpretation, aspects of Dionysus' character that the play emphasizes provide notable parallels to historical and literary demagogues.

First, while Pentheus' approach to leadership is similar to other portrayals of tragic tyrants, Dionysus is conspicuous in emphasizing propinquity with his maenads as a means of asserting his friendly connection to them.[22] On line 57, Dionysus calls the Bacchants his *fellow* travelers (ξυνεμπόρους), then follows that up by saying that he will soon be dancing *with* them (συμμετασχήσω, 63).[23] Pentheus, picking up on the arrangement, calls the maenads Dionysus' "*partners* in crime" (συνεργούς, 512). In another of Euripides' plays likely produced near the time of *Bacchae*, *Cyclops*, the chorus refers explicitly to similar companionship between Dionysus and his followers as a "friendship" (φιλίας, 81), and, in a disputed passage a few lines earlier, may go as far as to refer to him as a "friend" (φίλος, 73).[24] When Pentheus, on the other hand, speaks to or of his countrymen, it is clearly with a sense of his authority foremost. While he gives orders, as is fitting for a king, there is no corresponding indication of loyalty or camaraderie, either from Pentheus or from the countrymen he addresses. His first communication is to mock and threaten the city elders Cadmus and Teiresias (248–60), to which Teiresias responds by scolding and disputing him (266–327). And the first time that one of Pentheus' soldiers appears onstage, he makes it clear that he followed Pentheus' orders only against his better judgment (441–2).

The favors that Dionysus does for the maenads, based on his privileged position, also contribute to making the maenads feel drawn to him, much as apparent favors that demagogues, the *Knights'* Paphlagon, and *Hecuba's* Odysseus seem to have done for their statuses among their constituencies. The maenads appreciate that Dionysus shares his greatest resource, wine, with all alike, including the lowly: "Equally he gave unto the blessed and the lower one to have the harmless enjoyment of wine" (ἴσαν δ' ἔς τε τὸν ὄλβιον / τόν τε χείρονα δῶκ' ἔχειν / οἴνου τέρψιν ἄλυπον, 421–3). They also value that he protects them from peril, when they could not otherwise protect themselves (604–12): "Who would be my guardian, if you would chance upon a misfortune?" (τίς μοι φύλαξ ἦν, εἰ σὺ συμφορᾶς τύχοις; 611–12).[25] Someone looking for parallels to contemporaneous events might note Cleon's and Cleophon's use of their influential positions to push for material benefit for the Athenian poor, and Cleon's apparent depiction of himself as a fierce guardian of common Athenians.[26] In contrast with Dionysus' effectively inclusive and ingratiating political style is Pentheus' uncompromising authoritarianism, which is no more effective, in the end, against Dionysus and his band of outsiders than were elite attempts to squelch demagogic politics throughout the Peloponnesian War.

Furthermore, as with Odysseus in *IA*, and, arguably, as with Cleon as well, Dionysus' subordinates carry out his will not due to compulsion or deference to his authority, but because they feel enough of a sense of kinship with him that they *want* to do so. While Dionysus does give unilateral commands to the maenads (34, 412, 1079–81, 1088), they speak of the work they do for him as "sweet" (ἡδὺν, 66), and a messenger refers to the women's labors as "delightful" (τερπνοῖς, 1053), revealing a sense of personal pleasure in doing work for Dionysus. In other sources from the classical period, expressions of delight in working for a god are extremely unusual.[27]

The emphasis on these subordinates of Dionysus as the agents carrying out his plans also aligns the play with *IA* and the demagogic model more broadly.

Just as it is not Odysseus himself, but his influence over the army, that pushes Agamemnon to sacrifice his daughter in *IA*, and the Athenian masses whose votes made the demagogues' influence meaningful, so, too, is it Dionysus' female followers, both Lydian and Theban, whose actions most concern, occupy, then harm Pentheus at Dionysus' behest.[28] Pentheus' first word after claiming that he has heard of subversive mischief happening in the land is γυναῖκας (217), and it is the women's supposed rural wine-drinking and sex that has him most upset (217–25).[29] It is the women whom he first imprisons (226–7) or seeks to imprison (228–32) upon his return. Their escape from their shackles tempers Pentheus' success in arresting Dionysus (443–8). Their supernatural accomplishments in the wild press the issue of Pentheus' acceptance of Dionysus' worship (664–774). Finally, they are the ones who rip Pentheus to shreds (1095–1143), called into action by Dionysus (1078–81, 1088–94).

Further tying Dionysus' followers to demagogic dynamics of the time, language associated with these women—parallel to terms attached to the army in *IA*, and other "masses" of lower-class people elsewhere—suggests an implicit link to the common people of Athens.[30] They are either called words equivalent to "the rabble," or express support for that group, on four occasions during the play. The first reference appears in the parodos, when the Lydian chorus states that a womanly mob (θηλυγενὴς ὄχλος, *thelugenes okhlos*, 117), consisting of the women of Thebes, rests in the mountains, driven from their shuttles and looms by Dionysus (116–19). In a later stasimon, the Bacchants claim allegiance with the masses (430–1):

τὸ πλῆθος (*plethos*) ὅτι τὸ φαυλότερον ἐνόμισε χρῆ-
ται τε, τόδ᾽ ἂν δεχοίμαν

I accept that which the simplest masses believe and practice.[31]

The immediate appearance of a representative of the "simplest masses," a soldier directed to deliver Dionysus to Pentheus, supports this connection. Oranje (1984: 109) takes the soldier's expression of sympathy with the stranger (*Bacch.* 441–2) and his suggestion that there may be something divine to the stranger's actions (449–50) as a statement of commonality with the Bacchants and of opposition to Pentheus' dismissal of the divinity of Dionysus.[32] At the end of the play, that ideological connection of the Bacchants (among whose number the women of Thebes can now be counted) to the masses reappears during the maenads' culminating act of destruction while under Dionysus' power. The messenger relating Pentheus' demise twice refers to the women who are about to tear the king to shreds as an *okhlos* (1058, 1130).

Finally, even the portrayal of Dionysus in *Bacchae* has demagogic undertones.[33] For one, despite being a god, Dionysus, both in his own identity and in the persona he presents, is clearly portrayed as an outsider from the established power structure that he enters, as was *IA*'s Odysseus and, as well, were most demagogues. While Odysseus in *IA* is an outsider by choice, deciding that greater power lies in circumventing Agamemnon's authority, Dionysus in the *Bacchae* initially depicts himself as an outsider based on a complicated family background, implications of foreignness, and inexperience with elite norms, which were among the reasons that several demagogues were also seen (or at least depicted in comedy) as outsiders. Dionysus both expresses anger at being perceived in Thebes as the son not of Zeus, but of an ordinary man (*Bacch.* 26–9, 41–2), and also presents himself as a foreign stranger (ξένος, 233 *et passim*), at a time in history when undistinguished or alien parentage was a common slur against demagogues.[34] Also, it is not just the androgynous appearance of Dionysus' persona (233–6, 353, 457) that marginalizes him, but also what that appearance says about him: Pentheus notes that the stranger's hair is unsuited for wrestling (455), training in which sport is treated in Aristophanes' *Frogs* (729–33, 1069–72) as marking a person at this time as elite and well-disciplined, and thus suitable for leadership in Athens.[35]

The values typically associated with Dionysus, and his application of those values in this play, also have demagogic resonance. While Dionysus is widely considered the most versatile and elusive of gods in the breadth and paradox of his portrayals in myth and ritual, one commonality of many portrayals is his egalitarianism.[36] Versnel calls him "the democratic god *par excellence*," and his democratic appeal evens the status of poor and rich, weak and strong, ignorant and educated, old and young, and even, at times in Athenian history, alien and citizen, and slave and free.[37] Dionysus' approach in this play is presented by Teiresias in populist terms as lack of discrimination between worshipers (206–9):

οὐ γὰρ διήρηχ' ὁ θεός, οὔτε τὸν νέον
εἰ χρὴ χορεύειν οὔτε τὸν γεραίτερον,

ἀλλ' ἐξ ἁπάντων βούλεται τιμὰς ἔχειν
κοινάς, διαριθμῶν δ' οὐδέν' αὔξεσθαι θέλει.

No, for the god has not distinguished whether it is proper for someone young or old to dance, but wants to have honors in common from all, and setting apart no one, he wants to be glorified.

The chorus, in turn, treats his populism as open beneficence, in terms of the sharing of the gift of wine with both the fortunate and less fortunate, as noted above (421–3).[38] But while the chorus says he shares his gifts equally, Dionysus states early in the play that his purpose is not to *give* in equal portions, but to *insist* on equal devotion from those who do not already follow him (39–42). And the specific targets of his further offensive suggest a populist bent: he targets not everyone, but rather the reigning king and the king's mother and aunts, who are the daughters of the city's founder.

In sum, the *Bacchae* presents another scenario from late in the fifth century BCE in which a contrast between the effectiveness of two leaders is predicated on the sense of friendship that they inspire in their followers. That the portrayal of the effective leader (Dionysus) and his subordinates (maenads) also suggests a demagogic dynamic further parallels the depiction of Odysseus and the army in *IA*. It additionally reinforces the idea that leadership by winning "friends" was primarily associated with demagogues, even nearly two decades after Cleon's death.

IV. Xenophon, Clearchus, and Other Military and Political Leaders in Xenophon's Biographical Works

The continuing influence on Athenian politics of friendship-based techniques of cultivating humble supporters may be seen as well in even less obvious sources. Xenophon's works were most likely written several decades after the end of the Peloponnesian War, when people labeled "demagogues" became a less prominent part of the Athenian political scene, and several of Xenophon's works were primarily about people and historical events outside of Athens.[39] Xenophon himself lived out of the *polis*, most of that time in exile, for more than three decades following the Peloponnesian War, and he likely wrote many of his works during that time abroad.[40] However, as indicated in the discussion of the *Cyropaedia* in Chapter 3, he could not have avoided being influenced by his rearing in Athens during the age of the demagogues, and the fact that he was almost certainly writing his works primarily for an Athenian audience, quite possibly as a way to justify himself to his native compatriots, suggests that he would have written them in a way that would be familiar to Athenians.[41]

Demagogic influence is not obvious in all of his works or at all times in the works in which it seems to appear. The *Hellenica*, for instance, Xenophon's historical work that specifically covers the late Peloponnesian War and talks about Cleophon himself, gives only a few indications of friendship development with common Athenians as a primary method of coalition-building, by demagogues or others. Buxton (2016: 170) notes the "frustrating scarcity in [the *Hellenica*] of direct authorial commentary or generalizing reflection" on model leadership other than "in contexts devoid of larger political-military significance." Like Thucydides' history, which it followed, the *Hellenica*'s emphasis is far more on events than on people or relationships.

Xenophon's works that focus more on individual leaders, though, such as *Cyropaedia* and the *Anabasis*, dwell extensively on those individuals' actions that moved history, and on the techniques they used to lead large groups effectively. In those works, there is a notable emphasis on top leaders successfully winning the allegiance of subordinates by using techniques of individual friendship-building with them. As noted earlier, the *Cyropaedia* portrays Cyrus the Great as intentionally, and successfully, cultivating feelings of individual friendship with lower-class members of his army—by means of propinquity and homophily with those he met, and via transitivity with those whom he did not—to help him in his cause. The *Anabasis*, as well, and, to a lesser extent, the *Hellenica* and several of Xenophon's other works, also suggest leaders' efforts to provoke subordinates' feelings of friendship toward them by showing their regard for, equality with, and accessibility to those subordinates. The regular portrayal of these leaders demonstrating their affinity for, and identity with, their lower-class soldiers suggests internalization of effective practices of leaders that are consistent with the behaviors of Cleon; Euripides' Odysseus, Talthybius, Agamemnon, and Dionysus; and, I contend, Athenian demagogues who succeeded Cleon, but not consistent with the behaviors of the large majority of prior Athenian leaders. There are also enough indications of *philia* as a tie binding soldiers to generals to imply Xenophon's sense that

Athenians would have seen this as a common way for inferiors to feel toward superiors.

A. Leadership in Xenophon's Works: Prior Perspectives

While this is far from the first study of Xenophon's attention to leadership in his works, it is the first tying it to demagogic influence and tacit awareness of the efficacy of the sociological concepts described in Chapter 3. Christ (2020: 153–83), in particular, compellingly argues for a strong Athenian undercurrent in the mass–elite leadership dynamic in the *Anabasis*, and he brings up demagogues as among the figures providing models for Xenophon's success in his bid for leadership. But Christ treats oratory as the particularly Athenian method of winning over the army; while that certainly plays a role in effective political leadership, my focus will be on the aspects of their portrayed oratory, and other steps that Xenophon's leaders take, that win the trust and consequent friendly allegiance of individual soldiers.

Much of Xenophon's work tacitly addresses what makes an effective leader; the *Cyropaedia* and *Hiero* have it as among their chief foci, and Xenophon on several other occasions, either in his narrative voice or through characters, ponders the matter. He describes Socrates regularly conversing about what makes a good leader of people (ἀρχικὸς ἀνθρώπων, *Mem.* 1.1.16) or of soldiers (στρατηγός, 3.1.7). He has characters describe how good leadership looks, which is for subordinates to have enough trust in whoever is guiding them that they follow instructions gladly: Ischomachus expresses to Socrates his sense that the best leadership is "leadership of the willing" (τὸ ἐθελόντων ἄρχειν, *Oec.* 21.21), and Cyrus' father, Cambyses, tells him that the best form of leadership is "persuading the willing" (τὸ ἑκόντας πείθεσθαι, *Cyrop.* 1.6.21).[42] He considers it a worthy thing to do (without doing so himself in the transmitted text of the *Hellenica*) to consider what the Spartan admiral Teleutias did that "disposed those he led in such a way" (οὕτω διέθηκε τοὺς ἀρχομένους) that they showed him tremendous fondness at the end of his term of guidance of them (*Hell.* 5.1.4). Many contemporary scholars, across a range of fields, have followed up with inquiries into the skills that *do* make leaders in Xenophon's works effective, and in some cases, how those skills can be applied in the contemporary world.[43] Generally, those looking for influences on the skills that Xenophon highlights trace them to Socrates, to various military leaders, or to Xenophon's own experience running his estate.[44]

One of the techniques that scholars have observed Xenophon's featured leaders using to win over their subordinates, which may actually tie back to demagogic influence, is their cultivation and use of *philia*, though not of the personally felt type identified in Chapter 3.[45] Among recent treatments, Gray (2011: 291–329) provides a nuanced discussion of Xenophontic leaders' efforts to cultivate feelings of friendship with subordinates that is like that between personal friends. She highlights both "emotional" and "transactional" benefits that Xenophontic leaders aim to pass on to their followers, services that they can receive in turn from their followers, and terms of friendship (φιλέω, στέργω, εὖ ποιέω, and similar words and expressions) used regularly by leaders toward their followers and vice versa (294–7). She breaks down how the unequal statuses of leaders and subordinates can be overcome in friendly relations between them (298–314), in a manner similar to that laid out in Chapter 3. And she notes services that leaders and followers can provide one another (315–20). While friendliness and reciprocity, which Gray handles thoroughly, are key features of classical Greek friendship, though, Gray does not go into details of why these unbalanced relationships might have been processed by supporters as genuine emotional friendship, and not just transactions between people who feel positively inclined toward one another as allies or partners in mutually beneficial endeavors. Buxton's (2017) discussion also brings in the importance in leadership of "benevolence" (327) and "attention to [subordinates'] well-being" (334), and notes "reciprocal goodwill" (332) as an important force binding leaders and the led. He cites (173) examples such as Jason of Pherae's conspicuous rewarding of outstanding effort in his soldiers (*Hell.* 6.1.6, 15) and Teleutias' example of hard work that his soldiers were likely to follow (*Hell.* 5.1.15). Those things, however, while useful for achieving an objective, are not the same as friendship, which brings with it a different bond than situational loyalty does. Xenophon's works do, though, indicate ways in which his exemplary leaders take steps that likely encouraged many of the soldiers under those leaders' influence to see them not just as advocates, well-wishers, or panderers, but actually as *philoi*, through approaches that tie back to the sociological effectiveness of demagogic coalition-building styles, and even through references specifically to demagoguery. Those will be addressed shortly.

Tamiolaki (2016), too, observes personal dynamics between Xenophon's leaders and subordinates that further tie to the possibility of demagogic influence. She notes (32) that one of the things that makes *philia* in the context of Xenophontic leadership striking—as at, e.g., *Mem.* 2.6.13, when Socrates and Critobulus discuss how much the city of Athens liked (φιλεῖν) Pericles and Themistocles—is that it contrasts with the pederastic model that Pericles famously tells the Athenian people should be the way that they envision themselves relative to the *polis* (Thuc. 2.43.1). As pointed out in Chapter 3, Section V, that image appears in a range of other sources from the fifth and fourth centuries as well, among them works of Plato, in which Socrates uses *erastes* imagery to capture aspiring politicians Callicles' (*Gorg.* 481d) and Alcibiades' (*1 Alc.* 132a) feelings for a political body that they hoped to have a role in governing.[46] Xenophon was a follower of Socrates at the same time that Plato was; the fact that Plato has his Socrates using pederastic imagery in political circumstances while Xenophon has him employing *philia* imagery indicates, as one possibility, that Socrates was not entirely consistent in the political imagery he used. It may also, just as likely, be that the historical Socrates was not the only model upon which Xenophon was drawing in his construction of the ideal leader that he intended for Socrates to embody in the *Memorabilia*, and the character of Socrates here may be expressing an amalgam of ideas of different leaders that Xenophon admired.

Tamiolaki also observes, though, that the focus of affection in Xenophon's political imagery moves from the *polis* to the leader in a way that may reflect Persian models more accurately than Athenian ones (32–3). Alongside the passages cited above about Athenians' affection for Themistocles and Pericles, she includes *Cyropaedia* 1.6.24 and *Anabasis* 1.9.28, in which forms of φιλέω are used to capture what the Persian leaders are depicted as either wanting or receiving from their subordinates. These leaders focus their actions on becoming the sorts of people that those they lead might *like*, in a manner that Tamiolaki notes is parallel with private relationships (33).

Finally, Tamiolaki contends that portraying Athenian leader–subordinate relationship dynamics in this way distorts history. It makes pre- or early-Peloponnesian-War leaders seem more like Persian autocrats or like Xenophon's version of Socrates than they actually were, based on Xenophon's projections onto these Athenian leaders of what he observed or studied about those foreign ones, or what he remembered about his inspiring mentor (34–5).

These perspectives on *philia* in Xenophontic leadership as being characterized either by broad friend-like or affection-seeking behaviors in leaders, or on approaches that are defined as essentially Persian or Socratic, overlook some details that may tie cross-cultural Xenophontic leaders' actions at least in part to demagogic influences. First, leaders' practices that might initially be categorized imprecisely as showing "good will" or "care," as discussed above, take on more efficacy as friendship-developing when looked at through the sociological lenses applied previously to demagogues and others seeming to have taken up their practices. Second, leaders' focus on doing things to encourage their subordinates to "like" them is certainly not restricted to Persians, as the behavior of Greek leaders' behaviors will illustrate. Buxton (2016: 187) speaks of an "innovation" of Xenophon in the *Anabasis* in "expand[ing] the scope of aristocratic friendship from the army's leadership to its entire complement," and in such action standing out from Cyrus in *Cyropaedia*, who Buxton says "builds a reputation for channeling his vast wealth to those aristocrats who are proactive in advancing his interests as a means to motivate Greeks and Persians alike to perform spontaneous services in his presence (1.4.13–17 and 1.5.7–8, respectively)." While Cyrus' actions, as documented in Chapter 3, are far more likely to register as those of a *philos* to common Persian soldiers, through carefully planned practices, than Buxton observes here, Buxton's credit to Xenophon is still valid: *contra* Tamiolaki, *philia*-like behavior toward subordinates is certainly practiced by Xenophon's Greeks leaders, notably Xenophon himself in the *Anabasis*.

B. The Sociology of Demagogic Behavior in Xenophon's Works

On the sociological side of friendship development between leaders and subordinates, several behaviors of Xenophon himself (portrayed in the *Anabasis*) and other Xenophontic leaders could be recognized as encouraging propinquity with their soldiers, likely encouraging feelings of homophily in them, with suggestions of transitive connection to compound the friendship impact. One of those practices is open accessibility. In the *Anabasis*, for instance, Xenophon is reputed always to be open to a visit from his soldiers to talk about a war-related matter, no matter what the time is or what else he is doing (4.3.10).[47] Several other leaders in other works are similarly renowned for their willingness to speak to whoever would approach them: the Syracusan general Hermocrates (*Hell.* 1.1.30), the Spartan admiral Teleutias (*Hell.* 5.1.14), and the Spartan king Agesilaus (*Ages.* 9.2). This policy of accessibility encourages close personal contact with subordinates, with the friendship-building benefits of propinquity that come from it. It implicitly communicates a sense of homophily: people signal their likeness to others when they invite interaction with them. And it promotes a transitive sense, from soldiers who have not yet taken any of these leaders up on their policy, that they *could* do so, expanding the feeling of propinquity.[48] This accessibility to subordinates is also a trait that is seen, as noted above, in Cleon in the *agora*, in Agamemnon when he initially wins over the army in *IA*, and in Dionysus as he travels, dances, and works with his maenads. Also, in *Anabasis*, Xenophon personally tends to those who are weak or ill in the midst of their long march (4.5.7–9, 12–18). Again, this requires close physical contact, encouraging propinquity; willingness to tend to others physically suggests homophily; and an implicit message of transitivity follows such care: he would share that space and provide that care with any of the soldiers.

A range of other practices further suggests the efficacy of friendship-building in Xenophon's leaders' behavior. When there is a need for a fire, but entering the bitter cold from the warmth of the army's snow cover is an unpleasant prospect, Xenophon gets up and starts cutting wood, inspiring others to do the same (*Anab.* 4.4.12–13). On another occasion, when a soldier named Soteridas tells Xenophon that he is not equal (ἐξ ἴσου) to the other troops because he is riding while they walk, he gets down from his horse and takes up Soteridas' shield (3.4.47–8). After he has marched this way for some time, wearing his heavy cavalry breastplate, the message is clearly sent that he is not above the hard work that the infantry members do, and other soldiers malign Soteridas until he takes up his shield again (3.4.49). Xenophon dismounts again at 7.3.45 to join the hoplites on foot, and when Seuthes asks him why, since it would slow him down, Xenophon replies, "you do not need only me" (οὐκ ἐμοῦ μόνου δέῃ, 7.3.45), treating himself as equivalent to other soldiers, and claiming that the hoplites would likely be faster and happier with him along with them (7.3.46).[49] Through these actions, he intentionally shoulders the burdens of his soldiers, signaling his likeness to them and likely triggering feelings of homophily. When he gets off his horse, he directly puts himself in physical proximity to the soldiers, and by setting an example regarding the fire that other soldiers then follow, he is again near those others—there is propinquity. And again, transitivity can be implied. Similarly, the way that Teleutias' troops treat him in the *Hellenica* when he is to return home after completing his assignment with them shows that his cultivation of propinquity with them is likely one of the reasons that he is so celebrated by them, as noted earlier in this section. Xenophon specifies that every soldier present shakes Teleutias' hand (ἐδεψιώσατο), others festoon him with a garland and a fillet, and those who arrive late throw into the water after him the garlands they had intended to present to him (*Hell.* 5.1.3). In all of those cases, the soldiers know that Teleutias is open to close contact with them, almost certainly because he had shown such openness on many prior occasions.

Practices concerning money and praise, too, communicate Xenophontic leaders' sense of the value of cultivating homophily. In the *Anabasis*, both Xenophon and Clearchus express to their soldiers the value both claim to put on the well-being of those soldiers rather than on their own enrichment: Xenophon says that he always pays the soldiers before himself (7.7.39–40), and then is shown doing so (7.7.56); Clearchus, too, tells his troops that the money he received from Cyrus he used to advance his soldiers' interests (1.3.3–4). Additionally, Xenophon rebukes Seuthes for not providing the soldiers their promised pay (7.7.21). In this rhetoric and these practices, the attention to the material needs of subordinates before oneself likely cultivates feelings of homophily among them. Nussbaum (1967: 141) notes that such dedication to putting others' material well-being ahead of one's own is quite extraordinary for the time, and Xenophon's and Clearchus' practices signal that, despite their higher status, they put themselves behind the soldiers in line for compensation. Xenophon notes that he also pays the other generals and captains before himself (7.5.3), and tells the soldiers that he has received less, overall, for his efforts than the rest of the generals and even some of the captains (7.6.19). His putting those who are at his level, and even those who are below him on the leadership chain, ahead of himself further sends a message to his soldiers that he is the sort of person—like them, typically—whose interests are tended to after others' are, likely further cultivating in them a sense of homophily toward him. Those who followed him back to Greece would know that those practices were not simply inconsequential tokens; he returns from his expedition with so little gold that he has to sell his horse to pay his traveling expenses (7.8.1–3).

When Clearchus and Xenophon, separately, are in danger of losing their troops (Clearchus' troops to mutiny, Xenophon's troops to the Spartans), each one's defense of himself to the group reveals a philosophy of leadership based on principles of *philia*, with a specific emphasis on propinquity and homophily in their rhetoric. Clearchus, speaking of the dilemma he faces concerning continuing an expedition with Cyrus that his soldiers want to abandon, says that maintaining his friendship (φιλίᾳ) with Cyrus would require him to betray (προδόντα) his soldiers, an unpleasant prospect to him (1.3.5). He uses the same terms two sentences later, stating that he wishes no one to say of him that he betrayed (προδοὺς) the Greeks in choosing the friendship (φιλίαν) of the barbarians. While *philia* can refer to alliances that have little personal component, Clearchus surrounds that imagery with propinquity-based characterizations of his physical connection with his troops. Using the same and similar prepositions to those that Dionyus does in his expression to the maenads of the pleasing physical proximity to them that he hopes to maintain in the *Bacchae*, Clearchus speaks to his troops of punishing the Thracians "along with you" (μεθ᾽ ὑμῶν, 1.3.4), but that the current circumstances have made the soldiers no longer willing to "journey with" (συμπορεύεσθαι) him (1.3.5). Since they will no longer obey or follow him, he will follow "with [them]" (σὺν ὑμῖν, 1.3.6), and if he is "with [them]" (σὺν ὑμῖν, 1.3.6), he says, he will be honored by people they meet. The model of which he tries to convince his soldiers is that of a friendship of equals with his soldiers (likely aiming to provoke feelings of homophily in them), emphasizing his physical accompaniment of his soldiers on joint endeavors (reminding them of propinquity he has likely experienced with many of them).

Xenophon, too, addresses his troops in terms of friendly fellowship and reminds them of the services he has done for them that are like a friend's favors. Like Clearchus, he refers to his actions with them in terms of the work of companions in close proximity to one another: he has endured toils and dangers "with [them]" (σὺν ὑμῖν), and "with [them]" (σὺν ὑμῖν) has set up many trophies against the barbarians (7.6.36). Furthermore, in addition to pointing out the actions he has taken "on behalf/account of" (ὑπέρ, 7.6.35) and "in defense of" (πρό, 7.6.36) them, as someone who cares for someone else would do, he reminds the soldiers that they recognized him as a "benefactor" (εὐεργέτης) during hard times (7.6.38).[50] His terminology reflects Archedemus' terms for favors friends do for one another (εὐεργετούμενον ... καὶ ἀντευεργετοῦντα, "receiving good works ... and reciprocating good works in turn," *Mem.* 2.9.8). He also puts those favors (and appropriate reciprocation for them) in terms of *kharis* (7.6.23, 32), as did demagogic characters in Aristophanes' *Knights* and Euripides' *Hecuba* (see Chapter 3, Section VI).[51] Xenophon, like Clearchus, defines himself not just as someone who does well by his soldiers, as one does for friends, but also as someone who does things not at the head of his soldiers, but in physical concert with them.

Furthermore, the language that others use to describe Xenophon and his actions, and that he and Clearchus use to express their motivations and relationships with the soldiers, ties these two leaders to the tradition of Cleon and other demagogues, and further suggests a sense of friendship as a connection between themselves and their soldiers. When the Thracian Seuthes criticizes Xenophon to the Spartan delegation that is deciding what to do with him, he calls Xenophon φιλοστρατιώτης (*philostratiotes*, "friendly to the soldiers," 7.6.4), recalling the use of *philodemos* at *Knights* 786 and *Clouds* 1187. The Spartan Charminus soon thereafter claims that *philostratiotes* is not a particularly damning criticism (7.6.39).[52] An even more precise link to the age of Cleon comes from the Spartans Charminus and Polynicus, who respond to Seuthes' appraisal of Xenophon with the clarifying question, "so indeed [Xenophon] acts like a demagogue toward the men?" (Ἀλλ' ἢ δημαγωγεῖ ὁ ἀνὴρ τοὺς ἄνδρας, 7.6.4).[53] What it means to Xenophon himself to act in a way that Seuthes would characterize as he does becomes explicit in his explanation to Seuthes of why, unlike Heracleides, he aspires to exhibit merit, justice, and generosity toward his soldiers, rather than to accumulate wealth before all other priorities (7.7.41). Someone who possesses these qualities, Xenophon says, prospers "because he has many friends" (ὄντων φίλων πολλῶν), and "because others want to become" his friends (ἄλλων βουλομένων γενέσθαι, 7.7.42).[54] In this approach he stands out from Seuthes, whose subjects, Xenophon says, did not live under his rule due to *philia*, but rather necessity (7.7.29). And while the narrator makes a similar comment about Clearchus, that his severity meant that soldiers did not follow him out of *philia* (2.6.13),

Clearchus knows a way to grab their allegiance when he needs it most, when he is about to be abandoned. At that point, after laying out all that he has done in concert with his troops, he concludes by saying he thinks of them as his "fatherland and friends and allies" (πατρίδα καὶ φίλους καὶ συμμάχους, 1.3.6).[55]

V. Conclusion

Depictions of interactions between historical figures specifically labeled demagogues and other Athenians are not extant after the death of Cleon. But the sorts of engagements that are portrayed between Cleon (or a proxy of him) and Athenians (or actual or potential proxies of them) during Cleon's life appear in other media for decades following his death. Figures in Euripidean tragedy—primarily Odysseus and Dionysus—who share much in common with Athenian demagogues, lead in the same *philia*-focused ways, using propinquity and homophily to promote friendship development, that Cleon appears to as he is represented in Aristophanes. And Xenophon portrays leaders in several of his biographies and histories operating in similar ways to Cleon and the tragic characters who follow his practices. All of these cases provide the best evidence available from our extant sources that the sort of leadership cultivation that Cleon seems to have practiced made an impact on leaders who followed him; leadership based on *philia* seems to have taken root as something that leaders aimed to employ and that many subordinates came to expect.

Conclusion: Cleon and the Legacy of Leadership by Friendship

Athenian demagogues during the Peloponnesian War, beginning with Cleon, have long been recognized as standing out from their predecessors in power. As noted in Chapter 2, there are stereotypes from the ancient world of ways in which they differed from earlier leaders: they were from humble families, and in some cases had foreign parents; as owners of factories in which enslaved workers did manual work, they themselves were no different from menial workers; they won over common Athenians because their flamboyant, gesticulating rhetorical styles exploited the audiences' ignorance and lack of discrimination; and they won loyalty from poor Athenians by lobbying for measures that benefited those Athenians materially. More recent studies have suggested that the peers of the so-called demagogues recognized that the financial savvy they acquired because of their close engagement with the growth of their businesses would be useful in the management of Athens' growing empire. On the other hand, some analyses, both ancient and modern, have proposed that purported differences between those labeled "demagogues" and other Athenian politicians have been overstated, and that identities and tactics attributed to demagogues were in the range of normal for Athenian politicians that had been recognized from the democracy's beginning.

This study, though, establishes ways in which so-called "demagogues" both were and were not "new" sorts of politicians, as coined by Connor (1971). In their approach to cultivating supporters on whom they could rely, they were much like Athenian politicians had been for centuries, as laid out in Chapter 1: they leaned on friends. The way they made those friends, though, may be the innovation that most influenced Athenian leadership in the political sphere after them, and perhaps the military one as well. Chapter 2 addresses Connor's

(1971) insight that, beginning with Cleon, politicians whose families were less esteemed than those of their predecessors in positions of influence took advantage of their closer connection to common Athenians to win over that majority through their greater attention to the masses' interests, and though treating the masses—as a whole–as a *philos*.

This book builds on Connor's insight, in Chapter 3, by using sociological principles to demonstrate that the "friendship" that Cleon and other demagogues cultivated with common Athenians was not merely figurative. Using depictions of characters representing demagogues from comedy and tragedy from the time of Cleon, this book expresses how Cleon, as well as some of his political peers and successors, took advantage of what contemporary sociologists recognize as techniques of friendship-building to capitalize on those connections. By making himself available in public, Cleon was able to capitalize on the effect of propinquity in generating feelings of friendship among many Athenians whom previous politicians would not have viewed as "friend material." His efforts would not have worked, though, if not for a sense of homophily that the targets of his outreach might have felt with him due to the humble roots that they shared with him. Transitivity, in turn, would have led others who did not have opportunity to share space with Cleon, but who knew or closely identified with those who did, to feel a similar sense of friendly connection to the demagogue. When Cleon, then, was speaking in the assembly, he had more than just his skill as an orator on which to rely, but also the knowledge that many in the audience considered him a friend, on some level, whether or not he particularly felt that way toward them.

Where this reading of Cleon playing the role of leader as friend to humble Athenians is most obvious is in Aristophanes' *Knights*, with reflections in others of Aristophanes' comedies and in Euripides' *Hecuba*, all from the mid-420s BCE. All of those works depict demagogic figures engaging at close range with people of humble social status, likely reflecting styles of interaction in real life for which Cleon and others were known. To reveal the friendly engagements in *Knights* for what they are, though, Chapter 4 explores ways in which the comedy portrays what is ostensibly a competition between competing *erastai* for Demos, portrayed as an *eromenos*, as, more genuinely, a depiction of a straightforward *erastes* (Sausage-Seller) and a rival, Paphlagon (Cleon), who repeatedly shows that he is actually a friend, as Cleon seems to have portrayed himself in his engagements with common Athenians outside of the assembly.

This model of demagogic politicians encouraging common citizens to feel friendship toward them seems to have set a standard in Athenian leadership that extended beyond just the demagogues, as expanded on in Chapter 5. While later demagogues seem to have done things similar to those that Cleon did in their efforts to gain and hold power, literary depictions suggest that it was not just leaders from humble backgrounds who aimed to develop or solidify their power by making friend-like connections with the masses. While Odysseus in both *Hecuba* and *Iphigenia in Aulis*, and Dionysus in *Bacchae*, are depicted as similar in many ways to demagogues, Agamemnon in *Iphigenia in Aulis* is not, and Cyrus in the *Cyropaedia* is not, yet their success with their soldiers in the works in which they are depicted is dependent on making the soldiers feel as though they are the friends of these lofty figures. Throughout several of Xenophon's other histories and biographies, a demagogic style of earning allegiance by acting as a friend to one's subordinates becomes a common route to success.

The legacy of Cleon and other demagogues, then, seems not so much to be their leadership of the common citizenry as a whole as though it were a collective friend, but rather their influence that was gained through making members of that common citizenry, one at a time, feel as though they had not just an ally, but a friend, in a position of authority. For those leaders, leadership on a macro level started on the micro level of convincing individuals that there was more than just a transactional relationship between them, but a feeling of personal connection, which would almost certainly be felt much more acutely by the lower-status individual. The cultivation of political loyalty through personal engagement that many of them appear to have employed is what, in the modern world, is known as "retail politics"—on-the-ground, face-to-face, physical contacts between politicians and voters. And it worked then, with demagogues, for the same general reason that it works now, with politicians of all sorts: politics is largely built on relationships, and we all want a friend in power.

Notes

Introduction

1 *Oxford English Dictionary* (Second Edition) definitions: "1. In ancient times, a leader of the people; a popular leader or orator who espoused the cause of the people against any other party in the state. 2. In bad sense: A leader of a popular faction, or of the mob; a political agitator who appeals to the passions and prejudices of the mob in order to obtain power or further his own interests; an unprincipled or factious popular orator." The first example that the *OED* provides for this derogatory usage is from 1649.

2 E.g., Mercieca (2020), *Demagogue for President: The Rhetorical Genius of Donald Trump*; Fuchs (August 31, 2019), "Boris Johnson Takes His Demagoguery to the Social Media Sphere," *Truthout*; Shabir (May 10, 2017), "Is It Right to Brand Imran Kahn a Demagogue?," *The Nation* (Lahore, Pakistan); Tharoor (November 4, 2018), "Trump Finds a 'Like-Minded Demagogue' in Bolsonaro," *The Washington Post*; MacCallum (November 5, 2018), "Thus Spake Mungo: ScoMo—the Authentic Demagogue," *Echo Net Daily*.

3 E.g., Tye (2020), *Demagogue: The Life and Long Shadow of Senator Joseph McCarthy*; Horowitz (2015), *Sharpton: A Demagogue's Rise*; Hoeller (November 9, 2008), "Sarah Palin — A Demagogue in a Skirt," *Huffington Post*; Borman (1954), "Huey Long: Analysis of a Demagogue," *Today's Speech* 2.3.

4 Thuc. 4.21.3: μάλιστα δὲ αὐτοὺς ἐνῆγε Κλέων ὁ Κλεαινέτου, ἀνὴρ δημαγωγὸς κατ' ἐκεῖνον τὸν χρόνον ὢν καὶ τῷ πλήθει πιθανώτατος ("The one who most encouraged them was Cleon, son of Cleaenetus, a man, a demagogue of that time and most persuasive to the masses"). On Thucydides' use of ἀνήρ (*aner*, "man") along with another noun, see Hershkowitz (2018) 20–1, with his citations.

1 Friendship in Athenian Politics Prior to the Demagogues

1 Moore (1975: 45), Frisch (1976: 29), and Osborne (2004: 25) translate *philousi* as "like," Kalinka (1913: 79) renders it as "lieben," and Dakyns (1892: 287) stretches it to "love[]." Bowersock (1968: 497) puts it as "cultivate." All other translations in the paper are my own, unless otherwise noted. As to who is included among the "elite,"

see Ober (1989: 11–13), with agreement, elaboration, and refinement in Christ (2006: 154–5) and (2020: 2 n. 1).

The dating of the [*Ath. pol.*], written by an author once thought to be Xenophon (and thus often creatively referred to as "Pseudo-Xenophon), is unresolved, but sometime during the Peloponnesian War is likely, with recent analysis putting it in the mid-420s to mid-410s (Mattingly 1997; Balot 2001: 185 n. 24; Osborne 2004: 6; Rosenbloom 2004: 87; Marr and Rhodes 2008: 5). Ober (1998: 14 n. 1), Rosenbloom (2004: 87 n. 120), Mann (2007: 39 n. 2), and Marr and Rhodes (2008: 31–2) provide brief bibliographies of approaches to the dating issue, and Hornblower (2000: 366–7), Osborne (2004: 4–6), Gray (2007: 57–8), Mann (2007: 39–41), and Marr and Rhodes (2008: 3–6) discuss the rationales for different dating philosophies.

2 Konstan (1997: 28, 53, 55, 67–78) argues for family members not being included as *philoi*, and others discuss ambiguities of including family members as such (Goldhill 1986: 82; Heath 1987: 73–4). However, Konstan (1997: 60–6) himself lays out a collection of passages in which family members certainly appear to be referred to as *philoi*, and Millett (1991: 113), Belfiore (2000: 19–20), Christ (2012: 51), and van Berkel (2020: 27) make a compelling case for family members being included as *philoi* in the great majority of cases.

3 On dedication to the *polis*, that Athenians expected of one another, see Christ (2006: 1–2), with supporting citations. On their commitment to their friends and family far surpassing that to fellow citizens (though not necessarily to the *polis*, as a whole), see Dover (1974: 273–6); Millett (1991: 127–32); Christ (2012: 10–12).

4 Among those who discuss the ideology of helping friends and harming enemies are Earp (1929: 31–5), Dirlmeier (1931), Pearson (1962: 15–17, 86–9), Ferguson (1968: 53–75), B. Vickers (1973: 243–5), Dover (1974: 180–4), Vlastos (1980: 303–7), Blundell (1989: 26–59), Millett (1991: 127–32), Konstan (1997: 56–67), and Christ (2012: 10–11).

5 On the date of *Heracles*, see Diggle (1981: 116).

6 On the difficulty of applying precise dates to Plato's dialogues, other than likely written no earlier than following Socrates' death in 399 BCE and no later than Plato's death in 347, see Cooper (1997: vii–xiv).

7 See also, e.g., Sapph. 5. 6–7; Eur. *Med.* 809, Gorg. *Pal.* 25; Ar. *Av.* 418–21; Xen. *Mem.* 4.5.10.

8 On the dates of *Antigone*, see Lewis (1988) and Griffith (1999: 1–2, with n. 7). On the long tradition into which falls her attendance to the welfare of the family at the expense of the law, see Knox (1964: 76–7) and Christ (2012: 1). Konstan (2018: 159–85), however, perceives much more continuity between ancient affection for friends and for the state.

9 Cf. Adkins (1960: 231–2); Connor (1971: 48). *Crito* was written in the first half of the fourth century BCE; see n. 6 above.

10 For elaboration on Athenians' sense of their duties to the city and unfamiliar fellow citizens relative to their *philoi*, see Christ (2012: 48–93).

11 While I will use Plutarch as a source on a number of occasions in this article, like Hansen (1991: 280, with n. 145) and the others he cites, it is with full awareness of his limitations, and I have striven to corroborate him when possible. He is the most specific source on the lives of Cleon and Hyperbolus, though, and thus must be accounted for in a book on demagogues. Hershkowitz (2018: 97–8) notes that there are good reasons for using Plutarch (and other late critics, including scholiasts), mainly that he had much better access to a wealth of written source material from the time of the demagogues than has passed to the present day, so his accounts and analyses should carry "nearly the same weight as fifth- or fourth-century sources."

12 *Meno* was written in the first half of the fourth century BCE; see n. 6 above.

13 Hornblower (1991: 251 *ad* Thuc. 2.13.1); Mann (2007: 118).

14 For concise summaries of the role of the elite in Athenian politics prior to Pericles' death, tempered by the caution of Hignett (1950: 253–6) about the paucity of available sources from that time, see Bicknell (1972: vii) and Stockton (1990: 125–7). For more thorough coverage, see Littman (1990: 15–194). On the code of loyalty between upper-class *philoi* (including *hetaireiai* and *sunomosiai*, discussed in n. 19 below) in all matters, including politics, see Connor (1971: 18, 64), Davies (1981: 2, 97), Finley (1983: 40–1), and Ober (1989: 250); for illustration, see, e.g., Andoc. 1.54, 63; Xen. *Mem.* 2.6; Pl. *Men.* 71e2–5; and Plut. *Mor.* 807b, *Arist.* 2.5. For the effectiveness of political cooperation between aristocrats and coalitions they assembled, see n. 19 below. On the political value of friends, see Connor (1971: 64–5).

15 On *philia* as a tie binding political groups in the fifth century, including abundant citations, see Calhoun (1913: 128); Connor (1971: 64–6); Bicknell (1972); Rhodes (1995: 158–9); Mitchell and Rhodes (1996: 11–12); L. G. Mitchell (1997: 41–72). Hansen (1991: 283), however, reveals reservations about the influence of *philia* on politics in this period. On the breadth of relations that could be included under the heading of *philia*, see Fisher (1976: 5) and Millett (1991: 113–16). For the distinctions that Greeks would have made between the various relations that could be classified under the heading of *philia*, and the various roles that these groups would play in an individual's life, see Konstan (1996; 1997: 53–6). Konstan (2018: 163–71) explores ways in which *philia*, interpreted as feelings of affection, both did (in some cases) and did not (in others) bind groups from the level of individual family to a *polis* as a whole.

16 According to Aristotle, at least part of being *philoi* meant wishing well for one
   another (Ar. *Eth. Nic.* 1155b33–34), acting on behalf of the other purely because of
   this good will (*Eth. Nic.* 1156b7–17, *Rhet.* 1361b36–37), taking pleasure in loving
   one another more than in being loved (*Eth. Nic.* 1159a33–b1), and feeling a sense
   of personal chemistry with one another (*Eth. Nic.* 1166b33–34; Hutter 1978: 34).
   Konstan (1996; 1997: 53, 73; 2018: 39–53) emphasizes the importance of personal
   feelings in the relationship between those labeled *philoi*, who, he argues, were
   much more like "friends" in the contemporary Western sense than is commonly
   thought (e.g., Fisher 1976: 18). But even friendships in which interpersonal
   fondness was clear required a sense of mutual benefit between the parties (*Eth.
   Nic.* 1157b36; Fisher 1976: 5; Strauss 1987: 21; Blundell 1989: 45; Konstan 1997:
   56–9; 1998; 2018: 52), and *philoi* were widely sought and cultivated for the
   practical purposes they could serve for one another.

   Aristotle specifies (*Eth. Nic.* 1156a10–1156b6; *Eth. Eud.* 1236a30–1236b1) that
   two of the three types of friendship, those based on utility (διὰ τὸ χρήσιμον) and
   those based on pleasure (δι' ἡδονήν), derive primarily from the benefit that each
   friend sees himself or herself receiving from the other. While exchanges of favors,
   sometimes involving risking death or significant material loss for one another,
   were a part of friendships in which there was an obvious, or at least apparent,
   emotional connection (e.g., Lys. 1.23, 27; Pl. *Cri.* 45–6; Eur. *Or.* 1059–161; Dem.
   53.4–12), some people could be quite blatant in their intentions to befriend others
   solely because of the political benefit they hoped to derive from doing so (Lys.
   9.14; Xen. *Mem.* 2.9.3–4, *Anab.* 2.5.11; on the roles of friends in political life more
   broadly, see Connor 1971: 36–47 and Blundell 1989: 32, with citations in n. 32).
   For the centrality of reciprocity to friendship, see Heath (1987: 73–4); Blundell
   (1989: 32), with supporting citations in n. 36; Goldhill (1986: 82); Konstan (2018:
   52); van Berkel (2020: 53–4). On expectations of reciprocity in general between
   friends, see Blundell (1989: 26–59, with the citations in 32 n. 36).

   For a portrayal of friendship in Athens more focused on emotional
   connections than reciprocal benefit, see Konstan (1997: 72–82).

17 People seeking *philoi* solely for their power or prominence: Lys. 9.14; Xen. *Mem.*
   2.9.4, *Anab.* 2.5.11.

18 People avoided as *philoi* because of their poverty or challenging personal
   circumstances: Eur. *Med.* 561; *El.* 605–9, 1131; *Her.* 558–9, 561; Xen. *Symp.* 4.51.

19 On the range of roles that *hetaireiai* and *sunomosiai* played in the lives of elite men
   (primarily in the fifth and early fourth centuries), from dinner companions (Isoc.
   16.6) to legal allies (Thuc. 8.54.4) to political facilitators and enforcers (Thuc.
   8.65.1–3; Xen. *Hell.* 2.3.46), see Calhoun (1913); Sartori (1957); Connor (1971:
   25–9); Pecorella Longo (1971); Hutter (1978: 27–8); Hansen (1991: 281–2);

L. G. Mitchell (1997: 42–3, 46); Hershkowitz (2018: 165–6). Strauss (1986: 20), followed by Konstan (1997: 60) sums up their functions during the Peloponnesian War.

While Calhoun (1913: 23) contends that *sunomosiai* were likely not restricted to the elite, based on Socrates' comment that *sunomosiai* were something with which the majority of people (οἱ πολλοί, *hoi polloi*) concerned themselves (Pl. *Apol.* 36b), the other matters that Socrates lists as concerns of the majority—moneymaking, household management, generalships, public speech, public offices, and conspiracies—include the sorts of pursuits that would be overwhelmingly the concern of the leisure class, not the typical Athenian. Connor (1971: 28 n. 45) adds that the use of *hoi polloi* in this instance does not suggest that a true majority of people were involved in *sunomosiai*, but rather that *sunomosiai*, like the other matters, were concerns of a good number of people—in this case, most likely wealthy people. For the generally elite status of *hetaireiai* and *sunomosiai*, see, e.g., Thuc. 8.54.4; Ps.-Arist. [*Ath. Pol.*] 34.3; Stockton (1990: 23); Hansen (1991: 282); Jones (1999: 224–5); Munn (2000: 90).

20 Chroust (1954: 282–4, with nn. 13–23). On the role of *hetaireiai* in the invitation of Lysander into Athens, see Ps.-Arist. [*Ath. Pol.*] 34.3; Lys. 12.71–4.

21 See the analysis of Hornblower (2008: 375–6 *ad loc.*).

22 On the mutilation of the Herms and Alcibiades' supposed role in it, see Thuc. 6.27–8. On the profanation of the Mysteries and Alcibiades' alleged role in that, see Thuc. 6.60–61.4. On the likelihood of Alcibiades' actual involvement in these matters, see de Romilly (2019: 71–5). Mann (2007: 244–62) offers a careful analysis of the full matter of the Herms and Mysteries. Fornara (1971: 62–4) and de Romilly (2019: 37–88) document Alcibiades' period as *strategos*.

23 On his defection to Sparta and his efforts against his native city on Sparta's behalf, see Thuc. 6.61.6, 6.88.9–6.92, with de Romilly (2019: 89–103).

24 Chroust (1954: 288). On the complications of obligations to the *polis* and *philoi* more broadly, see Dover (1974: 301–6). See also n. 10 above.

25 For this connotation of δῆμος (*demos*), see LSJ⁹ s.v. II.1: "commons, common people." Finley (1962: 5) sees all uses of the term in literary texts to connote "the lower classes," a point of view that Hershkowitz (2018: 8 n. 12) contends the ancient sources do not corroborate. For the use of δῆμος (and of πλῆθος, addressed in the next note) to represent the common masses, see Rhodes (1981: 88–9). For the evolution of the use of δῆμος from the archaic period through the fifth century, see Donlan (1970) and Sealey (1973). On δῆμος in Herodotus and Thucydides, see Moggi (2005), and on the word in Thucydides specifically, see Frazier (2003) and Saïd (2013). Connor (1971: 101 n. 19 and 109–10 n. 34) points out the ambiguity of the word in different contexts and thus the difficulty of

precisely understanding its tone in any given passage: it could refer just to "the people," as in "the populace as a whole," or it could refer to just the lower classes of the populace, often with a derogatory sense.

26 Several scholars, however, find this presentation of the matter to be purely derivative of Herodotus (How and Wells 1912: 33 *ad* Herod. 5.66.2; Wade-Gery 1958: 138; Rhodes 1981: 243 *ad* [*Ath. Pol.*] 20.1), or that it resembles matters of the time of the composition of the [*Ath. Pol.*], or times close to it, more than the time of Cleisthenes (How and Wells 33 *ad* Herod. 5.66.2; Wade-Gery 1958: 138; Littman 1990: 218 n. 2).

   On the connotation of πλῆθος (*plethos*) as referring to common Athenians, see LSJ [9] s.v. I.2.b: "commons . . . populace, mob"; see also Connor (1971: 203); Rhodes (1981: 88–9); Ober (1989: 11, with n. 15); Reinders (2001: 39–55); and Major (2013: 73). For the evolution and varied employment of πλῆθος over time, see Roncali and Zagaria (1980) and Ruzé (1984: 259–63).

27 The expression Herodotus uses, to "make the *demos* one's *hetairos*," may well mean nothing more than that Cleisthenes was careful to consider the common people in his political action. On the uncertain meaning of the passage in Herodotus, see Seager (1963: 287–9) and Connor (1971: 90–1, with n. 5).

28 Connor (1971: 55–7).

29 Cf. Connor (1971: 51–2). Griffith (1999: 159 *ad loc.*) notes that Creon later shows a much more conventional conception of family loyalty (634, 641–4, 651–2).

30 Later in the same speech, Creon uses the phrase εὔνους . . . τῇ πόλει ("well-disposed to the city") to refer to the only type of person he would considerable honorable (209). Connor (1971: 103, with n. 23) points out that this is the first attestation of this expression, which becomes more common in the 420s as εὔνους τῷ δήμῳ ("well-disposed to the common people"). See more elaboration on that expression and its significance at Chapter 2, Section II.A.

31 Belfiore (2000: 143) notes Creon's implicit recognition that his error was in not counting kin as *philoi* and thus providing them appropriate privileges even when they are at odds with the law.

32 Much later sources who refer to Nicias as a demagogue: Plut. *Alc.* 13, *Nic.* 2.1–3.2, 4.1–3.

33 On the distinction and wealth of Pericles' family, see Davies (1971: no. 11811).

34 Cf. Stadter (1989: 96 *ad loc.*). On Pericles' practices, see Connor (1971: 121–2); Stockton (1990: 127).

35 On Pericles' methods of distancing himself from his *philoi* and most other casual interactions, and his objectives in and success with those approaches, see Azoulay (2014: 87–91).

36 On Pericles' claim about himself, see Hornblower (1991: 333–4 *ad* Thuc. 2.60.5).
   On the confidence-inspiring qualities of Pericles, see Mann (2007: 173) and
   Hershkowitz (2018: 107–8).

37 Socrates and Critobulus make similar claims about Themistocles (*Mem.* 2.6.13).
   See Tamiolaki (2016: 29) on the passage.

38 On the connection between Creon's speech and Pericles', see Gomme (1956: 167
   ad 2.60.2) and Rhodes (1988: 237 *ad* 2.60.2). For a further statement of this
   concept, see Eur. fr. 360 N².

39 Cf. Pl. *Gorg.* 515e, with Dodds (1959: 356–7 *ad* 515e5–7); Arist. *Pol.* 1274a8–12;
   Plut. *Per.* 9.2–3. On class connotations of πολλοί (*polloi*) in certain circumstances,
   see LSJ⁹ s.v. πολύς II.3.b: "people ... commonality ... multitude," with Ober (1989:
   11). Ps.-Arist. [*Ath. Pol.*] is dated to *c.* 330 BCE (Rhodes 1981: 51–8).

40 Others who argue for similar continuity between Pericles and those who
   succeeded him: Mann (2007: 75–96); Samons (2016: 206); Hershkowitz (2018:
   102–18). For a dispassionate account of the transition from Pericles to the
   politicians that succeeded him, see Rhodes (2016: 119–22).

41 See also Polybius 9.23.6.

42 Henderson (forthcoming, *ad* 191–3). On evidence for educations of those labeled
   demagogues and other prominent politicians, see Saldutti (2014: 49–68).

43 Hornblower (1991: 347 *ad* 2.65.10) notes that the implication that Pericles himself
   had no political rivals against whom he had to contend is inaccurate; Cleon was
   likely one, and Hornblower cites sources for implications of others.

44 Hornblower (1991: 345 *ad* Thuc. 2.65.8) takes Pericles' supposed indifference to
   public opinion to be hyperbolic, in the face of other classical accounts that
   Hornblower cites.

2 Cleon and the Rise of Friendship-Based Athenian Demagogy

1 For the date of *Knights* and the rest of his securely datable plays, see Dover (1993:
   1–2) and Anderson and Dix (2020: 3).

2 See Canfora (2006: esp. 31) for discussion of Thucydides' *History* as in progress for
   decades but, as a whole, likely not being circulated widely until after his death
   early in the fourth century BCE.

3 LSJ⁹ s.v. 1: "popular leader, as Cleon or Pericles"; 2: "more freq. in bad sense, leader
   of the mob, demagogue." On the evolution of the connotations of *demagogos* and
   its variants over time, see Connor (1971: 109–22 and 139–47). For a similar
   analysis that also takes into account every appearance of each of those forms and
   variants in extant literature, see Hershkowitz (2018: 7–82). In its early uses,

starting with *Knights*, the connotation seems much as Henderson (2019: 244) expresses it: "'leader of the mob,' a politician who for his own profit and advancement plays to the passions and prejudices of the masses, with whom he identifies, and attacks the elite, instead of leading the whole people by virtue of his superior (or at least exemplary) stature, proven ability, and rational arguments." In the fourth century, the connotation becomes closer to "rabblerousing," such as in Xen. *Anab.* 7.6.4 (see Connor 1971: 109–10, with n. 34), when Seuthes says of Xenophon, Ἀλλ' ἤ δημαγωγεῖ ὁ ἀνὴρ τοὺς ἄνδρας; ("so indeed he acts like a demagogue toward the men?"). Among the scholars who take δημαγωγός to be a neutral or respectable term in the fifth century, with the connotation turning negative only in the fourth, are Gomme (1974: 461), Dover (1993: 69 n. 1), and Hershkowitz (2018: 22 n. 50, with supporting points *passim*). On the breadth of connotations of δημαγωγ- roots throughout the fifth century, see Hershkowitz (2018: 9–26), and on a similar breadth throughout the fourth, see Rhodes (1981: 323–4) (noted as well in Rhodes 2016: 244 n. 3).

4　See also Connor (1971: 109–10) and Mann (2007: 29).

5　Rhodes (2016: 257–9, with additional primary and secondary citations); Henderson (2019: 244); Bartlett (2020: 250, with n. 3).

6　Expressions of patriotism, put in terms of friendly fondness—or criticism of someone's supposed lack of fondness—for his or her homeland begin to appear around this time. In addition to Pericles' reference to himself at Thuc. 2.60.5 as *philopolis*, "friendly to the *polis*," as noted in Chapter 1, Section III, Nicias expresses "care for the city," κήδεσθαί τε τῆς πόλεως (Thuc. 6.14.1); Theseus says "it is essential to be fond of one's country," φιλεῖν ... χρὴ ... πατρίδα (Eur. *Supp.* 506–8); and Bdelucleon is tweaked for being "*polis*-hating," μισόπολις (Ar. *Vesp.* 411).

7　Hornblower (1991: 419 *ad loc.*) observes that this first appearance of Cleon should not really be seen as an introduction, since he may have been active in Athenian politics for more than a decade prior.

8　See Connor (1971: 91–4) for analysis of this move.

9　On this step being fairly commonplace among Athenians, see Mann (2007: 104–8). See Saldutti (2014: 95–114) for a thorough analysis of Cleon's action along these lines and the tradition into which it falls.

10　Gomme (1956: 195 *ad loc.*) indicates that Thucydides was referring to Cleon, Nicias, and Alcibiades, and de Romilly (2019: 36) concurs on Alcibiades. Hornblower (1991: 347 *ad loc.*) considers this an understatement of the bureaucratic sophistication of Cleon and his peers.

11　While Isocrates 8.126–27 also indicates that Pericles' similar focus on the *polis* at his own expense actually led his wealth to diminish and the commonweal to benefit greatly, with the opposite being true for the demagogues, the messaging of the latter politicians was more effective. For prior friendships that Cleon may have maintained, see Chapter 3, Section III.

12 Connor (1971: 140). Connor (1971: 140–1) also notes similarities between the styles of Cleon and Alcibiades in accounts of attacks each one made against Nicias (Thuc. 4.27.5; Plut. *Alc.* 14.4), suggesting that Alcibiades, and likely other politicians of the time, took a cue from Cleon in their political styles. On the other hand, Thuc. 6.16.1–4 has Alcibiades boasting about his wealth and ancestry to the assembly, suggesting that he was not exclusively committed to leaving out those aspects of his background that might occasionally impress some of his constituents; cf. Ober (1989: 93–4) and de Romilly (2019: 36).

13 Connor (1971) lays out his argument of demagogic leadership being presented as *philia* at 91–108 (cf. the discussion at Scholtz 2004: 266–7 = 2007: 46–8, on literary uses of this trope). Among the many who accept his characterizations are Konstan (1997: 61); Munn (2000: 372 n. 20); McGlew (2002: 87); Rosenbloom (2002: 304 n. 88); Wohl (2002: 73); Scholtz (2004: 266 n. 9), refined at Scholtz (2007: 46 n. 9). Specific critiques of Connor's ideas in *New Politicians in Fifth-Century Athens* tend to be modest: Davies (1975), for instance, complains that Connor extrapolates too much from a limited number of sources and does not sufficiently problematize the sources he uses. Rhodes (1986: 132) notes that Connor does not explain the logistics of Cleon and other demagogues getting groups of common people to support their measures. Strauss (1987: 16, 38 n. 23) argues that Cleon certainly could not have *completely* abandoned his personal *philoi* to dedicate himself to common Athenians. And Hershkowitz (2018) charges that Connor gives too much credit to the demagogues for the supposed innovations in their uses of *philia* and in the paths they took to political prominence.

14 On Paphlagon as standing for Cleon, see Arg. Ar. *Eq.* A1, A2, A3, B; Braund (2005: 94–5); Rosen (2010: 246); Hershkowitz (2018: 10 n. 14). Cf. Osborne (2020: 27–30), though, who notes the limited evidence on which this one-to-one identification between Paphlagon and Cleon is made. Σ Ar. *Eq.* 149a lists Cleonymus, Hyperbolus, and Eubulus as those whom the Sausage-Seller may represent. Eubulus, though, as Rosenbloom (2004: 60 n. 16) points out, is an anachronism. Sidwell (2009: 157–64) contends that the Sausage-Seller was more likely a gloss for Alcibiades (though de Romilly 2019: 8 finds Alcibiades to be the diametric opposite of the Sausage-Seller), and Bowie (1993: 52–77) associates him and his rise to power with no one figure, but with various myths, rites, and heroes long familiar to Athenians.

The text I cite of *Knights* throughout the book is that of Wilson (2007). All translations are mine, though often influenced by Henderson's (1998) Loeb edition.

15 On the emergence and regularity of appearance of *philodemos*, and other expressions like it, during the age of the demagogues, see Connor (1971: 99–108); cf. Adkins (1960: 230–1) and Scholtz (2004: 266–7, with notes, refined at Scholtz (2007: 46–7, with notes).

16 *Clouds* was originally performed in 423 (Dover 1968: lxxxi, and Sommerstein 1982: 2, both with supporting sources).

17 *Wasps* was first performed in 422 (MacDowell 1971: 1).

18 Xen. *Hell.* 2.3.47; [Andoc.] 4.8; Plut. *Alc.* 21. On *misodemos* as a politically charged term at this time, see Connor (1971: 101–2). Similarly, in *Knights*, Paphlagon wishes to perish if he "hate[s] [Demos]" (σε μισῶ, 767).

19 Major (2013: 104) chooses a more literal translation of δημιζόντων, "Demos-izing," to capture the portrayed insincerity of such politicians' engagement with the *demos*.

20 On the introduction of *eunous toi demoi* to Athenian discourse, and on similar expressions used at the time and prior to it, see Connor (1971: 103–4). Creon, at *Antigone* 209, uses a similar expression, εὔνους . . . τῇ πόλει (*eunous . . . tei polei*, "well-disposed to the city") to refer to the only type of person he would considerable honorable (see also above, p. 104 n. 30).

21 Cf. similar language at [*Ath. pol.*] 1.7. Aristotle (*EN* 1155b31–34) uses εὔνους as well to indicate a feeling of good will for others for whom people have friendly feelings that they understand will not be reciprocated (cf. Konstan 2006: 173).

22 On the wealth of Cleon, see Davies (1971: no. 8674); on Nicias' wealth, Davies (1971: no. 10808A); on Hyperbolus', Davies (1971: no. 13910); on Cleophon's, Davies (1981: 42, with n. 6). On the consistently great wealth and social status of the leading politicians of the sixth and fifth centuries, see Rhodes (1981: 344–5). Connor (1971: 75–7) discusses the likelihood that the poor were, at the very least, not substantial contingents in the *philoi* and *hetairoi* of the rich. On disdain for the poor as friends, see Soph. fr. 85 N^2; Eur. *Med.* 561, *El.* 1131.

23 Finley (1962: 16) assumes that post-Periclean politicians' non-elite status must have given them a different outlook from their predecessors.

24 On the long-term wealthy, prominent family from which Alcibiades derived, see Davies (1971: no. 600), and de Romilly (2019: 4–8).

25 Davies (1981: 41–2), with the entries in Davies (1971) referenced in n. 22 above. On Cleophon's father, see Rhodes (1981: 355, with references), Davies (1981: 42), and Imperio (2020: 105, with notes 53 and 54).

26 Lane Fox (1994: 138); Saldutti (2014: 37–48); Imperio (2020: 95–8, 107–8). Cleon himself seems to have married a daughter of Dikaiogenes, a rather distinguished Athenian (Davies 1971: no. 8674 [Cleon] and no. 3773 [Dikaiogenes]; Azoulay

2014: 129–30). On uncertainty about the veracity of that supposed match, though, see Davies (1971: no. 320) and B. Mitchell (1991: 170).

27 On the continuous primarily elite status of *strategoi*, cf. ps.-Xen. [*Ath. pol.*] 1.3; Xen. *Mem.* 3.4.1; Arist. *Pol.* 1282a31–32. On the specialization and separation of *strategoi* and unelected politicians after 429, see Connor (1971: 143–7), Davies (1981: 120–5), Ober (1989: 91–3); cf. Lys. 13.7–8, Arist. *Pol.* 1305a10–15.

28 See Davies (1981: 41–2) on the role of the labor of enslaved people in the fortunes of Cleon, Hyperbolus, and Cleophon, and p. 43 on the characterization of business owners as themselves αὐτουργοί (those who physically labor for themselves, with little or no assistance). Cf. Ehrenberg (1962: 120) on this tactic. On common characterizations of demagogues along the lines noted above, see also Hershkowitz (2018: 212–13).

29 See also Rosenbloom (2004: 59–60). Cleon is also referred to by the name Paphlagon at *Nub.* 581 and *Pax* 314. Saldutti (2014: 17–26) explores the possibility that Cleon's mother may indeed have been of Paphlagonian ancestry herself. He is called or implied to be a tanner (βυρσοδέψης) or other sort of leather worker or merchant at *Eq.* 44, 47, 136, 139, 740, 852; *Nub.* 581; *Vesp.* 38–40; and *Pax* 270, 648. On the full extent of tanning imagery in *Knights*, with explanation of the process of tanning, see Lind (1990: 33–85).

30 Aristophanes refers to him as a lampseller (λυχνοπώλης, *Eq. 739*, with scholia; cf. 1314–15 with Σ 1315b), as "Hyperbolus of the lamps" (τῶν λυχνῶν, *Nub.* 1065, with Σ 1065a), and as a lampmaker (λυχνοποιός, *Pax* 690, with Σ 681b and Σ 692; cf. Σ *Eq.* 739a–b, 1304a–b). Andocides also identifies him as making lamps (λυχνοποιεῖ, fr. 5 Dalmeyda), and Cratinus (fr. 209 KA=196 K) sets him in the midst of lamps onstage. He is called a scoundrel in two different ways, both of which relate back to words for "work," and imply having the vices that a common worker has: μοχθηρός (Ar. *Eq.* 1304, with Σ 1315, and Thuc. 8.73.3) and πονηρός (Ar. *Pax* 684, *Thesm.* 837, and Plato Com. Fr. 182 KA=166 K; see also the following later sources: Philochorus *FGrH* 328 F 30; Androtion *FGrH* 324 F 42; Plut. *Arist.* 7.3, *Nic.* 11.5–6, *Alc.* 13.4, *Mor.* 855C9–10; Σ Ar. *Pax* 681b, Σ *Vesp.* 1007b; Σ Lucian *Tim.* 30 Rabe).

Plato Comicus refers to Hyperbolus at fr. 182 KA=166 K as a foreigner (ξένος), as does Andocides (fr. 5 Dalmeyda), who also calls him a barbarian (βάρβαρος). He is specified as being two separate nationalities in other contemporaneous sources: at Plato Com. fr. 185 KA=170 K, he is a Lydian (Λύδος), and at Polyzelus fr. 5 KA=791 K, a Phrygian (Φρύξ); Σ Ar. *Pax* 692 calls him a Syrian (Σύρος) as well. The name that Eupolis gives a thinly disguised Hyperbolus as title character in *Maricas* is Old Persian, also a reference to Hyperbolus' supposed foreign background (Cassio 1985; Morgan 1986).

His father is referred to as tattooed (ἐστιγμένος) and employed as a slave in a public mint (ἐν τῷ ἀργυροκοπείῳ δουλεύει τῷ δημοσίῳ, Andoc. fr. 5 Dalmeyda), yet his name is the entirely Athenian Antiphanes (Davies 1971: no. 13910), making these allegations of enslavement complete fabrications. Aristophanes slanders Hyperbolus' mother himself at *Thesm.* 836–45, and at *Nub.* 551–9 discusses how Eupolis (*Maricas*), Phrynichus, and Hermippus (*Artopolides*, says the scholiast) did so as well.

31 Cleophon portrayed as a lyremaker (λυροποιός): Σ *Ran.* 681=Plato Com. *Cleophon*, fr. 61 KA=60 K; Andoc. 1.146; Aeschin. 2.76; Σ Ar. *Thesm.* 805. Depictions of Cleophon's foreignness and lower-class status, and the foreignness of his parents: Ar. *Ran.* 678–82: Κλεοφῶντος, ἐφ' οὗ δὴ / χείλεσιν ἀμφιλάλοις δεινὸν / ἐπιβρέμεται / Θρηικία χελιδὼν / ἐπὶ βάρβαρον ἑζομένη πέταλον ("Cleophon, upon whose bilingually babbling lips a Thracian swallow roars a terrible tune as it sits on a barbarian leaf"); Σ *Ran.* 679, discussing Plato Comicus' portrayal of Cleophon: τοῦτον δὲ κωμῳδεῖ ὡς ξένον καὶ ἀμαθῆ καὶ φλύαρον καὶ δυσγενῆ. Θρᾷκα γὰρ αὐτὸν ἔλεγεν (Plato "lampoons him as a foreigner, an ignoramus, a babbler, and a man of low birth; for Plato said that he is Thracian"); Σ *Ran.* 681= Plato Com. *Cleophon*, fr. 61 KA=60 K: Θρηκία χελιδὼν·Ἵνα διαβάλλη αὐτὸν ὡς βάρβαρον. Κωμῳδεῖται δὲ ὡς υἱὸς Θράσσης ... καὶ Πλάτων ἐν Κλεοφῶντι δράματι βαρβαρίζουσαν πρὸς αὐτὸν πεποίηκε τὴν μητέρα. Καὶ αὐτὴ δὲ Θρᾷσσα ἐλέγετο ("'A Thracian swallow': in order for [Aristophanes] to malign him as a barbarian. He is mocked as the son of a Thracian ... And Plato in his play *Cleophon* had Cleophon's mother speak in barbaric fashion to him. She also is said to be Thracian"); Σ 1504: ὡς ξένος δὲ ὁ Κλεοφῶν κωμῳδεῖται ("Cleophon is mocked as a barbarian"); Σ 1532: μαχέσθωσαν οὖν, φησὶ, Κλεοφῶν καὶ οἱ ἄλλοι, ὅσοι τούτῳ ὅμοιοί εἰσι ξένοι, ἐν ταῖς πατρίσιν αὐτῶν, καὶ μὴ ἐν τῇ Ἀττικῇ κινείτωσαν πολέμους· οὐ γάρ ἐστιν αὐτῶν πατρὶς αὕτη ("Therefore, [Aristophanes] is saying, let Cleophon and the others, as many as are foreigners like he is, fight in their own native lands, and may they not stir up battles in Attica, for it is not their native land"). The foreign characterization of Cleophon's father, Cleipiddes, is particularly noticeable in that he was undoubtedly Athenian, having been elected general in 428 and a candidate for ostracism in the 440s (Rhodes 1981: 355, with bibliography).

32 See Henderson (2019: 246) for classical citations confirming the consistent characterization of demagogues as being of the working class, regardless of the reality of their family backgrounds. The imputations of foreignness were a trope used against many politicians; Ostwald (1986: 215), Ober (1989: 266–70), and Yunis (1996: 52 n. 28) are among the scholars who point out an Athenian tendency to undermine politicians by questioning their citizenship.

33 Brunt (1961: 144), Connor (1971: 126 n. 68), and Davies (1981: 126–7) touch on the value of these entrepreneurs' financial and administrative skills, and the credibility this might have earned them.

34 Ar. *Eq.* 51, 255, 797–800; Σ *Vesp.* 88, 300; Sommerstein (1981: 147 *ad Eq.* 51; 186 *ad* 799–800); Anderson and Dix (2020: 77 *ad* 50–1, 103 *ad* 255–7, 165 *ad* 799–800).

35 Thuc. 3.19.1, with Gomme (1956: 278–9) and Hornblower (1991: 404 *ad loc.*); Ar. *Eq.* 773–6, 923–6; Sommerstein (1981: 193 *ad Eq.* 924); Anderson and Dix (2020: 161 *ad Eq.* 773–6, 178 *ad* 923–4 and 925–6); Munn (2000: 74, with 372 n. 25).

36 For evidence of Cleon's attacks on the cavalry, see Fornara (1983: 131), and Fornara (1973) for interpretation of the evidence. Cf. Ar. *Eq.* 222–9; Munn (2000: 77). On further perceptions of Cleon as being committed to the financial well-being of the common people, sometimes at the expense of others, see Ar. *Eq.* 52, 773–6, 1019, 1100–14, 1166–7, 1171–2, 1177, 1181–2, 1190, 1192; and Munn (2000: 73).

37 Cf. Munn (2000: 109).

38 Xen. *Hell.* 1.7.2; Ps.-Arist. [*Ath. Pol.*] 28.3, with Rhodes (1981: 355–6 *ad loc.*); Munn (2000: 156). Both Ps.-Aristotle ([*Ath. Pol.*] 28.3, 34.1) and Aeschines (2.76) refer to the *diobelia* as a sop to the poor to win their political favor. On the amount of food that two obols could buy, see Markle (1985: 280). See also Azoulay (2014: 248 n. 6), building on p. 128, on purposes of the *diobelia* and the years that it was in effect.

39 On the range of associations of *demos* during the Peloponnesian War, with a common connotation of Athenians of the lower class, see Reinders (2001: 28–242), and pp. 168–203 for the reflection of this connotation in the portrayal of Demos in *Knights.*

40 Thompson (1981: 159), Ostwald (1986: 202), Henderson (1990: 281–2), and Rhodes (1995: 157; 2016: 254), among many others, concur.

41 On the designation of politicians by that term, see Ar. fr. 205 KA=198 K; *Ach.* 37–9, 679–80; *Eq.* 59–60, 324–5, 356–8, 879–80; *Th.* 529–30; cf. *Pl.* 31–2, 377–9, 567–70; Eup. frr. 102, 103 KA=96, 98 K; Pl. Com. fr. 202=186 K; Eur. fr. 597.4 N; Connor (1971: 116–17, with n. 51); Hansen (1983: 41–2, 47–8); Ober (1989: 105–8); Arthurs (1993). Rhodes (1986: 140–1) expresses the importance of oratory in late fifth-century Athens, with abundant supporting citations. On persuasive speech as one likely factor in Cleon's rise to prominence, see Rhodes (2016: 254).

42 Finley (1962: 10–16), backed by Rhodes (2006: 120), argues that attention-getting speech was hardly the sole possession of the demagogues. Cf. Aristotle's similar claim that almost every tyrant was a demagogue (*Pol.* 1305a9–10), which suggests that appeal to the masses via persuasive speech was not a new phenomenon.

43 On Cleon's physical presentation, see Ps.-Arist. [*Ath. Pol.*] 28.3.3–7; cf. Theopomp. *FGrH* 115 F 92.1–2; Plut. *Nic.* 8; *Ti. Gracch.* 2; Cic. *Brut.* 28. Aeschines (*In Tim.* 25)

claims that speakers prior to Cleon made no use of gestures, with their hands hidden in their cloaks. On his unusual use of his voice, see also Ar. *Eq.* 137 and 311 and *Vesp.* 36. On the possibility that the line about the "foreign guests" referred to the 292 Spartans he captured at Sphacteria, see Wade-Gery (1958: 233–5); cf. Connor (1968: 49–50).

44 Ps.-Arist. [*Ath. Pol.*] 34.1 and Σ Ar. *Ran.* 1532.

45 Among the other nicknames that appear in literature is Archedemus as γλάμων, "Bleary Eyes" (Lys. 14.25; Ar. *Ran.* 588; Eup. fr. 9 KA). On Archedemus as a demagogue, see Σ Ar. *Ran.* 419, 420a; Xen. *Hell.* 1.7.2; cf. Connnor (1971: 35 n. 1). Connor (1971) notes several more colorful nicknames at p. 139, with n. 3. Among them is Syracosius, who is nowhere specifically noted as a demagogue, but who fits into that class due to his political activity while never, apparently, holding office (Roberts 1982: 360). Ar. *Av.* 1297 indicates that he earned the nickname κίττα ("jay"), and Eup. fr. 220 KA, has him running about on the speakers' platform howling like a dog.

46 Humphreys (1983: 29): "the *demos* voted for people rather than policies." Strauss' (1987: 27) adjustment: "The *demos* was not indifferent to policies, but it never abstracted them from personalities."

47 I am only considering uses of the term in the fifth century and early fourth, in order not to misrepresent the meaning of the term as it evolves over time.

48 Herod. 1.214.20, 2.123.2, 3.3.2, 3.9.6, 3.9.7, 4.95.20.

49 Eur. *Thyestes* fr. 392 Collard and Cropp; Eur. *Antiope* fr. 185.4–5 Collard and Cropp.

50 Aristophanes uses the term twice in *Thesmophoriazusae* to refer to the trustworthiness of actions of characters who do not appear to reflect any specific figures in contemporaneous Athens. *Thesm.* 267–8: Euripides tells Mnesilochus, Ἢν λαλῇς δ᾽, ὅπως τῷ φθέγματι / γυναικιεῖς εὖ καὶ πιθανῶς ("If you speak, be sure that in your voice you act like a woman well and convincingly"). *Thesm.* 463–4: the chorus describes an anonymous woman's testimony against Euripides as οὐδ᾽ / ἀσύνετ᾽, ἀλλὰ πιθανὰ πάντα ("not stupid, but all convincing").

51 On class connotations of πλῆθος, see n. 26 in Chapter 1, Section II.C.

52 On the demagogic implications of προστάτης τοῦ δήμου during the Peloponnesian War, see Connor (1971: 110–15) and Hershkowitz (2018: 5, 15–25). On class connotations of πολλοί in certain circumstances, see n. 39 in Chapter 1, Section III. Hornblower (2008: 407 *ad* Thuc. 6.35.2) calls the description of Athenagoras "an echo of the Athenian Kleon."

53 Ar. *Eq.* 628–9: λέγων / πιθανώταθ᾽ ("speaking persuasively"). On Paphlagon as a stand-in for Cleon, see n. 14 above.

54 Eur. *Or.* 906: πιθανὸς ἔτ᾽ αὐτοὺς περιβαλεῖν κακῶι τινι ("persuasive enough to involve [the Argive masses] in some evil"). On the equation of Tyndareus' hired

speaker with Cleophon or other demagogues, see Σ *Or.* 904, Ebener (1966: 47), Schein (1975: 60), Willink (1986: 231 *ad* 902–16), and Rosenbloom (2011: 420).

55 *Demoi* has been dated between 417 and 410: see Olson (2017).

56 Alcibiades apparently did much to win over the Athenian people with his considerable rhetorical skills (Plut. *Alc.* 10.2; cf. de Romilly 2019: 9), but Thucydides (6.16.1–4) also has Alcibiades boasting about his wealth and ancestry to the assembly (cf. de Romilly 2019: 36), about the latter of which, at least, the demagogues could never do. De Romilly (2019: 36) also notes the massive advantage in political matters that being from a prominent family, like Alcibiades', was. On the demagogues' status as outsiders, see, e.g., Rosenbloom (2011: 414), and above, Section II.B.

Examples of elites stacking the assemblies during the Peloponnesian War through their own connections or through various coalitions, thus blunting the impact of each speaker on his audience: Thuc. 6.13.1, 8.66.1; Xen. *Hell.* 1.7.8; *Lys.* 12.44, 75–6; Plut. *Nic.* 11.5, *Alc.* 13, *Per.* 11.2. On these practices, see Sealey (1956: 241–2); Connor (1971: 134–6); Strauss (1987: 28–31); Stockton (1990: 130); Hansen (1991: 280); Rhodes (1995: 158–9); L. G. Mitchell (1997: 42–3); Rhodes (2016: 247). On fifth- and early-fourth-century elites explicitly referencing their contributions to the cities' coffers or prestige in public speeches (with abundant references), obviously expecting that doing so would positively predispose audiences toward them, see Davies (1981: 92–8). On Athenians' use of status and wealth in general to grant them political power for centuries prior to the Peloponnesian War, see Davies (1981: 88–131).

57 On the perceived distance between being *pithanos* and being truthful, see, for example, Eur. *Thy.* fr. 392 Collard and Cropp, and Pl. *Apol.* 17a3.

58 Thuc. 2.65.10: ἐτράποντο καθ' ἡδονὰς τῷ δήμῳ καὶ τὰ πράγματα ἐνδιδόναι. Plut. *Alc.* 13.5: ἐχρῆτο δ' αὐτῷ πολλάκις ὁ δῆμος ἐπιθυμῶν προπηλακίζειν τοὺς ἐν ἀξιώματι καὶ συκοφαντεῖν. Cf. Munn (2000: 109).

59 On the development of ingroups and ways that they can be brought more tightly together through attacks on members of the group, see Brewer (1999); Castelli, Tomelleri, and Zogmaister (2008); and Knowles and Tropp (2018).

60 See Henderson (forthcoming, *ad* 191–3) for pejorative connotations of what is portrayed as a deficient education.

61 I will elaborate on all of these disparagements in Chapter 3.

62 See Carey (1994: 75) on the peculiarity of *Knights*, based on the evisceration of Cleon, having won at the Lenaea, yet Cleon still having won election as general a short time later. On Aristophanes' prospective reasons for attacking Cleon in *Knights*, including a wish to derail his election as general, and possibly as well in retaliation for Cleon's slander suit against Aristophanes for *Babylonians* (on which,

see *Ach.* 377–82; Σ *Ach.* 378; cf. *Ach.* 502–3, 515–16, 659–64), see Sommerstein (1981: 2); Henderson (1990: 298); (1998: 221, cf. *Eq.* 973–6); and Hesk (2000: 256); and for the efficacy of Cleon's efforts, Yunis (1996: 52, with n. 29). For consequences Aristophanes might have suffered for his portrayal of Cleon in *Knights*, see *Vesp.* 1284–91, with elaboration by MacDowell (1971: 299 *ad loc.*) and Henderson (1998: 223).

On Aristophanes' apparent politics and his treatment of Cleon, also see, e.g., de Ste. Croix (1972: 355–67, 71); Lind (1985); Sommerstein (1986); Edmunds (1987: 1, 15–16, 59–66); Atkinson (1992); Olson (2002: xxix–xxxi, xlvi–xlvii, l–li); Sidwell (2009); and Rosen (2020).

63 On these connotations, see Marr and Rhodes (2008: 24–5).

64 Along the lines of ingroup building and separation from an outgroup during the time of the demagogues, the Old Oligarch suggests that it was impossible for Athens' democracy as it was to attend to the interests of anyone who is not "of the people" (τοῦ δήμου), and that the wealthy who chose to operate in such a system (*sc.* the demagogues) could only be intending to do wrong (ἀδικεῖν, [*Ath. pol.*] 2.20).

65 See also Isocrates' contrast of great Athenian politicians Aristides, Themistocles, and Miltiades with Hyperbolus and Cleophon (8.75).

66 Christodoulou (2013: 246, with notes 115 and 116), following J. Price (2001: 239), accepts that the demagogues' styles of leadership and their specific guidance were, indeed, at the root of a number of Athens' difficulties following Pericles' death. Gomme (1956: 194–5 *ad* 2.65.10) specifies that the apparent subjection of political decisions to the whim of the people does not necessarily imply bad policy, just *inconsistent* policy.

67 Regarding the finger-pointing in the wake of the Sicilian Expedition, Thucydides certainly holds the voters accountable for their role in the disaster, as Gomme, Andrewes, and Dover (1981: 5 *ad* 8.1.1) emphasize, but perhaps not entirely fairly: Hornblower (1991: 348 *ad* 2.65.11) points out that the Athenian people underestimated the force that would be opposing them, in large part, as Finley (1962: 1–2) highlights, due to the great amount of false information presented to the assembly, often to serve the goals of the presenters.

68 For the date of *Frogs*, see Dover (1997: 1).

69 Redheads (πυρρίαι) were stereotypically Thracians (e.g., Xenophanes B 16) and enslaved (Dover 1997: 64 *ad* 730; Henderson 2008: 64 n. 97). Thracian ancestry was also regularly derogatorily attributed to Cleophon (Ar. *Ran.* 678–82, with Sommerstein 1996: 214 *ad* 680–1, Dover 1993: 69, and Stanford 1968: 130 *ad* 679 ff.; Σ *Ran.* 679; Σ *Ran.* 681= Plato Com. *Cleophon*, F 61 KA=60 K), and

Sommerstein (1996: 220 *ad* 730) and Dover (1993: 283 *ad* 730) take this particular reference as a shot at Cleophon.

70 Eupolis fragments 384 KA=117 K and fr. 219 KA=205 K express what appears to be similar class bias, though in a way that does not as explicitly connect demagogic leaders and the *demos*. Fr. 384 KA, which may be from *Demoi*, *Poleis*, or *Maricas*, and thus datable to anywhere from 422 to 410, defames generals (στρατηγοί) as no longer being "from the greatest families, leaders in wealth and birth" (all Eupolis translations by Storey 2011), but now "scum of the earth" (καθάρματα). And fr. 219 KA, from *Poleis*, may be making a similar indictment of class standing of generals in saying that those who would not previously have been viable candidates as "wine inspectors" (οἰνόπτας) are now being chosen as generals. On a date of Eupolis' *Maricas* to 421, see Imperio (2020: 102); on a date of *Poleis* from 422 to 419, see Storey (2011: 180–1); on arguments for various dates of *Demoi* between 417 and 410, see Olson (2017).

71 Tajfel and Turner (1986).

72 On this sub-genre of Old Comedy, see Lind (1990: 235–52) and Sommerstein (2000).

73 This event can be dated to 416 or 415; see Munn (2000: 380 n. 2) for a bibliography of the discussion as to which. Rosenbloom (2004) argues for the ostracism in 415 as a response to Alcibiades' Olympic victory in 416 and studies closely the efforts at the time to make Hyperbolus seem less than fully worthy of this prestigious punishment. See Mann (2007: 230–43) for further analysis of Hyperbolus' ostracism.

74 Cf. Ar. *Nub.* 1065–6: "Hyperbolus procured many talents through his insolence" (Ὑπέρβολος ... τάλαντα πολλὰ / εἴληφε διὰ πονηρίαν). See Hornblower (2008: 968–72 *ad* 9.73.3) on the uncertainty about motivations for Thucydides' scornful appraisal of Hyperbolus, and further analysis of Hyperbolus and potential reasons for his ostracism.

75 For compendia of extant records of Hyperbolus, see Connor (1971: 81–2), Storey (2003: 200–1), and Imperio (2020: 102–3, with nn. 41 and 46). Those records are extensive enough to suggest his prominence in Athens (Connor 1971: 79–84; Munn 2000: 109–10; Storey 2003: 201).

76 Connor (1971: 79–84) and Munn (2000: 109–10). See de Romilly (2019: 50–1 and 76) on Alcibiades' role in Hyperbolus' ostracism.

77 Some of the ridicule Cleon endured was for the sorts of things for which anyone in the public eye might be tweaked: his extreme litigiousness, for instance, is ridiculed in *Wasps* as a whole, and *Peace* 314 mocks his style of speech (cf. *Ran.* 576–7). The vast range of disreputable sexual behaviors tied to him in *Knights* are

the same sorts that were attached to all sorts of public figures, as will be explained in Chapter 4. He was a fixture of ridicule in Aristophanes' plays year after year (*Knights*, produced in 424 BCE; *Clouds* in 423; *Wasps* 422; and *Peace* 421), all of which were written, and all but *Peace* performed, while Cleon was alive and almost certainly watching.

78 Osborne (2020: 38): "The repeated emphasis on Pylos in *Knights* focuses on the theft of Demosthenes' victory." See also knocks against his administrative approaches to warfare at *Eq.* 438, 466–7, 834–5, 1070–1 and *Pax* 269–70. Cf. Paphlagon's defenses of Cleon's performance at Sphacteria at 702, 742–3, 844–6, 1051–3, 1166–7, and 1171–2.

79 See the positive reception (noted above, Section II.C.2) that the Athenian assembly gave him (Plut. *Nic.* 7.7, *Mor.* 799d) for his line that he "needed to entertain some foreign guests" (ξένους ἑστιᾶν μέλλοντα, Theopomp. *FGrH* 115 F 92.6), an apparent reference to the Spartans captured at Sphacteria. On Cleon's election as *strategos* in 423/422 and 422/421, see Fornara (1971: 61–2).

80 On Thucydides' (perhaps unfairly) derisive portrayal of Cleon (particularly at 3.36.6; 4.20–2, 27–8; 5.6–7, 10–11), see, e.g., Gomme (1974: 637–8 *ad* 5.7.2, 3.652 *ad* 5.10.9); Woodhead (1960; 1962); Westlake (1968: 70–5); Pouncey (1980: 79); Connor (1984: 116–17); Pope (1988: 283–4); Hornblower (1991: 419 *ad* 3.36.6); (1996: 185–6 *ad* 4.27.3, 483 *ad* 5.7.2); Flower (1992: 48–9); Lang (1995: 50); Spence (1995); Gruber (2001); Wohl (2002: 74–5); Hershkowitz (2018: 18). On personal grievance that may have motivated Thucydides' harsh treatment of Cleon, see Mann (2007: 88, with his sources). Lafargue (2013: 51–9) lays out both Thucydides' oversteps in criticism but also reasonable acknowledgments of lucky breaks that went Cleon's way.

81 Hornblower (1991: 420 *ad loc.*) thinks that βιαιότατος may not have been intended to mean "most violent" as much as "most forceful" here.

82 Cf., e.g., Archidamus (1.79.2): ἀνὴρ καὶ ξυνετὸς δοκῶν εἶναι καὶ σώφρων ("a man considered to be both sagacious and prudent"); Pericles (1.139.4): ἀνὴρ κατ᾿ ἐκεῖνον τὸν χρόνον πρῶτος Ἀθηναίων, λέγειν τε καὶ πράσσειν δυνατώτατος ("a man first among the Athenians at that time, most capable both in speech and action"); even Brasidas (4.84.2): ἦν δὲ οὐδὲ ἀδύνατος, ὡς Λακεδαιμόνιος, εἰπεῖν ("he was not lacking as a speaker, as Lakedaimonians go").

Alcibiades' introduction (6.15.2–4) is the only one that rivals Cleon's for negativity, in fact attributing Athens' downfall to Alcibiades (de Romilly 2019: 30, 87). But even this claim more severely indicts Alcibiabes' peers: Thucydides says that Alcibiades' questionable personal habits turned οἱ πολλοί against him, leading them to put their trust in other politicians, and before long they had ruined the city. On the time period and the peers of Alcibiades Thucydides might have had in mind with his two comments in this passage about the city's downfall, see Gomme, Andrewes, and Dover (1970: 242–5 *ad* Thuc. 6.15.3 f.).

83 Cf. Woodhead (1960: 292) and Westlake (1968: 8).

84 J. F. Johnson (2016: 59) describes Thucydides' portrayal of Cleon as of "a vigorous opponent to the Athenian disposition to compassion," reflecting (56) the vindictiveness that Aristophanes projects onto him as well through the character of Philocleon in *Wasps*.

85 On the unrealism of Cleon's demands of Sparta, see Hornblower (1996: 178 *ad* 4.21.3). Rawlings (1981: 230) notes that Thucydides' disapproval of Cleon's advice to continue the war and drive away the Spartan ambassadors is clear through his refusal to present Cleon's reasoning in the form of direct speech. Ostwald's (1986: 298) much more sympathetic approach: Cleon "seems to have been genuinely concerned to implement a policy he regarded as good for his city."

86 On the peculiarity of Thucydides' attribution of motives to Cleon, see Westlake (1968: 72–3) and Hornblower (1996: 185–6 *ad* 4.27.3).

87 Hornblower (1996: 185–6 *ad* 4.27.1) notes the lack of objectiveness that Thucydides employs in his portrayal of Cleon in this section.

88 Hornblower (1996: 435–6). As part of his Thracian campaign against Brasidas, Cleon leads the Athenian recapture of Torone (5.5.3) and takes Galepsos (5.5.6). It is possible that he took more cities as well along the way and that Thucydides suppressed them in his quest to vilify Cleon (West and Meritt 1925; Gomme 1974: 636 *ad* 5.6.1; Woodhead 1960: 304–5; de Romilly 1963: 166; Westlake 1968: 77; B. Mitchell 1991: 176–82; Spence 1995: 426–32).

89 Hornblower (1996: 448 *ad* 5.10.9): "The most famous and extreme instance of a discreditable motive attributed on the evidence of overt action."

90 Gomme (1974: 652 *ad* 5.10.9) suggests that Cleon's death may not have been as cowardly as Thucydides makes it seem. His retreat is not an act of individual panic, but rather an enactment of his decision that the army should pull back. He could have retreated with the left wing, which was more quickly out of harm's way, but chose to lead the right, which put him in greater individual peril.

91 Additional criticism of Cleon from decades to centuries after his death: Isoc. 15.316–17; [Arist.] *Ath Pol.* 28.1, 3–4; Diod. Sic. 12.55.8; Cic. *Brut.* 28; Plut. *Mor.* 806f–807a; *Nic.* 2.2–3, 8.3; *Comp. Nic. Crass.* 2.3, 3.1, 3.4; *Demetr.* 11.2.

92 On Cleon's two elections as *strategos*, see Fornara (1971: 61–2).

93 As Whedbee (2004) has highlighted, while eighteenth- and nineteenth-century historians typically accepted the critical approaches of Thucydides and Aristophanes (72–8), Grote (1888: *passim* in volumes 5 and 6) provided the first serious defense not just of the virtues of Cleon and other demagogues, but also of the limits of the damage that they could have caused (Whedbee 2004: 78–85). For

further reinforcement of Grote's innovative perspective on Cleon, see Kierstead (2014: 196–8) and Liddel (2014: 236–7). I owe these citations to one of Bloomsbury's anonymous readers.

3 The Sociology of Making Individual *Philoi* among the Masses

1   Rosenbloom (2002: 305 n. 89). For a broader account of negative perceptions of demagogues as manipulative flatterers who are incapable of genuine friendship, see Rosenbloom (2002: 304–6, with notes). Cf. Yunis' (1996: 45) claim that "the politician who leads and manipulates the mob for his own advantage is a demagogue," and Finley's (2004: 164) that "[t]he demagogue is driven by self-interest, by the desire to advance himself in power, and through power, in wealth."

2   On this situation as reflective of the active role of *philoi* in all matters of an individual's life, including political, see Strauss (1987: 23). De Romilly (2019: 149): Alcibiades was "surrounded by a security escort of friends, ready to repel any attempt against his person." Konstan (1997: 65) lays out the layers of significance of different parties in Alcibiades' return: "it was the Athenian majority ... that was decisive in Alcibiades' successful return to Athens. His personal friends and relatives were on hand mainly to provide protection."

3   See also, e.g., Schutte and Light (1978: 263), Bradley and Karney (2010: 232–3), and Preciado et al. (2012).

4   Bustos and Johnson (2018: 21); R. Johnson (2022).

5   As with all of Xenophon's works, the date of the *Memorabilia* is uncertain, but somewhere in the range of 371 BCE seems likely. Christ (2020: 37 n. 3) cites some of those who have engaged in the debate over it. On the possibility that Xenophon exaggerated the poverty of Archedemus, see Christ (1998: 87–8).

6   Millett (1989: 33) suggests that Archedemus' designation of himself as a *philos* of Crito is merely an attempt to maintain appearances, while what Archedemus gains from the arrangement between the two is far more typical of a *kolax* than a *philos*. Christ (2020: 70 n. 109) contends, though, that the narrator's reference to Archedemus as a φιλόχρηστος (2.9.4)—which LSJ translates as "loving goodness or honesty," but in this context likely has a connotation tied to χρηστοί, "of good family" (LSJ II.c.2), i.e., the elite—suggests that Archedemus is being treated as worthy of association with that group because of his ability and willingness to do useful favors for these elite individuals.

7   Pisistratus is also reputed to have left his fields open for the needy to eat from their produce if necessary (Athenaeus 12.532f1–2, *FGrH* 115 F 135), and to have given loans to poor farmers in need (Ps.-Arist. [*Ath. Pol.*] 16.2–3). On the poor as

Pisistratus' chief supporters, see Rhodes (1981: 184–8). Cimon's generosity: Theopompus, *FGrH* 115 F 89; Ps.-Arist. [*Ath. Pol.*] 27.3. Cimon's wealth: [*Ath. Pol.*] 27.2–3.

8 Wade-Gery (1958: 237–8), Connor (1968: 33), and Davidson (1997: 275) also treat Cimon's actions to the poor as generosity motivated by ambition (φιλοτιμία), with no notation of personal interactions as part of his appeal.

9 Ps.-Arist. [*Ath. Pol.*] 27.3 also has Cimon leaving his fields open and inviting strangers to dine at his house, but Pseudo-Aristotle treats the invitation to dine as limited to Cimon's demesmen.

10 See also the example of Hippias, whom Thucydides (6.57.2) notes was πᾶσιν εὐπρόσοδος ("approachable to everyone"). Hornblower (2008: 450 *ad loc.*) notes the quality in Hippias as only a "Hellenistic royal virtue."

11 On friendship as activity, rather than a state, see also Konstan (2018: 44–7 and 150–1).

12 Calhoun (1913: 7, with more examples in the text and at n. 3). Examples: Thuc. 6.65.1, Xen. *Hell.* 1.7.8, *Hell. Oxy.* 1.2. See also Connor (1971: 68), Strauss (1987: 19), and L. G. Mitchell (1997: 43) on these citations, and Connor (1971: 73–5) on the tendency for political groups not to be identified by the group, but rather the individual at its center.

13 See Hornblower (2008: 334–5 *ad* Thuc. 6.13.1) for discussion of the extent to which the passage can be treated as evidence for "packed assemblies."

14 On one type of *philoi* as those who are politically like-minded, whatever their personal feelings for one another, see Arist. *Eth. Nic.* 1161a25–26, Konstan (1997: 62–5), and Christ (2012: 50–1).

15 For examples, see Chapter 2, Sections II–III.

16 Sommerstein's (1981: 89) translation: "You see what a phalanx of young leather-mongers there always is around him; well, next to them live the sellers of honey and cheese." Henderson (1998: 335): "You see what a pack of young leather sellers surround him, and around them live the honey sellers and cheese sellers." Roche (2005: 104): "A gang of young and husky tanners screen him in a medley of fellows selling honey, selling cheeses." Barrett (2020: 205): "For you see the sort of gang of young leather-sellers he has, and dwelling around them are honey-sellers and cheese-sellers."

17 See Nicias' and Alcibiades' marshaling of friends and supporters to avoid ostracism for themselves and push it forward for Hyperbolus (Plut. *Alc.* 13.4–7; *Nic.* 11.1–5; *Arist.* 7.3–4). See also Hansen (1991: 280–7); Rhodes (1994: 92–8); L. G. Mitchell (1997: 46, with n. 34) on the veracity of this story; de Romilly (2019: 50–1).

18 Sommerstein (1981: 190 *ad Eq.* 852–3) sees the portrayed occupations of the vendors in *Knights* as demeaning distortions, as many other things are in the play,

of their genuine, more dignified stations in life, designed to undermine Cleon by making him appear to have disreputable political associates. Other scholars, however, who have addressed this scene (e.g., Rosenbloom 2002: 306, with n. 93; Tylawsky 2002: 26–7; Fisher 2008: 200) treat it just as Aristophanes portrays it: as insincere flattery between Cleon and the commons who come near him, a pantomime carried out so that the masses receive tangible benefits and the demagogues attain prominence and, with it, wealth. Taking another approach, Edmunds (1987: 15–16) associates these companions with "the typical bodyguard of a tyrant."

19 On what is known about these associations and why they seem to have been treated as demeaning to Cleon, see Connor (1971: 129–31), Fisher (2000: 374, 388 n. 81), and Tylawsky (2002: 22–6). One more associate of Cleon's, Thudippus, was close enough to Cleon to have named his son after the demagogue (*PA* 7251–2), but their patterns of interaction with one another are not extant.

20 Commentators on these passages (Platnauer 1964: 133 *ad Pax* 756; MacDowell 1971: 266 *ad Vesp.* 1033; Olson 1998: 222 *ad Pax* 756–7) mention the flattery model without elaborating it.

21 Sealey (1956: 241) goes so far as to label them as part of Cleon's *hetaireia*, which could imply respectable class status for all of them (see Chapter 1, Section II.B). Plutarch is clear in his association of the "hundred heads of flatterers" with *hoi polloi* (*Mor.* 807a2–9) and his other associates with *ho demos*, though (807a10–12).

22 On a date of *Hecuba* to 425 or the few years following, see Sutton (1980: 108–20, esp. 114–20); Cropp and Fick (1985: 23 and table 3.5); Ley (1987); Collard (1991: 34–5); Zeitlin (1991: 71); Mossman (1995: 10–11, with n. 19); Gregory (1999: xii–xiv); and Marshall (2003: 228, with nn. 9 and 10).

23 For the action of this role expressed as a verb, see Pseudo-Aristotle [*Ath. Pol.*] 28.1: Περικλῆς προειστήκει τοῦ δήμου ("Pericles stood before the people").

24 Passages where a form or derivative of κόλαξ (*kolax*, "flatterer") is attached to a demagogue or his behavior: Ar. *Eq.* 48; *Vesp.* 45, 419, 592; Arist. *Pol.* 1292a17, 1313b40–41. Passages where *kolax vel sim.* is not used, yet demagogues, or figures appearing to represent them, are treated as insincerely acting as well-meaning friends to masses of non-elite individuals: Eur. *Hec.* 132, 257; *Supp.* 412–15; *Or.* 907; Thuc. 2.65.10, 3.42.6, 7.8.2. For more on interpretations of Cleon as a flatterer of the *demos* and his followers, see Tylawsky (2002: 23–6) and Fisher (2008: 200). Landfester (1967: 57–9), Dover (1972: 91–2), and Brock (1986: 18–21) lay out where, in *Knights*, suggestions of flattery from Cleon's stand-in Paphlagon to

Demos (beyond the use of ἐκολάκευ' at 48) appear in the play, and Scholtz (2004: 274–9), refined at Scholtz (2007: 54–9), shows how the pederastic relationship that the play treats as binding Paphlagon and Demos is linked elsewhere to flattery.

25 See Chapter 2, Section II.C.1, with notes, for the very tangible measures Cleon took to benefit that constituency.

26 On *kolakeia* and its connotations, see Ribbeck (1883). Konstan's (1997: 98–103) discussion of flattery focuses almost exclusively on the practice in the Hellenistic world; most sources on the subject are post-classical. This is most likely, argues Konstan (1997: 101), since the democratic ethos of Athens discourages treating someone else as a superior, as is implicit in flattery. Scholtz (2004: 277 n. 45), though, disputes that interpretation.

27 Scholtz (2004: 277, with citations in n. 45), refined at Scholtz (2007: 57 and n. 52), talks about the difficulty of telling a friend from a flatterer, and Davidson (1997: 275) discusses the difficulty of drawing lines between the appropriateness or inappropriateness of behaviors in all sorts of relationships.

28 Davies (1975: 377) contends that the labeling of Cleon's followers as *kolakes* rather than *philoi* in *Knights* and elsewhere, while Archedemus is called a *philos* of Crito in Xenophon's *Memorabilia*, is purely a function of the hostility of Cleon's portrayal, versus the neutrality of Archedemus'; their circumstances are very similar.

29 See also Finley (1983: 77–8, with n. 27). Sommerstein (1981: 190 *ad* 852–3), followed by Rhodes (1994: 93), suggests the portrayal of the vendors around Cleon was a reference to "the fairly common practice whereby organized groups of supporters of a particular politician sat together in a compact block in the Assembly," but Anderson and Dix (2020: 171 *ad* 582–54) find that unlikely.

30 Fisher (2000: 374) thinks they would have thought of themselves as his "friends," Strauss (1987: 16, cf. 38 n. 23) as his *philoi*, and Hershkowitz (2018: 170–1) as his "political *philoi*."

31 Ar. *Rhet.* 1381a25–28, with Konstan (2018) 41.

32 Jones (1964: 118–60); Boissevain (1974: 85); Schutte and Light (1978: 263–4); Moskowitz (2004: 339).

33 Aristotle (*EN* 1158a10–11, 16–17) states that it is not possible to be fully a friend to many people, and that those who try to make it seem as though they have many friends come off as true friends to none, but only as political friends (1171a15). And indeed, no politician or other sort of leader of many is going to come across as a close friend to hundreds or thousands of supporters. However, contemporary sociology, as applied in this chapter, nuances Aristotle's expressed sense of individuals' perceptions of friendship with those at a different status level. There is,

reasonably, no expectation of individual reciprocity, but there is an emotional attachment from the lower-status "friend" to the higher-status one that makes the lower-status one *feel* as though the actions of each that affect the other have a personal component to them.

34 The converse is shown to be true as well in the case of Electra's husband in Euripides' *Electra* (45–6, 247–57): poor people were not desirable friends in part because of their inability to assist friends materially, but also because there was no prestige in being associated with them.

35 On dynamics of Athenian friendship, see note 16 in Chapter 1, Section II.B.

36 Roisman and Luschnig (2011: 90 *ad* 23–4, 95 *ad* 44–6, 132 *ad* 247).

37 E.g., Marsden (1988); McPherson, Smith-Lovin, and Cook (2001); Schwartz (2007); Amichai-Hamburger, Kingsbury, and Schneider (2013). Cf. Arist. *Eth. Nic.* 1158b29–1159a12.

38 Xen. *Mem.* 2.9.4–7; see Section II, above.

39 E.g., Rothbart and Taylor (1992); Haslam et al. (2006); D. L. Hamilton (2007: 1081–5).

40 On the wealth of Cleon, Hyperbolus, and Cleophon, see n. 22 in Chapter 2, Section II.A. While Cleon's father, Cleaenetus, gained enough wealth through his tannery to perform a liturgy at the City Dionysia in 460/459, the generations prior to Cleaenetus were undistinguished both in wealth and in status. On the path that these non-elite families took to achieve their wealth, see Connor (1971: 158–60) and Davies (1981: 41–2). Cf. Henderson (1990: 281), who is less convinced than the others that these demagogues' family backgrounds were quite as humble as they are often made out to be.

41 See notes 29–31 in Chapter 2, Section II.B for citations.

42 Other associations of the Sausage-Seller with the *agora*: *Eq.* 181, 297, 634–8, 1257–8. Cf. Rosenbloom (2002: 306).

43 Henderson (forthcoming, *ad* 217–20) sums up these characterizations as "You have all the endowments that made Cleon successful"; see also Neil (1901: 35 *ad* 217–18). To give this critical presentation of demagogues' qualities context, Hershkowitz (2018: 14), following Lossau's (1969: 85) similar appraisal of expectations versus reality in Aristophanes' uses of προστάτης and Canfora's (1993: 10–12) summation of *Eq.* 118–93 and 211–19, suggests that it was not people doing demagogic things (δημαγωγικά, *demagogika*, 217) in general who were weak in these areas, but only that the *current* ones were, and it was the incongruity between expectation and reality that contributed to the humor of Demosthenes' claim. Henderson (forthcoming, *ad* 191–3) makes a similar point.

44 LSJ⁹ s.v. I.A.1. On connotations of vulgarity, see LSJ⁹ s.v. II.1–2; cf. Suda α 308 and Hershkowitz (2018: 12). On connotations of persuasive speaking ability, LSJ⁹ s.v.

III.1. On traits of people designated as ἀγοραῖοι, see Connor (1971: 154–5, with n. 39) and Rosenbloom (2002: 305–7); cf. Ostwald (1986: 214–15), and the classical citations at Rosenbloom (2004: 60 n. 15). A rather neutral use of this term appears at *Eq.* 297, when Hermes, patron of merchants, is called Ἑρμῆν τὸν Ἀγοραῖον.

45 On ἀγοραῖος as referring to the petty traders in the *agora* as a segment of the *demos*, and a set of characteristics and behaviors associated with that class, see Connor (1971: 154–5), Rosenbloom (2002: 305; 2004: 60), and Saldutti (2014: 27), with their primary citations, particularly Ar. *Ran.* 1013–17; Pl. *Prot.* 347c2–d7; Xen. *Mem.* 3.7.6; Arist. *Pol.* 1289b33, 1291b18–30, 1319b26–28, 1328b39–41; *EN* 1158a21; Suda α 308; Photios α 33. See Mann (2007: 178–9) for ways in which his portrayal and speech in Thucydides reveal common touches that could endear him to the majority Athenians.

46 Halliwell (2020: 113): "Aristophanic comedy represents, and of course manipulates, the micro- rather than the macro-world of Athenian politics."

47 Greek conceptions of the dynamics of "friends of friends": Strauss (1987: 29); Blundell (1989: 47–8, with the sources she cites, especially Arist. *Rhet.* 1381a7–9, 13–17; *Eth. Nic.* 1171a4–6); and Konstan (1997: 63). See also Strauss' (1987: 19) conjecture that Conon's friendship with Epicrates of Cephisia might have provided him influence over the *demos*, whose favor Epicrates had earned.

48 Holland and Leinhard (1971); Manhart (2000: 178–81); Kilduff and Tsai (2003: 42). On homophily as a key factor in the growth of perceptions of friendship through transitivity, see Louch (2000) and Flynn, Reagans, and Guillory (2010).

49 Modern online culture provides a model of such tangential friendly feelings, with individuals in a virtual community of otherwise unconnected peers treating the interactions of any one of them with a prominent figure that they all revere as a reason for a feeling of deeper connection, even friendship, toward that prominent figure; see, e.g., Erikson (2008).

50 Bishop and Cushing (2008: 259, 262–3); Bustos and Johnson (2018: 23); R. Johnson (2022).

51 Though a precise year of birth for Xenophon is unknown, 430 or shortly thereafter is likely (Anderson 2001: 10; Waterfield 2005: xiii; Gray 2010: 8, with n. 34; Hobden 2020: 5; Christ 2020: 3), putting him in his twenties during the period of power of Cleophon and other demagogues at the end of the Peloponnesian War.

His numerous works with Socrates as his main character indicate that he was out in the public square and interested in the issues of his time during his upbringing and early adulthood as an Athenian, and his *Hellenica* indicates that he was attentive to events and trends in Athens from that period in his life. His works certainly imply that he had not forgotten about Athens; Tuplin (2017: 339–46) documents each explicit mention of Athens in Xenophon's works. Christ (2020)

makes a compelling case for the Athenocentrism of Xenophon's works; his
argument is particularly distilled on pp. 1–15.

Gera (1993: 23–5) dates the *Cyropaedia* to sometime in the 360s, summing up
many perspectives on the matter; Higgins (1977: 48, with 156 n. 22) narrows the date
to 362, and Carlier (1978: 137 n. 13) and Gray (2010: 7 n. 32) put it at 361 or shortly
thereafter. Though these dates would put publication a few decades after the peak
period of the demagogues, it seems reasonable both that Xenophon's rearing in Athens
during this period influenced his sense of how politics and friendship work, and that
he perceived that his audience, primarily Athenian, at the time of publication would
also have been familiar with the interplay of friendship and politics as he presents it.

Many of the ideas, examples, citations, and language in the following section
were previously published as Simmons (2018). They are included by permission of
Archaeopress.

52 On Xenophon's deviation from historical precedent in his portrayal of Cyrus the
Elder to make it relevant to audiences in both Sparta and Athens, see, e.g., Higgins
(1977: 44–5); Carlier (1978: 143); Hirsch (1985: 61–100); Cartledge (1987: 39–59);
Due (1989: 38–42, 117–46, 234–42); Stadter (1991); Nadon (2001: 16–17, 30–42);
and Sancisi-Weerdenburg (2010).

53 Reisert (2009: 24–32) explores how shrewd and deliberate Cyrus is in his
employment of friendship to win from his followers the dedication he needs from
them to achieve his aims. The details of this depiction are almost certainly
Xenophon's own creation, designed to appeal to his audience, some of which was
in Sparta, but the large majority of which was in Athens, where reading was a
more common behavior, and to where Xenophon either intended to return, or
already had. Higgins (1977: 128–43), in particular, followed by Carlier (1978: 137
n. 13), argues that Xenophon wrote *Cyropaedia*, and arguably all of the rest of his
works, in Athens after his exile was rescinded in 368, and that his works clearly
reveal his Athenian sympathies.

54 Years later, after Cyrus has secured his empire and become quite a bit more
complacent, he is a bit more blunt about this process: "by enriching people and
doing good deeds for them, I win good will and friendship from them, and from
those things I reap security and glory" (πλουτίζων καὶ εὐεργετῶν ἀνθρώπους
εὔνοιαν ἐξ αὐτῶν κτῶμαι καὶ φιλίαν, καὶ ἐκ τούτων καρποῦμαι ἀσφάλειαν καὶ
εὔκλειαν, 8.2.22). See Buxton (2016: 185) on the bald self-interest of this attitude.

The text of the *Cyropaedia* I cite is Marchant (1910). All direct translations of
passages from the *Cyropaedia* are my own, though often overlapping with or
influenced by Ambler (2001).

55 Reisert (2009: 24–32), too, explores Cyrus' shrewd and deliberate employment of
friendship to win from his followers the dedication he needs to achieve his aims.

56 The expression *andres philoi* seems to have been adapted from a similar Persian
   expression. Herodotus has Gobryas use the same words to address a small group
   of other prominent Persians conspiring against Smerdis the Magus (3.73.2), and in
   the *Anabasis*, Xenophon portrays Cyrus the Younger referring in the same way to
   other noble Persians and the trusted Greek Clearchus (1.6.6). Yet, while these
   Greek authors may have been transmitting tropes of Persian speech, each author's
   lack of comment on the patterns of use of this expression for his Greek,
   predominantly Athenian, audience suggests that it would have translated clearly
   enough to local norms not to require explanation. Furthermore, the development
   and use of friendship is such an enormous part of the *Cyropaedia* that, if the
   approach to friendship portrayed in this work was not familiar to the Greeks
   reading it, it is difficult to imagine that the work would have survived.

57 Xenophon has Artabazus lay out Cyrus' systematic efforts to become *philoi* with
   people whose friendship would benefit him (7.5.48–54). Cyrus, too, speaks of the
   value to kings' sovereignty of faithful friends, and the need to win those friends by
   good works (8.7.13). On the overlap between kings' *philoi* and their advisors or
   other leading officials in other Persian circumstances, see Konstan (1997: 96).

58 *Cyr.* 1.5.7, 1.11.2, 2.2.27, 2.4.22, 3.2.4, 4.2.38, 4.22.1, 4.3.4, 5.2.23, 5.3.2, 5.5.44,
   6.3.15, 7.5.20, 7.5.39, 8.4.32, 8.6.3.

59 For Cyrus' conscious efforts to win over "the multitude" (τὸ ... πλῆθος) so that
   they would fight and risk their lives on his behalf, see *Cyr.* 7.5.55. From early in
   life, he shows a keen awareness that, although the affection of subjects can be won
   in the same way that the love of friends can, "subjects" and "friends" are clearly in
   two different categories (1.6.24).

60 Cyrus had been encouraged by one of the Persian Peers to make the invitation
   personally, since the common Persians were likely to receive the invitation more
   favorably if it were delivered by the king's son, rather than someone of a lower
   rank (2.1.13).

61 Due (1989: 196 n. 60) notes this practice as an effort to be accessible, which he
   shows as well at 7.5.37–40 (Due 204).

62 On the impact of these invitations on people's sense of loyalty and attachment to
   Cyrus later in the work, see Reisert (2009: 30).

63 The other exception is at 3.3.7, where Cyrus refers to a group of officers and "all
   the others he was honoring" (πάντων ὅσους ἐτίμα) as *andres philoi*; again, he
   makes it seem as though merit can vault a common soldier into friendship with
   him.

64 On the psychological effects of one's level of satisfaction with the "ingroups" of
   which one is a part, see, e.g., Tajfel and Turner (1986); Mischenko and Day (2015);
   van Veelen, Eisenbeiss, and Otten (2016).

65 Due (1989: 183) and Nadon (2001: 75) note the confidence that Cyrus instilled in Pheraulas through their interactions.

66 On the role of reciprocal assistance as a key component of friendship, see Chapter 1, Section II.B above, particularly n. 16. On the role of *kharis*, specifically, in friendship, see, e.g., Blundell (1989: 32–6), L. G. Mitchell (1997: 18–21), Konstan (2006: 157–64 and 167), and Konstan (2018: 109 and 116–17). Davies (1981: 92–7), Millett (1991: 123–6), Konstan (1997: 81–2) and point out that *kharis* is also regularly referenced in the context of gratitude for good works between individuals and the *polis* as a whole, but even then the relationship between individual and state is clearly seen as analogous to that between friends or family members (Blundell 1989: 44, with classical citations).

67 On the engagement of *Hecuba* as a whole with the issues of its time, see Gregory (1999: 58 *ad* 107, with citations of other scholars who discuss tragedy's contemporaneous flavor). More specific reference to Odysseus' demagogic characterization will come as I engage with specific passages.

The text of *Hecuba* that I use is Diggle's (1984).

68 Anderson and Dix (2020: 162 *ad* 773–6) translate χαριοίμην as a neutral "please." Henderson (1998: 323) and Barrett (2020: 199) both have it as "gratify"; forms of χάρις may have an implication of sexual gratification (Dover 2016: 44–5), but that is not, typically, what an *erastes* (as Paphlagon nominally is) does for an *eromenos*.

69 Collard (1991: 63) translates *demokharistes* as "people-flatterer," Mitchell-Boyask (2006: 36) as "crowd-pleasing," and Kovacs (1994: 411) as "demagogue." On this passage, and the term *demokharistes*, as linking Odysseus' behavior to that of contemporaneous demagogues, see Mossman (1995: 38) and Gregory (1999: 63 *ad* 131–3). The word before *demokharistes* is ἡδυλόγος (*hedulogos*), which Montiglio (2011: 9) translates as "smooth talker," further tying Odysseus to a skill commonly attributed to demagogues.

70 Other classical sources in which *demegoros* denotes a demagogue: Xen. *Hell.* 6.2.39, 6.3.3, *Anab.* 2.6.15, *Symp.* 2.14; Plato *Prot.* 329a, *Gorg.* 482c, 494d, 520b, *Leg.* 908d. On the portrayal of Odysseus here as reflective of demagogues of the time, see Σ *Hec.* M and Mⁱ *ad* 254; cf. Tierney (1946: 58 *ad* 254); Connor (1971: 98 n. 16); Kovacs (1987: 81); Collard (1991: 146 *ad* 254–7); Mossman (1995: 38); Gregory (1999: 76–7 *ad* 254–7); Montiglio (2011: 9–10).

71 On this meaning of *pros kharin*, see LSJ⁹ s.v. χάρις VI.2.b. Mitchell-Boyask (2006: 41) translates the phrase as "currying favor."

72 For *pros kharin* taken as "pleasing," see Connor (1971: 98 n. 16); Collard (1991: 69).

73 See J. F. Johnson's (2016: 114) explanation of Odysseus' abrogation of his reciprocal *kharis* benefit to Hecuba. On *kharis* in the play as flattery, see Scholtz (2004: 275, with notes 39–40), refined at Scholtz (2007: 55, with notes 43–4).

4 Distinguishing Desire from Friendship in Leadership Models in Aristophanes' *Knights*

1 Anderson and Dix (2020: 157 *ad* 732) interpret the image as unambiguously positive and uncomplicated by sexual implication: "To be a 'lover' of the demos (cf. φιλόδημον, 787) implies idealized love and devotion to the city." See below, Section V, with nn. 68–74, for discussion of the image of the political *erastes* in other sources.

2 Scholars who take this point of view, though with some hesitation, include Connor (1971: 96–8) and Monoson (2000: 66, 86). Crane (1998: 318–19) speaks of "Kleon" being the *erastes* of Demos in *Knights*, without specifically going into whether he thinks that this character's feelings are representative of those of the historical Cleon. Sommerstein (1981: 181 *ad* 732), Hornblower (1991: 311 *ad* Thuc 2.43.1), and Wohl (2002: 93) note Rogers' and Connor's interpretation that Cleon may genuinely have used such language, though do not specifically endorse it.

3 See also Landfester (1967: 52), Sommerstein (1981: 181 *ad* 732), and Halliwell (2020: 125).

4 Wohl (2002: 86) treats the image as not likely Cleon's own, but rather taken from a speech of Pericles, recounted at Thucydides 2.43.1, which will be discussed below in Section V. Rhodes (1988: 225 *ad* Thuc. 2.43.1), too, considers Pericles' expression, if genuinely his and not a creation of Thucydides', a likely source of the pederastic language in *Knights*. Ludwig (2002: 144–5) contends that, while it is possible that Aristophanes was quoting Cleon, it is at least as likely that he, like Thucydides, was just tapping into a generic tradition of erotic rhetoric in the late fifth and early fourth centuries. Others with similar views: Neil (1901: 175 *ad* 1341–2); Burckhardt (1924: 40); Gomme (1956: 135–7 *ad* Thuc. 2.43.1); Dover (1972: 91); Hornblower (1991: 311 *ad* Thuc. 2.43.1); cf. Olson (2002: 117 *ad Ach.* 143–4). Scholtz (2004: 265–6; 2007: 45–6) contends that there is reason to be skeptical about the sincerity of any such political pederastic imagery (more of which will be addressed below). For one, he observes, none of the records in extant oratory, history, or philosophy of *eros* being expressed for a civic body (more examples of which, again, I will note below) includes a speaker (including Cleon) making such a declaration in his *own* voice; there is always someone else exhorting *eros* from others, projecting *eros* onto others, or expressing that *eros* as an actor in a play. Scholtz (2004: 269; 2007: 48–9) suggests that orators' attribution of excessive fondness for the Athenian people to other speakers was a common rhetorical trope to bring attention to the vulgarity of such speakers. Holmes (2011: 15 n. 34), however, assumes that political pederasty must have been a sincere motif in oratory, based on the extent to which Aristophanes plays on it in his comedies.

Scholtz (2004: 271–4; 2007: 51–4) touches on aspects of the political pederasty model in *Knights* that verge on *philia*, but his focus in the whole 2004 article and in the "He Loves You, He Loves You Not" chapter (pp. 43–70) of the 2007 book is on the way that *Knights* problematizes contemporaries' uses of pederasty as a metaphor for Athenian politics.

5	Phiddian (1995: 13–14): "[A]ll parody refunctions pre-existing text(s) and/or discourses, so it can be said that these verbal structures are called to the readers' minds and then placed under erasure. A necessary modification of the original idea is that we must allow the act of erasure to operate critically rather than as neutral cancellation of its object. Parodic erasure disfigures its pre-texts in various ways that seek to guide our re-evaluation or refiguration of them." Hodgart (1969: 121–2): "The mimic must create a likeness, so that his audience shall recognize it; but he must not stop at a mere impersonation, he must go on to produce a ludicrous distortion in which the compulsive gestures and tics of the victim are exaggerated: a newly-created character is built out of them and superimposed on the original likeness." Cf. Connor (1971: 96); Dentith (2000: 39). Pelling (2000: 123–40), too, discusses the nuances of exaggeration that would acceptably generate humor in Athenian audiences.

6	For possible explanations as to why the mask did not resemble Cleon, see Dover (1975: 64); Sommerstein (1981: 154–5 *ad* 231–3); Edmunds (1987: 68 *ad* 230–3); and Anderson and Dix (2020: 99 *ad* 231–3).

7	Demos refers to Paphlagon and the Sausage-Seller as such as well at 1163.

8	Ar. *Rhet.* 1380b35–81a1, with Konstan (2006: 171–2) and (2018: 40). *Pace* Landfester (1967: 53), who takes the use of *phileo* by a self-proclaimed *erastes* as implicitly investing the term with erotic connotations. Others whose translations or interpretations treat *phileo* as consistent with the erotic feelings of an *erastes*: Scholtz (2004: 272): "[Y]ou're special to me, Demos . . . I love you"; Scholtz (2007: 52): "I love you, Demos . . . I'm the one who's hot for you"; Anderson and Dix (2020: 156–7 *ad* 732): "Paphlagon's profession of love for Demos (773, 791, 799, 821; cf. 1341–2) is transmuted into erotic love for a decrepit old man."

On the inherent instability of pederastic relationships, see Arist. *Eth. Nic.* 1157a3–10 and Konstan (1997: 38–9).

9	Other than its appearances in *Knights* at 732, 769, 821, and 1341, and the citation from *Lysistrata* included in the text, *philo se* (whether in that order or the opposite, whether elided or not, and whether or not with intervening words) occurs only at HH 4.382 (Hermes to Zeus), Eur. *Med.* 327 (Creon to Medea), Ar. *Av.* 1010 (Peisetaerus to Meton), Lys. F 369.16 Thalheim (uncertain referent), Pl. *Phaedr.* 228e1 (Socrates to Phaedrus), and Pl. *Euthyd.* 284e7 (Dionysodorus to Ctesippus), and in every case the context is an expression of friendly fondness (or lack of it).

10 On women's means of expressing their feelings for male lovers, see Dover (2016: 49–50, 52) and Davidson (2007: 30). On the language *eromenoi* used for expressing feelings for *erastai*, see Halperin (1986: 63–6 and his citations), and also Dover (2016: 53, 123–4). Pl. *Symp.* 182c5–7 illustrates what each party in a pederastic relationship was supposed to feel for the other, and Xen. *Symp.* 8.21 talks about a boy's supposed lack of desire. At *Eq.* 746–8, for example, as Scholtz (2004: 272; 2007: 52) also notes, when Paphlagon wants Demos to decide which *erastes* he will favor, it is *phileo* that he expects Demos to feel for the chosen one (καὶ μὴν ποιήσας αὐτίκα μάλ' ἐκκλησίαν, / ὦ Δῆμ', ἵν' εἰδῇς ὁπότερος νῷν ἐστί σοι / ὑνούστερος, διάκρινον, ἵνα τοῦτον φιλῇς, "Furthermore, Demos, convene the assembly right away, and distinguish between us, so that you can see which of us is better-spirited toward you, and <u>cherish</u> him"); Scholtz treats *phileo* as "love," though, and something that can be euphemistic for sexual gratification. Henderson (1998) translates φιλῇς with "cherish," and Barrett (2020) chooses "befriend"; the same translations for both apply at 1052, when the prophecy that Paphlagon relates commands that Demos φίλει him.

11 On the other hand, neither are ἐρῶ σου (or σ') and ἐπιθυμῶ σου (or σ') (the significance of which I will explain shortly) extant in classical literature, but the absence of the two of them in this form, coupled with the absence of *philo se* as an expression of *erastai*'s passion, underscore the importance of seeing how these words are used in other constructions to understand the significance of Paphlagon's choice of words to express his feelings for Demos.

12 Paphlagon's uses of forms of *phileo*, other than at 732: πῶς ἂν ἐμοῦ μᾶλλόν σε φιλῶν, ὦ Δῆμε, γένοιτο πολίτης; ("How could there become a citizen caring for you more than I, Demos?" 773); καὶ μὴν εἴ πού τις ἀνὴρ ἐφάνη τῷ δήμῳ μᾶλλον ἀμύνων / ἢ μᾶλλον ἐμοῦ σε φιλῶν, ἐθέλω περὶ τῆς κεφαλῆς περιδόσθαι ("And, indeed, if some man somewhere seemed to protect the *demos* more or to care for you more than I, I am willing to wager my head," 790–1); οὔκουν ταυτὶ δεινὸν ἀκούειν, ὦ Δῆμ', ἐστίν μ' ὑπὸ τούτου, / ὁτιή σε φιλῶ; ("Isn't it awful, Demos, that I am hearing this from him, all because I care for you?" 820–1). Demos indicating Paphlagon's expressed feelings: σὺ δ', ὦ Παφλαγών, φάσκων φιλεῖν μ' ἐσκορόδισας ("You, Paphlagon, have aggravated me with your claims to care for me," 946).

13 Like *phileo*, *stergo* can also mean "love," but typically of the sort within families or between friends (LSJ⁹ s.vv. I–II). The Sausage-Seller's uses of forms of *phileo* or *stergo*, other than at 1341: κἄγωγ', ὦ Δῆμ', εἰ μή σε φιλῶ καὶ μὴ στέργω, κατατμηθεὶς / ἑψοίμην ἐν περικομματίοις ("As for me, Demos, if I don't care for and cherish you, let me be chopped up and boiled in mincemeat," 769–70); οὐχὶ φιλεῖ σ' οὐδ' ἔστ' εὔνους ("He [Paphlagon] does not care for you, nor is he well-disposed," 779); πῶς σὺ φιλεῖς, ὃς τοῦτον ὁρῶν οἰκοῦντ' ἐν ταῖς φιδάκναισι /

καὶ γυπαρίοις καὶ πυργιδίοις ἔτος ὄγδοον . . .; ("How do you care for him [Demos], while seeing him living in storage jars, crannies, and holes in walls for the eighth year now . . .?" 792–3); οὐ γάρ σ' ἐχρῆν, εἴπερ <u>φιλεῖς</u> τὸν δῆμον, ἐκ προνοίας / ταύτας ἐᾶν αὐτοῖσι τοῖς πόρπαξιν ἀνατεθῆναι ("For if you truly care for the *demos*, you would not intentionally have allowed these [shields] to be hung up with their handles," 848–9); σκύτη τοσαῦτα πωλῶν / ἔδωκας ἤδη τουτῳὶ κάττυμα παρὰ σεαυτοῦ / ταῖς ἐμβάσιν, φάσκων <u>φιλεῖν</u>; ("Selling as many hides as you do, have you ever given him [Demos] a gift of patches for his shoes, since you claim to care for him?" 868–70).

14 769: "I'm . . . a friend"; 773: "feels . . . friendship"; 779: "isn't your friend"; 791: "who is a better friend"; 821: "I feel friendly affection"; 848: "you're a friend"; 870: "you are his friend"; 946: "be my friend."

   Moreover, on five of the seven occasions when the Sausage-Seller uses *phileo* (or the equally benign στέργω, *stergo*) in regard to Demos, he is just passing on what he claims Paphlagon says to the object of his affection, or what Paphlagon's true feelings supposedly are (779, 792, 848, 870, 1341).

15 The speaker at Lysias 3.5 uses the same expression (εὖ ποιῶν) to express his method of winning over an alluring boy, and he is similarly clear about his (and a rival's) feelings for the boy: ἐπεθυμήσαμεν ("we desired [him]").

16 Dover (2016: 43–4, 49–50). Others who discuss these and other terms and their implications in various relationships involving friendship and/or romantic love are Davidson (1997: 19–36) and, specifically to Aristophanes' plays, Robson (2013a). While the examples below are from works released in the fourth century BCE, several decades after *Knights*, they provide the most thorough record of the terminology of pederasty and friendship in classical Athens and show consistency with the terminology used in *Knights* and other works of its time.

17 Ἐράω to express the passion of an *erastes*: *Symp.*, e.g., 178d5, 179a3, 179b4, 180a5, 181a5–6, 181d4, 181d7, 182a1, 182d6, 182d8, 183b2, 183c2–3, 183e1–2, 184a4, 186d6, 197b8, 198d7; *Phaedr.*, e.g., 231a6, 231c1, 232a1, 232a4, 232a6, 232b2, 232d4, 233c7, 234b2, 234b7–8, 236a8, 237b4–5, 237d5, 240e8, 243c4, 249e3, 255c2, 255d3. Ἐπιθυμέω to express the passion of an *erastes*: *Symp.*, e.g., 192d6, 192d8, 200a3, 200e2–3; *Phaedr.* 255e2. Both used together to express such passion: e.g., *Symp.* 200a5–6. *Symposium* and *Phaedrus* were written in the first half of the fourth century BCE; see n. 6 in Chapter 1, Section II.

18 On the speeches of Lysias and Socrates here, see Ferrari (1987: 88–102).

19 On the ranges of meaning of *eros* and *philia*, particularly in Phaedrus, see Nicholson (1999: 210–12).

20 See Hyland (1968: 36–8) for an explication of the differences between the three verbs, as highlighted in the passage. On the relations between friendship and

desire in *Lysis*, as expressed by these three words and their cognates, see Penner and Rowe (2005: 104 n. 18; 110–11; 115 n. 44; 186–7 with n. 8; 211–12; 229–30; 249 with nn. 34 and 35; 307–12; 325 n. 63). *Lysis* was written in the first half of the fourth century BCE; see n. 6 in Chapter 1, Section II.

21 Rowe (1986: 147–8 *ad Phaedrus* 233c7): "the lover himself can be *philos* as well as *erastes* to the boy, ... but *qua* lover he would normally be distinguished from the *philos*." *Pace* Landfester (1967: 53) and Robson (2013a: 254). See also Dover (2016: 50, 91–7) for pederastic courtship practices in general.

22 *Symp.* 179c1–3: Alcestis vaulted above Admetus' parents in her friendship (τῇ φιλίᾳ) due to her passion for him (διὰ τὸν ἔρωτα). *Symp.* 182c3–4: Pausanias explains that gratifying *erastai* is discouraged by the Persian governments in Ionia, since *eros* tends to engender strong friendships (φιλίας ἰσχυρὰς ... φιλεῖ ... ὁ ἔρως ἐμποιεῖν). *Symp.* 209c5–7: Diotima says that *erastai* and *eromenoi* who have reached a level of closeness that they have procreated in soul reach a far surer friendship (φιλίαν βεβαιοτέραν) than that which comes with human children. The speaker in [Demos.] 61.6 also treats *philia* as a component of a pederastic relationship, and also as a development of a relationship that was instigated through the desire (in this case expressed as ἀγαπῶ) that led the *erastes* in this essay to pursue Epicrates, his *eromenos*.

23 On the scholarly dialogue over meanings of *eros* and *philia* in the *Symposium*, see Sheffield (2006: 155–7).

24 For an in-depth study of *eros* and *philia* in both of these authors, see A. W. Price (1997).

25 Forms or cognates of *phileo* also appear at times as euphemisms for sexual passion when the circumstance or individual scruples would discourage explicitness; see, e.g., Halperin (1986: 71) on Xen. *Mem.* 2.6.28, and Dover (2016: 49) on Xen. *Symp.* 9.6. Exigencies of meter or *variatio* can also lead to such substitution (Dover 2016: 50). None of these situations, however, is applicable in *Knights*.

26 See also, e.g., Dover (2016: 16); Hornblower (1991: 311 *ad* Thuc. 2.43.1); Ludwig (2002: 147–8); Scholtz (2004: 264); Scholtz (2007: 44). *Pace* Davidson (2007: esp. 123–4), who finds expressions for love of different sorts to be more flexible than many scholars take them to be.

27 Henderson (1991: 69) and Hubbard (1991: 67–8) both note how reserved Paphlagon is in his references to sexuality, compared to the completely uninhibited Sausage-Seller.

28 Henderson (1991: 67) also reads *Eq.* 1032–4, spoken by the Sausage-Seller about Paphlagon, as suggesting cunnilingus. On common practices of, and attitudes toward, cunnilingus, see Henderson (1991: 51–2, 67, 185–6) and Dover (2016: 101–2). As for male performance of fellatio on another man, it is a pathic activity,

the willing performance of which, as with acceptance of anal penetration, can be tantamount to prostitution, and consequently potentially disenfranchising (Dover 2016: 99, 106; Henderson 1991: 52, cf. 209–15). The Sausage-Seller also wishes that Paphlagon would "bite his own dick" (τὸ πέος οὑτοσὶ δάκοι, 1010); though Hubbard (1991: 68) treats this as an example of fellatio, this encouragement of autosexuality seems more in line with the rhetoric of sexual violence to imply a physical threat; see notes 32–44 below for other examples and analysis of such.

29 On comic exploitation of sexuality, see Dover (2016: 135–53); on obscenity, primarily sexual, in Aristophanes' plays, see Henderson (1991: 56–107). On comic treatment of passive homosexuality as nearly a prerequisite for participation in politics, see Henderson (1991: 209) and Ludwig (2002: 43). Underscoring the political connection of the pathic behavior attributed to the competing demagogues in *Knights*, the Sausage-Seller claims that Paphlagon put a premium on disenfranchising passive sodomites only in order to reduce the number of candidates who might oppose him politically (878–80). Other accusations of pathic behavior among politicians: e.g., Eup. fr. 104 KA; Pl. Com. fr. 186.5 K; Ar. *Nub.* 1093–4, *Eccles.* 102–4; Pl. *Symp.* 192a. *Nub.* 1088–92 goes further than that, implicating prosecutors and tragedians as pathics, and Adesp. fr. 12 K links all elites to that behavior (on fr. 12 K, see Henderson 1991: 216–17 and Hubbard 1998: 53). And it is not just the elite: *Nub.* 1094–100 marks the majority of spectators at the performance as passive homosexuals, and numerous other passages implicate nearly the full male population in pathic behavior: *Ach.* 79, 104, 635; *Eq.* 1263; *Pax* 11 (with scholia), 101; fr. 694 Edmonds. See Davidson (1997) 167–82, though, for an argument that the many derogatory references to sexual passivity among politicians and others is to their decadence in general, rather than specifically to their acceptance of penetration as their main offense; passive penetration, in Davidson's interpretation, just highlights behavior that is more broadly unrestrained.

30 It should be noted that being the active member of any homosexual pairing appears to have been accepted in Athens, at least among the elite (Fowler 1996; Hubbard 1998: esp. 49–50, 59, 64, 69–70; Hubbard 2000: 8) and pederasty was not a problem if the *eromenos* and his family approved of the pairing (Henderson 1991: 215), as seems to be the case in this play, based on the Sausage-Seller's claims that Demos has spurned others to give himself to Paphlagon and people like him (736–40).

31 Sommerstein (1981: 162 *ad* 355) takes κασαλβάσω as metaphorical for "overwhelm" or "put to flight."

32 On anal rape as a symbol of dominance over an opponent, see Dover (2016: 105–6, with notes) and Henderson (1991: 218–19). The Eurymedon vase (R1155)

is another apparent example of violent anal intercourse used figuratively (Schauenburg 1975); see Golden (1984: 315 n. 34) for references to other similar vase images.

33 On the sexually violent implications of the *Wasps* passage, see van der Valk (1967: 128–9) and Henderson (1991: 175).

34 On possible rape imagery in this passage, see Maxwell-Stewart (1976), Edmunds (1987: 68), Henderson (1991: 68), and Anderson and Dix (2020: 104–5 *ad* 261–3).

35 On connections between imagery of sexual violence tied to Cleon and any implications of the demagogue's own sexuality to be taken from them, Henderson (1991: 218) is explicit: "These are all figurative uses of the image of anal penetration and are not meant to imply that Cleon was a pederast in real life."

36 Sommerstein (1981: 99, 195 *ad* 963) takes *molgos* as representing the dead flesh that Demos would supposedly become if he were to trust the Sausage-Seller, and Bartlett (2020: 213 n. 172) takes it to mean that Demos would be flayed alive. Both of them, along with Neil (1901: 135 *ad* 962), Henderson (1998: 347, with n. 74), and Anderson and Dix (2020: 180 *ad* 963–4), treat it as also referring to a well-known oracle. Sommerstein and Neil allude as well to the sexual meaning of *molgos* that I explain above, and with which Henderson (1991) deals (see n. 40 below). Neil (1901: 135–6 *ad* 963–4), Sommerstein (1981: 99, 195 *ad* 964), Henderson (1998: 347, with n. 75), Scholtz (2004: 273; 2007: 53), and Anderson and Dix (2020: 180 *ad* 963–4) all take *psolos* to refer to someone who is circumcised, and thus shamefully out of step with Greek convention.

37 Henderson (1991: 212, with references); cf. Dover (2016: 204).

38 Scholtz (2004: 273–4, with n. 33; 2007: 53, with n. 37) agrees with Henderson's interpretation.

39 On the attractiveness, to classical Athenian men, of anal penetration of boys in the age range of *eromenoi*, see, e.g., *Ach.* 1102, 1121; *Eq.* 1384–91; *Pax* 11; *Ran.* 145–8; *Plut.* 149–54. Halperin (1990a: 88–90) and Dover (2016: 99, 137, 145–6) cite a number of post-classical sources as well. Halperin (1990a: 90, with sources at 182 n. 24) also notes that male prostitutes were generally below the age of majority. On the extent to which anal penetration might have been an accepted part of pederasty among at least some couples, see the sources cited in n. 50 below.

The reference to Demos as a *molgos* in this passage seems to counter one potential explanation for Aristophanes' reticence in this play to make Paphlagon too lustful an *erastes*, namely that it would be awkward to have a character express a wish to sexually dominate the Athenian *demos*, and the portrayal of the *demos* as an *eromenos* can only work because the pairing is so implausible. As noted above in Section I, Demos' age and appearance make him an unlikely *eromenos*, so the audience can laugh about the relationship, as long as it is portrayed no more graphically than it is. It could potentially be rather uncomfortable to conceive of Demos (and the *demos*) as a victim of pederastic violation, or worse (in that culture), someone willingly accepting homosexual penetration (Hornblower 1991: 311 *ad* Thuc. 2.43.1; Monoson 2000: 86–7; cf. Dover 2016: 146). The *molgos* image, however, suggests that Aristophanes was not above such implications, in the same way that other sources from the time (cited below in Section V) portray imagery of pederastic attraction toward the *demos* or *polis* openly implying sexualized desire.

40 See also Henderson (1991: 204, 218) and Dover (2016: 204).

41 The observation of the sexual significance of the Sausage-Seller's goods comes from Hubbard (1991: 68, with n. 19).

42 Henderson (1991: 158); Anderson and Dix (2020) 219 *ad* 1384–6.

43 Anderson and Dix (2020: 206 *ad* 1263) take it as, instead, playing on other connotations of χάσκω that can make Κεχηναίων construable as "slack-jawed, clueless" Athenians.

44 Henderson (1991: 68, 209, 211).

45 Henderson (1991: 68) treats the Sausage-Seller as "at one with the people" in his passivity.

46 Underscoring the inequality of the portrayed relationship, Paphlagon calls Demos by the diminutive "Demidion" at 726 (ὦ Δημίδιον <ὦ> φίλτατον). Σ *Ach.* 404 A notes that such nomenclature is a practice of lovers (ἐρῶντες) toward their *eromenoi* (Landfester 1967: 52).

47 There is certainly an implicit reciprocal agreement between the partners in a pederastic relationship (Dover 2016: 91; cf. Ludwig 2002: 30), and Halperin (1986) contends that passion was something that the pair shared in common far more than is commonly believed. See Hubbard (1998: esp. 48–9 and 70–2) for a forceful argument in favor of a more egalitarian conception of homosexual love in classical Athens than is commonly perceived, and see Mommsen (1975: 56–60), Hupperts (1988), Golden (1991: 333), de Vries (1997), Kilmer (1997: 15–26), and Fisher (2001: 33) for black-figure vase depictions of deviations from the standard unbalanced perception of *erastai* and *eromenoi*. Robson (2013b: 39, 43, with his classical sources) even argues for the *eromenoi* having power over their *erastai*, due to the desire that *eromenoi* have the capability of provoking in their *erastai* (see similar ideas in Golden 1984: 313–16 and Hubbard 2003: 10). In any case, though, the roles of an *erastes* and an *eromenos* in classical Athens are typically quite distinct, and the *erastes* is generally conceived of as the dominant partner: see Arist. *Eth. Nic.* 1157a6–9, *Eth. Eud.* 1238b36–9; Pl. *Symp.* 184d–e; Dover (2016: 16, 52–3); Konstan (1997: 38–9). The passivity of Demos in his role as *eromenos* in this play is noteworthy, though, in that the *demos* is supposed to be the dominant

figure in Athenian democracy (Landfester 1967: 59; Wohl 2002: 75; Scholtz 2004: 274, with n. 36; 2007: 53, with n. 40). The fact that *eromenoi* commonly saw their *erastai* as a means to political advancement (Ludwig 2002: 29–31), however, may explain some of the initial imbalance between the parties in this play; the agency imputed to Demos by the Sausage-Seller at play's end (1365–83), as well as Demos' implicit status as having his own *eromenos* (1384–6), seems to suggest that he has served his apprenticeship and has now moved into the independence of male adulthood (Landfester 1967: 101). Wohl (2002: 73–123) provides another explanation of the *erastes–eromenos* relationship in the play, treating the erotic model as a new conception of a political relationship, one based on a politician's desire to govern being reciprocated by the people's desire to take part in the process of running the state (93). My interpretation differs from hers, though, since I do not detect any expression of desire deriving from the personified Demos, and such an absence of passion is completely consistent with the accepted dynamics of pederasty at the time (see n. 21 above).

48 See Dover (1972: 90) and (2016: 91–3) for gifts in pederastic courtship. As for Cleon's legislative actions, see Chapter 2, Section II.C.1.

49 See Chapter 3, Section VI for discussion of Paphlagon's use of χαριοίμην at 776 in the sense of doing a reciprocal friendly favor for Demos, and on the expectations of reciprocity in friendship more generally.

50 Cohen (1991: 171–202, esp. 183–7) follows Gouldner (1965: 49) in treating the sexual interaction between partners as a competitive "zero-sum game," with honor only possible for the *erastes* if he seduces the *eromenos*, and honor only possible for the *eromenos* if he resists such seduction. Dover (2016: 52–4, 94–106) treats the expected sexual behaviors of each partner in less competitive terms, though, and lays out ways in which an *eromenos* may acceptably "gratify" his *erastes* in certain circumstances. Cantarella (1992: 17–27) and Davidson (2001) go further in contending that sex, even penetrative sex, was an expected part of a pederastic relationship, and they lay out scenarios through which an *eromenos*' concession to sex would in no way have been a mark against his honor. Fisher (2001: 43–4) lays out the range of attested sexual practices in pederasty and the likelihood of a fair amount of negotiation among individual couples as to what they would be willing to do. Lear and Cantarella (2008: 106; cf. 190) contend that vase paintings' portrayals of intercrural sex rather than anal was simply a "visual euphemism."

51 There are, of course, the semi-mythical examples of *erastai* killing tyrants on behalf of their *eromenoi* (Thuc. 6.54.1–4, 56.1–57.4; Phainias of Eresus *FGrH* 1012 F 16), which are as much cautionary tales of the lengths to which tyrants can push people as they are exempla of pederastic relations. Even Thebes' Sacred Band, which Plutarch portrays as being based on 150 *erastes–eromenos* pairs, was

predicated on the pairs defending one another (Plut. *Pel.* 18–19). That model may also be just as fanciful as Plato's presentation of an ideal army of such couples in the *Symposium* (178d–179b). Ogden (1996) contends that Plutarch's portrayal of the Sacred Band's pairings as pederastic, rather than merely homosexual between consenting adults, may be based on Plutarch's Athenocentric model of pederasty as the only appropriate form of homosexuality; Ogden cites records (and hints) of military sexuality among Athenians and others to suggest that battlefield sexuality in the ancient world was not as refined as Athenian pederasty, in its idealized form, was.

52 Notable values of goods apparently did pass, at least at times, from men to boys whom at least the men thought of as *eromenoi* (e.g., Isaeus 10.25; Xen. *Mem.* 1.3.11, *Oec.* 2.7), and it is based on examples such as these that Ogden (1996: 108; 2010: 38), following Buffière (1980: 631–4), characterizes gifts from *erastai* to *eromenoi* as "extravagant." However, for Aeschines (1.137), a boy's acceptance of μισθός (*misthos*, "pay") as part of his relationship with a man marks him as a πόρνος (*pornos*, "prostitute") rather than an *eromenos*. For others, though, the line between standard courtship gifts and *misthos*, and between behaviors that might be typical of *pornoi* rather than of *eromenoi*, is not quite so distinct, but is an important negotiation: Ar. *Av.* 705–7, *Plut.* 149–59; Dem. 61.4–5; Henderson (1991: 217); Konstan (1993: 7–8); Davidson (2007: 71–4); Dover (2016: 103–9).

53 Dover (2016: 92–3) lays out typical gifts in courtship, with abundant classical sources; cf. Bennett and Tyrrell (1990: 247) and Ogden (2010: 38). While Hubbard (2003: 19) observes from vase paintings that there appears to be some correlation between the value of an *erastes*' gift and an *eromenos*' receptivity to that *erastes*, the gifts that pique the interest of the *eromenoi* that Hubbard notes are hares and roosters. On personal nurturance as a role of *erastai*, see, e.g., Pl. *Symp.* 178c3–e3, 217a2–5, b4–5, with Scholtz (2004: 273; 2007: 53). See Dover (2016: 202–3) on the educative role of the *erastes*.

54 Anderson and Dix (2020: 215 *ad* 1340–2) take this passage as another example of "ἐραστής in its patriotic sense."

55 Neil (1901: 175 *ad* 1341–2); Landfester (1967: 101).

56 767: περί σου μάχομαι μόνος ἀντιβεβηκώς ("I alone stand firm and fight for you"); 790: τῷ δήμῳ μᾶλλον ἀμύνων ("defended the people more"); 799: αὐτὸν θρέψω 'γὼ καὶ θεραπεύσω ("I will feed and serve him"); 1038: περὶ τοῦ δήμου ... μαχεῖται ("fight on the people's behalf"). Cf. in *Wasps*, the chorus calling Cleon κηδεμών ("protector," 242), and Bdelucleon mocking him for his claims to "fight" (μαχοῦμαι) for the Athenian masses (666–7).

57 This canine image is attached consistently enough to Cleon in other sources (*Vesp.* 894–994, 1031; *Pax* 313) to suggest that he may genuinely have used it in his

political oratory. Later politicians Demosthenes (Plut. *Demosth.* 23.5) and Aristogeiton ([Dem.] 25.40) apparently used the image as well for themselves. For imagery of canine protection and dedication not in themselves being associated with pederasty, see Xen. *Mem.* 2.9.7, addressed below.

58 Refer to n. 52 above for Aeschines' claim (1.137) that accepting *misthos* for providing affection is what marks a boy as a *pornos*. Anderson and Dix (2020: 200 *ad* 1192) point out that one of these gifts, hare's meat (λαγῷ[α]), is a common gift of an *erastes* to an *eromenos*; it is not as though Paphlagon does *nothing* like an *erastes*.

59 Bennett and Tyrrell (1990: 243–4); they back up their reading by pointing out that three obols, the rate that Paphlagon notes in the play that he (or, rather, Cleon) instituted for jury pay (Ar. *Eq.* 51, 797–800), was also a fee for a common prostitute at the time (Henderson 1991: 138). Scholtz (2004: 280; 2007: 60) also treats Demos' behavior as like that of a prostitute, but in a clearly figurative sense of self-compromise (cf. Aeschin. 1.22, 29, 54–5). Female courtesans (ἑταίραι) can accept gifts of money or other contributions to their sustenance (R589, Beazley *ARV*² 449; R627, *ARV*² 468; R632, *ARV*² 469; R728, *ARV*² 566; R817 *ARV*² 832; Alciphron 4.8–9; Philostr. *Ep.* 23), since their status is already low enough that survival is a more pressing issue than pride (Konstan 1993: 6–8). On the other hand, the expected approach of *eromenoi* to monetary gifts is illuminated in R638 (*ARV*² 471): there, a boy walks away from a bag full of coins that had apparently been on offer, and instead carries off what appear to be small fruits or nuts (Dover 2016: 92 n. 59).

60 Aristotle (*Eth. Nic.* 1155b33–1156a5, *Eth. Eud.* 1236a14–15) notes that *philia* requires *displays* of good will, not just claims of personal fondness. On obligations of friends to assist one another, see Eur. *Or.* 652–4, 665–7, 717–21, 735, 740, 748, 794, 802–3; Xen. *Mem.* 2.9.8; Konstan (1997: 56–9). On expectations of reciprocal benefit between friends, see *Eth. Nic.* 1157b36; Fisher (1976: 5); Strauss (1987: 21); Blundell (1989: 26–59, with the citations in 32 n. 36); Millett (1991: 118); Konstan (1997: 57–9); Konstan (1998). On ways to maintain reciprocity in unequal friendships, see Arist. *Eth. Nic.* 1163a24–1163b18. On friendship not as a state, but as an ongoing demonstration, see Konstan (2018: 44–7 and 150–1).

61 See Chapter 3, Sections II and III.

62 For discussion of the nuances of flattery in classical Athens, particularly as perceived between demagogues and non-elite Athenians, see Chapter 3, Section III.

63 On the murky lines that separate all sorts of behavior that are morally acceptable from those that are morally unacceptable, see Davidson (1997: 275).

64 It is unlikely that Aristophanes drew the line where he did to avoid offending Cleon; if he had feared that implications of portrayed sexual behavior would be

the thing that would particularly bring punishment down on him from Cleon, he would not likely have implicated Cleon in active and passive anal penetration and cunnilingus, as laid out above in Section III.

65 Connor (1971: 98 n. 15) proposes the possibility that Aristophanes was exploiting the irony of Cleon's expressing *eros* for the *demos* and antipathy toward elite pederasty more broadly. A more common interpretation of the reference to "put[ting] a stop to the pathics by erasing Grypus from the rolls" (ἔπαυσα τοὺς βινουμένους, τὸν Γρῦπον ἐξαλείψας, *Eq.* 877) is to take it as referring to Cleon's strict enforcement of laws against participation in public life for anyone who has acted as a male prostitute (e.g., Neil 1901: 126 *ad* 875–7; Sommerstein 1981: 191 *ad* 877; Edmunds 1987: 73 *ad* 877–80; Hubbard 1998: 56; Scholtz 2004: 278, with n. 52; 2007: 58–9, with n. 60; Dover 2016: 141). On the law itself, see Aeschin. 1.1, 3, 14, 19, 19–21, 28–32, 40, 46, 51, 72–3, 87, 119, 134, 154, 160, 164, 188, 195; Dem. 22.21–4, 30–2; Dover (2016: 23–34); Halperin (1990a: 94–5); Winkler (1990: 54–64). On the ambiguity of line 877, see Osborne (2020: 35–6).

66 Cf. the chorus' similar criticism of Demos at *Eq.* 1111–20. Cleon's criticism of the people's ἡδονή for the simple gratification of oratory stands in interesting apposition to Thucydides' earlier claim (2.65.10) that Cleon and other like politicians governed according to the "pleasure" (ἡδονή) of the people, suggesting the Aphrodisiac aspect of power in the masses' hands. Wohl (2002: 90–7) goes into connections between the language of sexuality in Cleon's reported speeches and the sexual dynamics of politics in *Knights*. Hornblower (1991: 420 *ad* 3.36.6) notes the irony of Cleon's scolding of Athenian citizens' marveling at speakers' rhetorical manners when he owes a significant part of his political success to his oratorical techniques.

67 See also Wohl (2002: 97), and the sources cited there, on the irony of Cleon using sophisticated techniques of persuasion to try to convince the Athenian people not to be swayed by others' similar techniques.

68 Monoson (2000: 67); Ludwig (2002: 147–8); Scholtz (2004: 264); (2007: 43–4); Dover (2016: 16).

69 On the erotic component of θεωμένους here, see Hornblower (1991: 311 *ad loc.*); Halperin (1990: 267); Crane (1998: 319). For analysis of the nuances of Pericles' use of the image, see Wohl (2002: 30–72). For a thorough look at Pericles' imagery in its social context, see Scholtz (2007: 21–42). Yates (2005: 42) says *Knights* "represents Pericles' metaphor of citizen as *erastes* turned upside down."

70 Dodds (1959: 261 *ad Gorg.* 481d2) comments only on the idea of "wisdom as an object of passion." See also Socrates' fear that Alcibiades would become a δημεραστὴς (*demerastes*), as many of the best Athenians were trying to be (Pl. *1*

Alc. 132a). *Gorgias* was written in the first half of the fourth century; see n. 6 in Chapter 1, Section II. *First Alcibiades*, which is likely spurious, was probably written in the 350s or shortly thereafter (Cooper 1997: 558).

71 Sommerstein (1980: 164 *ad Ach.* 144); Olson (2002: 117 *ad* 143–4, cf. 106 *ad* 104); Robson (2013a: 255–8).

72 Dunbar (1995: 177 *ad Av.* 135; 260–1 *ad* 324; 635 *ad* 1279). See also Yates (2005: 41–5) on the imagery of political pederasty in each of these primary sources, and Holmes (2011: 14–17) on that imagery in Aristophanes' plays.

73 Monoson (2000: 86): "For [the *erastes–eromenos*] metaphor to work, the audience must supply an image of the honorable lover who behaves admirably toward his beloved." Wohl (2002: 90): "the demagogue is a lover who aims to educate and improve his beloved." Ludwig (2002: 144, cf. 148): "an orator could recommend himself to the people on analogy with courtship, adducing the devotion, sacrifice, and subservience of one stricken by eros." Dover (1972: 91): "lovers try to outbid one another in generosity to the person whom they love." (Dover offers a point of view a few years later, though—Dover 2016: 103–9—that recognizes limits to the generosity that would be appropriate for *eromenoi* to accept.) See also Connor (1971: 96–8) and Sommerstein (1981: 181 *ad* 732). Stewart (1997: 80) proposes that the conflation of admiration of the city and lust for it that first shows up in literature of the 430s BCE arose from the attractive portrayals of the young men who represented the city on the Parthenon frieze, which citizens would first have seen in the late 430s. He suggests that Pericles himself may have popularized the concept.

74 Other places where either pederasty or *eros* are used in a political context: Herod. 1.96: Οὗτος ὁ Δηιόκης <u>ἐρασθεὶς</u> τυραννίδος ἐποίεε τοιάδε ("This Deioces did these things <u>since he lusted</u> for tyranny"); 3.53: Τυραννὶς χρῆμα σφαλερόν, πολλοὶ δὲ αὐτῆς <u>ἐρασταί</u> εἰσι ("Tyranny is a perilous possession, yet many people are <u>lovers</u> of it"); Soph. *OT* 601: οὔτ' <u>ἐραστὴς</u> τῆσδε τῆς γνώμης ἔφυν ("I am no <u>lover</u> of this proposition [i.e., becoming tyrant]"); Ar. *Vesp.* 473–4: ὦ μισόδημε / καὶ μοναρχίας <u>ἐραστὰ</u> ("O people-hater and <u>lover</u> of monarchy"); Eur. *Phoen.* 358–9: ἀναγκαίως ἔχει / πατρίδος <u>ἐρᾶν</u> ἅπαντας ("all people must <u>passionately love</u> their native land"); Isoc. *De pace* 65: δυναστείας ὑπὸ πάντων <u>ἐρωμένης</u> ("imperial power <u>lusted after</u> by all"); 113: οἱ πρωτεύοντες καὶ δόξας μεγίστας ἔχοντες τοσούτων κακῶν <u>ἐρῶσιν</u> ("the foremost men, those holding the greatest reputations, <u>lust after</u> such evil things [i.e., tyranny]"). Other metaphorical uses of *erastes* or related terms for sexual passion in contexts related to politics, but not specifically a part of it: Thuc. 6.13.1; Eur. *Heracl.* 37–78; Ar. *Nub.* 1459; *Pax* 191, 988. Ludwig (2002: 124–69) explores metaphorical uses of *erastes*, *eros*, etc. across situations and genres in the archaic and classical periods.

5 Later Developments of the "Leader as *Philos*" Model

1 For details of Hyperbolus' and Cleophon's backgrounds, actions in public life, and reception by their peers, see Chapter 2, Sections II–IV.

2 For details of the portrayal of Athenian leadership and its negative consequences in Aristophanes' *Frogs*, see Chapter 2, Section III.A. For the stereotype of demagogues as outsiders from the elite due to their class standing, see Chapter 2, Section II.B. For stereotypes of demagogues (and many other politicians) as outsiders because of purported foreign ancestry, see Chapter 2, Section II.B n. 32.

3 On *demotikos* as a politically charged term, see Wankel (1976: 1.138 *ad* Dem. 18.6), and Scholtz (2004: 269, with nn. 21–3), refined at Scholtz (2007: 49, with nn. 21–3).

4 Konstan (1997: 61). Other sources characterize Alcibiades as using demagogic approaches, despite his wealth and status. Plut. *Alc.* 10.2 has Alcibiades using his considerable rhetorical skills to win over the mass of Athenians, though he had plenty of resources in wealth and family status that he used to political advantage at other times (Thuc. 6.16.1–4; Ober 1989: 93–4; de Romilly 2019: 4–10). Connor (1971: 140–1) sees him using rhetorical techniques like those of Cleon to attack Nicias at Thuc. 4.27.5 and Plut. *Alc.* 14.4.

5 Lys. 20.23, 28.12, 30.9; Isoc. 16.36, 18.48, 18.62; Dem. 18.6, 58.30, 59.93; Aeschin. 1.173, 3.168, 3.176, 3.248; Din. 1.9, 1.44, 1.78–9, 3.22; Lycurg. 39.

6 On arguments for 405 BCE as a likely performance date, see Stockert (1992: I.63) and West (1981: 77 n. 23). It is likely that the play was incomplete at the time of Euripides' death, and that Euripides the Younger and, quite possibly, at least one later reviser contributed to the text as we have it now (e.g., Page 1934: 9, 130–216; Kovacs 2003; Gurt 2005). However, most of the lines employed for this book's argument pass the scrutiny of even the most attentive of the interpolation scholars (Page and Kovacs). Moreover, for the purposes of this argument, it matters little who actually wrote various parts of the play, as long as they did it within a few decades of the original date of Euripides' composition, and Page (1934: 211), while acknowledging the difficulty of precisely ascribing a date to any of the non-Euripidean elements in the play, finds many of the interpolations he notes as likely to have been added early in the fourth century. If portions were written for performance by someone other than Euripides, it would only underscore the extent to which the model of leadership in the play reflected that which was in common circulation in Athens at the time of the demagogues and in decades thereafter—in large part, I contend, based on the influence of Cleon. Kovacs (2003: 84–9) explains his doubts about the Euripidean authorship of the first episode, which is the focus of the first two paragraphs of this section, but does not put a date on the interpolations that he observes.

7   On the subtlety required to treat tragedies as works reflecting their historical periods, see Pelling (1997b) and (2000: 164–88). Among others who have discussed tragedies as reflections of their historical and social contexts: Debnar (2005), Boedeker and Raaflaub (2005), and the many authors in Markantonatos and Zimmermann (2011), with Markantonatos in that volume taking on *IA*'s engagement with Athens' political environment. Rosenbloom (2011) explores tragedy and comedy as vehicles for dealing with cultural anxiety about demagogues, typically with an oligarchic slant.

8   Konstan (1997: 53–4) brings up how *demotai* are in some cases put on a level similar to *philoi* (Lys. 6.53, 27.12; Ar. *Eccles.* 1023–4). In those cases, however, the *demotai* are clearly being thought of as peers, fellow citizens or fellow demesmen (LSJ⁹ s.v. II and III). Here, though, in this Panhellenic army, demes and citizenship in general are irrelevant, and reading *demotai* as though it refers to people whom Agamemnon considered his peers would take away from the main effect of Agamemnon's behaviors while aiming for leadership: he clearly considered himself to be above those with whom he was interacting, making his appearance of being humble (ταπεινὸς) so ironic. The main definition of *demotes*, "one of the people, a commoner" (LSJ⁹ s.v. I), seems clearly the most applicable, particularly given turns of events later in the play.

9   Kovacs (2003: 84) describes ἐκ μέσου in 342 as "odd and hard to translate," and it may be, but it is consistent with the way that Odysseus is described as being positioned as he speaks to the soldiers at 528–9: ἐν Ἀργείοις μέσοις ("in the middle of the Argives"). It may be that Euripides (or whoever wrote this passage) meant for Menelaus to be expressing a similar image of Agamemnon's manner of leadership when he won over the soldiery: he led while in their midst, as I express below that Odysseus seems to have done, rather than standing apart from them.

    The text of *IA* that I use is Diggle's (1994).

10 Stockert (1992: II.292 *ad* 337) and Wasserman (1949: 176) liken this approach to winning over the soldiers to an Athenian politician striving to win an election. Goff (2004: 352): "the play makes Agamemnon into a fifth-century politician who courts the people for his office, rather than receiving it as his kingly inheritance (337–45)." Michelakis (2006: 79–80), too, sees reflections, in the Panhellenic army and its leaders, of the influence of the Athenian masses on the city's politics at the time of the play's composition.

11 Stockert (1992: II.295 *ad* 344 ff.) characterizes this as part of a "φίλος-Topos," shown also at Eur. *Supp.* 867–8, Ar. *Plut.* 834–7, and Plut. *Cim.* 10. However, if it is, this instance of that topos underscores how far the concept of friendship has come to be stretched in the age of the demagogues. In the example from *Supplices*, Adrastus eulogizes Capaneus as "a true friend to his friends, whether they were

present or not" (φίλοις τ' ἀληθὴς ἦν φίλος παροῦσί τε / καὶ μὴ παροῦσιν), and in
Plutus, the Just Man says that one of the ways he found it best to use his fortune
was to help his friends when they were in need (κἀγὼ μὲν ᾤμην, οὓς
τέωςεὐηργέτησα δεομένους, ἕξειν φίλους/ ὄντως βεβαίους, εἰ δεηθείην ποτέ· / οἱ
δ' ἐξετρέποντο κοὐκ ἐδόκουν ὁρᾶν μ' ἔτι). It is not specified, but one might
imagine that the "friends" to whom Capaneus and the Just Man feel loyalty are not
soldiers whom they commanded in an army. And in the case of Cimon, though he
is generous to his demesmen and other fellow-citizens, as explained in Chapter 1,
the sources never indicate that he referred to those people as *philoi*, though he
treated them in a way that might have led them to think of Cimon as their friend.
In any case, if there is a "φίλος-Topos" of which the author of this passage was
aware, this passage extends that topos beyond the reach of its previous instances.

12 See Michelakis (2006: 45) for analysis of the dramatic impact of having onstage
characters attribute such power to another whom the audience never sees.

13 Stockert (1992: I.207–8 *ad* 106 ff.) characterizes the expression in these two lines
as "untragbar," and Page (1934: 138), followed by Kovacs (2003: 82), highlights
these lines as a prime example of what he sees as the post-Euripidean
interpolation in this play. Michelakis (2002: 129–30 *ad* 104–14), however, brings
up other scholars' defenses of the passage, while acknowledging reasons that some
find the passage inconsistent with other elements of the plot. For particularly
spirited defenses of the authenticity and coherence of the entire prologue,
including these lines, see Knox (1972) and Foley (1985: 102–5).

14 Michelakis (2006: 44–5) also notes the power that Odysseus wields over the army,
bringing up the last two of the three passages I cite in this paragraph. While
Ryzman (1989: 114, with n. 10) points out that Agamemnon's fears of Odysseus
razing Argos may be exaggerated (cf. *IA* 525), she also agrees that the full extent of
Odysseus' power is frighteningly uncertain to Agamemnon and Menelaus (cf.
527).

15 Kovacs (2003: 97), like Page (1934: 187–8), sees no reason to consider this passage
as anything but Euripidean.

16 Stockert (1992: II.349 *ad loc.*). Kovacs (2003: 84–9) is dubious of the authenticity
and coherence of much of the episode from 303 to 542 and brackets the majority
of it in his Loeb edition (1994). Page (1934: 158), however, though he considers
404–542 to be much interpolated, finds nothing un-Euripidean about 526.

On Odysseus as resembling an Athenian demagogue in his actions, approach,
and terms used to describe him in this play, see Stockert (1992: II.349 *ad* 526–7)
and Michelakis (2006: 80). Such a portrayal, and the use of the word *okhlos* to
characterize the masses over whom he holds sway, is consistent with his portrayal
in *Hecuba* (cf. Stockert *ad* 526), as I will detail below.

17 For the class connotations of ὄχλος, see LSJ⁹ s.v. I.1: "crowd, throng"; I.2: "populace, mob": I.3: "mass, multitude," with Hunter (1988), Ober (1989: 11). *Okhlos* used in this way during the Peloponnesian War: e.g., Thuc. 8.48.3, [Xen.] 2.10, Eur. *Hipp*. 988–9, Ar. *Vesp*. 540; *polloi* used in this way: e.g., Thuc. 8.97.2, [Xen.] 3.13, Ar. *Eq*. 943–5, Eur. *Or*. 772; *plethos* used in this way: e.g., Thuc. 4.21.3, [Xen.] 2.18, Eur. *Hec*. 884, Ar. *Vesp*. 667; *demos* used in this way: e.g., Thuc. 8.48.6, [Xen.] 1.3, Eur. *Supp*. 423–5, Ar. *Ran*. 779. On all those terms used in Thucydides, plus others, see Saïd (2013). For a whole host of terms used in the political arena during the Peloponnesian War, see Grossmann (1973).

Euripides' use of these terms (with *polloi* counted only if it is used pronominally to refer to masses of common people) seems to be a particular marker of class tensions in Athens (in the world outside the plays) that accompany particularly strong demagogic influence. While most of his plays use the terms rarely or not at all, they come up peculiarly regularly during Cleon's period of influence (*Hippolytus*, from 428, uses *okhlos* four times; *Hecuba*, from 425 or shortly thereafter, uses the four terms a total of thirteen times; *Andromache*, from c. 425, uses them five times in all; and *Supplices*, from c. 423, uses them thirteen times) and during Cleophon's similar period at the end of the Peloponnesian War (*Orestes*, from 408, uses the terms thirteen times; *IA*—as noted above—eight; and *Bacchae*, as will be discussed below, six).

Michelini (1999–2000: 54–6), following Mellert-Hoffmann (1969: 9–90), thinks the army is treated as an *okhlos* because it is a Panhellenic contingent, with the chaotic range of values and interests that would accompany such a force. Opposing her contention, based on their sense that Panhellenism is not at all an issue until Agamemnon raises it at play's end, are Siegel (1980: 302 n. 6) and Funke (1964: 288–9); cf. Lawrence (1988: 108 n. 12).

18 While Page (1934: 157) observes a range of anachronisms and infelicities in 528–42, he also points out that a few emendations can make the text seem perfectly Euripidean (157–8). On this passage as consistent with the fear, paranoia, and passivity that Agamemnon shows throughout the play, see Lawrence (1988: 93–4) and Siegel (1981: 263–4).

19 Simmons (2006: 201); Lush (2015: 216).

20 See Montiglio (2011: 10–11) on qualities of Odysseus in the *Iliad* that might look demagogic, in retrospect, but that are not held against him in the epic.

21 An objection could be raised that analyzing *Bacchae* as a reflection of Athenian practice is problematic because there is a biographical tradition that has Euripides completing *Bacchae* in Macedon, with plans to produce it there (Phld. *Vit.* col. 13.4; *Vit. Eurip.* 115 N²; Csapo 1999–2000: 414; Atkinson 2002: 5). However, the scholarly consensus is that *Bacchae* is clearly a play that reflects Athenian

structures and issues (Zeitlin 1990: esp. 131 and 134–9), whether, as is likely, he produced it in Athens (Lefkowitz 1981: 103; Scullion 2003), or even if he happened to have completed it in Macedon (Winnington-Ingram 1948b: 152 n. 1; Dodds 1960: xl; Segal 1978: 189).

Furthermore, the details of the story of Dionysus' entrance to Thebes in other sources vary enough from those in the *Bacchae* that it seems as though Euripides felt considerable freedom to shape the tale and its characters as he wished. For analysis of portrayals of the tale of Dionysus, Pentheus, and their interaction that differ from Euripides' portrayal of them in the *Bacchae*, see Webster (1967: 269) on Ar. Byz. *Hyp. Bacch.*; Webster (1967: 268–9) on Philippart (1930: pl. 12, no. 150); R. Hamilton (1974) on Aesch. *Eum.* 25–6; Yunis (1988: 77–8); March (1989). On the liberties that Euripides, in general, takes with his mythical source material, see Scullion (1999–2000), and March (1987) on the practice happening widely among tragic poets.

22 For an overview of reactions to the authoritarian practices of Pentheus, how they fit in the context of other doomed leaders in tragedy, and modern scholarly appraisal, see Mills (2006: 58–64).

23 Seaford (1996: 162 *ad* 115): "More than most gods, D. is imagined as *present* among his worshippers," a phenomenon on which Henrichs (1993: 19–22) elaborates. Ringer (2016: 317): "Dionysus encourages identification between himself and his worshipers." Cf. *Bacch.* 32 (with Seaford 1996: 152 *ad loc.*), 469–70, and 500–2, and Soph. *Ichneutae* 223–8.

The text of *Bacchae* that I use is Diggle's (1994).

24 On the date of *Cyclops*, see Seaford (1982). On other possible readings of *Cyclops* 73, see Seaford (1984: 116 *ad* 73–4).

25 Dodds (1960: 127–8 *ad* 421–3) goes through portrayals of Dionysus as a sharing god.

26 For Cleon's and Cleophon's efforts to assist Athens' poor, see Chapter 2, Section II.C.1.

27 Versnel (1998: 196–7).

28 Gould (2001: 242): "If, in the end, Dionysus is revealed as god, it is not in himself, but in the actions of women." Cf. Winnington-Ingram (1948: 30).

29 While Pentheus' interest in the women has long been taken to be voyeuristically sexual (for a start, see Dodds 1960: 97 *ad* 222–3), their effectiveness in unsettling the social order and carrying out Dionysus' will goes well beyond their function as a window onto Pentheus' psyche.

30 For the significance and pattern of usage of *okhlos, plethos, hoi polloi*, and *demos* in Athens during the Peloponnesian War, see n. 17 above.

31 Dodds (1960: 129–30 *ad* 430–3) also recognizes this association, but projects the allegiance also onto Euripides, contending that Euripides "may well have felt at times a deeper kinship with the intuitive wisdom of the people than with the arid cleverness of the intellectuals." Seaford (1996: 185 *ad* 430) focuses on φαυλότερον as reflecting "the democratic nature of Dionysiac cult."

32 Cf. McDonald (1989: 46–7) on ll. 877–81: "Euripides' chorus now represents the bourgeois ethic, which in its 'democratic' excesses resembled . . . the mob with which Euripides was familiar in his own time." Bierl (1991: 72) and Goff (2004: 214), too, both identify the maenads in this play as essentially democratic figures.

33 Though many of the demagogic traits that I will attribute to Dionysus in this play may be consistent with traditional depictions of the god, the fact that he appears at all here may be a reflection of Euripides' view of the times. Fewer than four percent of tragedies of which even a title is extant seem to have included Dionysus, a perplexingly low rate, both since he was the god of the theatre, and since the same small body of stories was staged over and over again (Scullion 2002: 110–11). And his stories had not been dramatized at all for nearly a decade before Euripides began his composition, with the most recent securely dateable one before Euripides' *Bacchae* being Xenocles' *Bacchae*, produced in 415 (*TrGF* I² DID C 14). Iophon also had at least one Dionysus play (Suda ι 451), but its/their date(s) are unknown. For a summary of other depictions of Dionysus in tragedy, see Mills (2006: 34–6).

34 See Chapter 2, Section III.A for discussion of the chorus leader in Aristophanes' *Frogs* (produced in 405, the year after Euripides' death and, accordingly, his last work on the *Bacchae*) maligning Athens' shift in political power that had led to "aliens, redheads, and lowlifes from lowlife families" (τοῖς δὲ . . . ξένοις καὶ πυρρίαις / καὶ πονηροῖς κὰκ πονηρῶν, 730–1) holding more power than those born into elite families (718–37). On foreign ancestry attributed to Cleon, Hyperbolus, and Cleophon, see notes 29–31 in Chapter 2, Section II.B.

35 Dover (1993: 283 *ad Ran.* 729); Sommerstein (1996: 220 *ad Ran.* 729). On common Athenians' resentful animosity toward those trained in wrestling, see Ps.-Xen. [*Ath. pol.*] 1.13, with Marr and Rhodes (2008: 81 *ad loc.*). On the implications of the stranger's hair (and skin) for his reception as an outsider by Pentheus, see Seaford (1996: 187 *ad* 455–8) and Mills (2006: 51 and 132 n. 5).

36 On the god's diversity of association and function, see, as a start, and for further references, Henrichs (1984); Burkert (1985: 161–7); Goldhill (1990: 126); Carpenter and Faraone (1993); Segal (1997b: 12–13); Seaford (2006); Cole (2007); Griffith (2013: 187).

37 Versnel (1998: 167). Cf. Leinieks (1996: 327) on Dionysus' emphasis on democracy as liberation, universality, and unity, and Mills (2006: 25) on the common scholarly

association of Dionysus with common people rather than the elite. Other evidence of Dionysus' appeal even to the humblest: Dodds (1960: 127–8 *ad* 421–3); Ar. *Ran.* 405–7.

38 Seaford (1996: 170 *ad* 206–9, 184–5 *ad* 421–3).

39 Hershkowitz's (2018) analysis of fourth-century authors' uses of terms related to demagogues reveals some reference to figures contemporaneous to the authors, though with minimal elaboration on the behaviors of the noted figures that led to their designation and little repetition of an individual in more than one source (50–75). See Hershkowitz's (2018: 85–9) chronological list of those referred to by at least one source as being a demagogue or having done something noted as demagogic for confirmation of that diminishing reference to new demagogic figures after the Peloponnesian War.

While dating the *Anabasis*, as with the rest of Xenophon's works, is difficult, there are compelling arguments for placing it sometime around or shortly after 370 BCE, with a final version perhaps completed after his return to Athens from exile (e.g., Stoneman 1992: xii; Dillery 1995: 59; Cawkwell 2004: 47–8), though Millender (2012) argues for a date in the late 380s, based on the significance it would have had to an Athenian audience at that time. For a summary of the few reasonably secure points by which to date Xenophon's work, see Lee (2017: 33–4).

40 He was certainly in Persia for the beginning of Cyrus the Younger's campaign against Artaxerxes II in 401, may have left Athens after the fall of the Thirty Tyrants in 404/403 (Lane Fox 2004: 11), was exiled sometime following the conclusion of the Long March in 394 (Gray 2010: 13), and was recalled to Athens in 368. On Xenophon's exile, see, e.g., Rahn (1981), Tuplin (1987), and Green (1994). For dating of the *Cyropaedia* to sometime in the 360s, see note 51 in Chapter 3, Section V.

41 For the *Anabasis* as a justification of Xenophon (despite the failure of the expedition he led), perhaps in order to encourage his recall to Athens or acceptance in the city (if he was already there when he wrote or finished the work), see, e.g., Mesk (1922–3); Erbse (1966: 399); and Cawkwell (2004: 59 n. 31). On Athenians as a significant part of Xenophon's intended audience, see n. 51 in Chapter 3, Section V.

42 Among those who discuss this emphasis on "leading the willing" as the goal of a leader are Breitenbach (1950: 47–104); Due (1989: 147–206); Gray (1989: 8, with 199 nn. 23–4); (2011: 5–24); Buxton (2016).

43 A few of the studies of leadership techniques and ideal leadership in Xenophon: Wood (1964); L. Strauss (1975: 135–9); Carlier (1978); Ruderman (1992); Dillery (1995: 164–76); Aupperle (1996); Howland (2000); Humphreys (2002); O'Flannery (2003); Gray (2007: 3–14); (2011); Buxton (2016; 2017); Flower (2016; 2017);

Huitink and Rood (2016); Keim (2016); Pownall (2016); Tamiolaki (2016); Ferraio (2017: 74–9); Marincola (2017: 108–12); Hobden (2020: 23–38).

44 Luccioni (1947: 44–56); Breitenbach (1950: 144); Wood (1964: 59–60); Dillery (1995: 5–6); Brock (2004: 256–7); Gray (2011: 7–8); Buzzetti (2014); Buxton (2016); Tamiolaki (2016). Christ (2020: 179–80) proposes that Pericles, too, was to be understood as a model for Xenophon in the *Anabasis*.

45 E.g., Wood (1964: 52–3); Rubin (1989: 400); Reisert (2009: 24–32); Gray (2011: 291–329); Buxton (2016; 2017); Tamiolaki (2016: 29–35).

46 Very similar imagery appears at Ar. *Ach.* 143, *Av.* 1279, and other sources documented in Chapter 3, Section V.

47 This accessibility is also noted by Humphreys (2002: 141).

The text of the *Anabasis* I cite is Brownson's, revised by Dillery (1998); translations are my own.

48 On the value of leaders' accessibility in Xenophon's works, see Flower (2012: 134).

49 This behavior is cited also by Humphreys (2002: 141). On these last two instances of leadership by personal example, see Nussbaum (1967: 115) and Flower (2012: 132–3). On his consideration for all soldiers, regardless of rank or background, in these and similar circumstances, see Flower (2012: 136).

50 See also 6.1.26 and 7.6.35 for Xenophon's expressed wish that his actions bring about the best possible outcome for the troops. See 5.8.26 for soldiers' recollections of Xenophon's beneficial actions on other occasions, and 7.2.9, 7.7.5, and 7.8.23 for soldiers' happiness with him and gratitude toward him.

51 Christ (2020: 177–8) puts the use of *kharis* here in terms of Athenian defendants' expression to jurors that they deserved favors (i.e., acquittal) based on favors they had done for the city. On that practice in Athenian forensic oratory, see Christ (2012: 71–2).

52 On the Spartans', and perhaps even Xenophon the author's, perception of this term as a compliment to Xenophon the leader, see Breitenbach (1950: 72); Nussbaum (1967: 124); Due (1989: 204); Buxton (2016: 184). See above, Chapter 2, Section II.A for a discussion of *philodemos* during the time of Cleon. On the validity of portraying Xenophon as *philostratiotes*, see Buzzetti (2014: 259–94).

53 Connor (1971: 110 n. 34) notes this as the first instance of δημαγωγός (*demagogos*) or one of its derivatives being used in a derogatory sense. Christ (2020: 167) agrees that the term may be understood pejoratively, but feels that the narrator is characterizing Xenophon's actions in terms of demagogues' renown as speakers who, in that role, express their friendly connection to "the people." Hershkowitz (2018: 50–1, with n. 96), however, thinks the context complicates such a straightforward appraisal. Hornblower (1996: 178), in turn, takes Xen. *Hell.*

5.2.7 to be an earlier decisively negative portrayal of demagogues: ἀριστοκρατίᾳ δ' ἐχρῶντο, ἀπηλλαγμένοι δ' ἦσαν τῶν βαρέων δημαγωγῶν ("they enjoyed an aristocratic government and were rid of the troublesome demagogues," translated by Brownson and Dillery 1998). Hershkowitz (2018: 51–2) disputes that as necessarily a pejorative usage of *demagogos* as well.

54 Flower (2012: 166) notes the similarity of approach to leadership between Xenophon and Cyrus the Great in the *Cyropaedia*.

55 On the emphasis in the *Anabasis* on the creation of a community among the mercenaries from disparate places and cultures, see Ma (2004: 336–41).

Works Cited

Adkins, A. W. H. (1960), *Merit and Responsibility: A Study in Greek Values*, Oxford: Clarendon Press.

Adkins, A. W. H. (1972), *Moral Values and Political Behavior in Ancient Greece*, New York: W. W. Norton & Co.

Ambler, W., trans. and notes (2001), *Xenophon: The Education of Cyrus*, Ithaca, NY: Cornell University Press.

Amichai-Hamburger, Y., M. Kingsbury, and B. H. Schneider (2013), "Friendship: An Old Concept with a New Meaning?," *Computers in Human Behavior*, 29: 33–9.

Anderson, J. K. (2001), *Xenophon*, 2nd ed., London: Duckworth.

Anderson, C. A., and T. K. Dix, eds., intro., comm., and notes (2020), *A Commentary on Aristophanes' Knights*, Ann Arbor: University of Michigan Press.

Andrewes, A. (1962), "The Mytilene Debate: Thucydides 3.36–49," *Phoenix*, 16: 64–85.

Arthurs, J. (1993), "The Term Rhetor in Fifth- and Fourth-Century B.C.E. Texts," *RSQ*, 23: 1–10.

Atkinson, J. E. (2002), "Curbing the Comedians: Cleon versus Aristophanes and Syracosius' Decree," *CQ*, 42: 56–64.

Atkinson, J. E. (2002), "Euripides' *Bacchae* in its Historical Context," *Akroterion*, 47: 5–15.

Aupperle, K. E. (1996), "Spontaneous Organizational Reconfiguration: A Historical Example Based on Xenophon's *Anabasis*," *Organizational Science*, 7: 445–60.

Azoulay, V. ([2010] 2014), *Pericles of Athens*, trans. J. Lloyd, Princeton: Princeton University Press.

Azoulay, V. (2018), *Xenophon and the Graces of Power: A Greek Guide to Political Manipulation*, Swansea: Classical Press of Wales.

Balot, R. K. (2001), *Greed and Injustice in Classical Athens*, Princeton: Princeton University Press.

Bartlett, R. C., trans., intro., comm., and notes (2020), *Against Demagogues: New Translations of the Acharnians and Knights*, Berkeley: University of California Press.

Basta Donzelli, G. (1978), *Studio sull' Elettra di Euripide*, Catania: Universita di Catania, Facolta de Lettere e Filosofia.

Beazley, J. D. (1963), *Attic Red-Figure Vase-Painters*, Oxford: Clarendon Press.

Belfiore, E. S. (2000), *Murder among Friends: Violation of* Philia *in Greek Tragedy*, New York: Oxford University Press.

Bicknell, P. J. (1972), *Studies in Athenian Politics and Genealogy*, Wiesbaden: Franz Steiner.

Bierl, A. F. H. (1991), *Dionysos und die griechische Tragödie*, Tübingen: G. Narr.

Bishop, B., and R. Cushing (2008), *The Big Sort*, Boston, MA: Houghton Mifflin.

Blundell, M. W. (1989), *Helping Friends and Harming Enemies: A Study in Sophocles and Greek Ethics*, Cambridge: Cambridge University Press.

Boedeker, D., and K. A. Raaflaub (2005), "Tragedy and City," in R. Bushnell (ed.), *A Companion to Tragedy*, 109–27, Malden, MA: Blackwell.

Boissevain, J. (1974), *Friends of Friends: Networks, Manipulators and Coalitions*, New York: St. Martin's.

Borman, E. G. (1954), "Huey Long: Analysis of a Demagogue," *Today's Speech*, 2.3: 16–20.

Bowersock, G. W., ed. and trans (1968), "Pseudo-Xenophon: Constitution of the Athenians" in E. C. Marchant and G. W. Bowersock (eds. and trans.), *Xenophon: Scripta Minora*, Loeb Classical Library, 459–507, Cambridge, MA: Harvard University Press.

Bowie, A. M. (1993), *Aristophanes: Myth, Ritual and Comedy*, Cambridge: Cambridge University Press.

Bradley, T. N., and B. R. Karney (2010), *Intimate Relationships*, New York: W. W. Norton & Co.

Braund, D. (2005), "Pericles, Cleon, and the Pontus: The Black Sea in Athens *c.* 440–421," in D. Braund (ed.), *Scythians and Greeks: Cultural Interaction in Scythia, Athens, and the Early Roman Empire*, 80–99, Exeter: University of Exeter Press.

Breitenbach, H. R. (1950), *Historiographische Anschauungsformen Xenophons*, Freiburg: Paulusdruckerei.

Brewer, M. B. (1999), "The Psychology of Prejudice: Ingroup Love or Outgroup Hate?," *Journal of Social Issues*, 55.3: 429–44.

Briant, P. (1987), "Institutions perses et histoire comparatiste dans l'historiographie grecque," in H. Sancisi-Weerdenburg and A. Kuhrt (eds.), *Achaemenid History II: The Greek Sources*, 1–10. Leiden: Nederlands Instituut voor het Nabije Oosten.

Brock, R. W. (1986), "The Double Plot in Aristophanes' *Knights*," *GRBS*, 27: 15–27.

Brock, R. W. (2004), "Xenophon's Political Imagery," in C. Tuplin (ed.), *Xenophon and His World*, 247–58, Stuttgart: Franz Steiner.

Brownson, C. L., trans., revised by J. Dillery (1998), *Xenophon: Anabasis*, Loeb Classical Library, Cambridge, MA: Harvard University Press.

Brunt, P. A. (1961), Review of V. Ehrenberg, *The Greek State*, Oxford: Blackwell, 1960, *Classical Review*, 11: 143–4.

Bustos, C., and R. Johnson (2018), "Hope from the Heartland: How Democrats Can Better Serve the Midwest by Bringing Rural, Working Class Wisdom to Washington," *Cher PAC*, 10 January. Available online: https://medium.com/@cherpacpress/hope-from-the-heartland-how-democrats-can-better-serve-the-midwest-by-bringing-rural-working-e5ff746f9839.

Buxton, R. F. (2016), "Novel Leaders for Novel Armies: Xenophon's Focus on Willing Obedience in Context," in R. F. Buxton (ed.), *Aspects of Leadership in Xenophon*, 163–97, *Histos* Supplement 5, Newcastle upon Tyne: Histos.

Buxton, R. F. (2017), "Xenophon on Leadership: Commanders as Friends," in M. A. Flower (ed.), *The Cambridge Companion to Xenophon*, 323–37, Cambridge: Cambridge University Press.

Buzzetti, E. (2014), *Xenophon the Socratic Prince: The Argument of the Anabasis of Cyrus*, New York: Palgrave Macmillan.

Calhoun, G. M. (1913), *Athenian Clubs in Politics and Litigation*, New York: Burt Franklin.

Canfora, L. (1993), *Demagogia*, Palermo: Sellerio.

Canfora, L. (2006), "Biographical Obscurities and Problems of Composition," in A. Rengakos and A. Tsakmakis (eds.), *Brill's Companion to Thucydides*, 3–31. Leiden: Brill.

Carey, C. (2014), "Comic Ridicule and Democracy," in R. Osborne and S. Hornblower (eds.), *Ritual, Finance, Politics: Athenian Democratic Accounts Presented to David Lewis*, 69–83, Oxford: Clarendon Press.

Carlier, P. (1978), "L'idée de monarchie impériale dans la Cyropédie de Xénophon," *Ktema*, 3: 133–63.

Carpenter, T. H., and C. A. Faraone, eds. (1993), *Masks of Dionysus*, Ithaca, NY: Cornell University Press.

Cartledge, P. (1987), *Agesilaos and the Crisis of Sparta*, Baltimore: Johns Hopkins University Press.

Cassio, A. C. (1985), "Old Persian *Marīka-*, Eupolis *Marikas* and Aristophanes *Knights*," *CQ*, 35: 38–42.

Castelli, L., S. Tomelleri, and C. Zogmaister (2008), "Implicit Ingroup Metafavoritism: Subtle Preference for Ingroup Members Displaying Ingroup Bias," *Personality and Social Psychology Bulletin*, 34.6: 807–18.

Cawkwell, G. (2004), "When, How, and Why Did Xenophon Write the *Anabasis*?," in R. Lane Fox (ed.), *The Long March: Xenophon and the Ten Thousand*, 47–67, New Haven: Yale University Press.

Christ, M. R. (1998), *The Litigious Athenian*, Baltimore: Johns Hopkins University Press.

Christ, M. R. (2006), *The Bad Citizen in Classical Athens*, Cambridge: Cambridge University Press.

Christ, M. R. (2012), *The Limits of Altruism in Democratic Athens*, Cambridge: Cambridge University Press.

Christ, M. R. (2020), *Xenophon and the Athenian Democracy: The Education of an Elite Citizenry*, Cambridge: Cambridge University Press.

Christodoulou, P. (2013), "Thucydides' Pericles. Between Historical Reality and Literary Representation," in A. Tsamakis and M. Tamiolaki (eds.), *Thucydides Between History and Literature*, 225–54, Berlin: DeGruyter.

Cizek, A. (1975), "From the Historical Truth to the Literary Convention: The Life of Cyrus the Great Viewed by Herodotus, Ctesias and Xenophon," *L'Antiquité Classique* 44: 531–52.

Cole, S. G. (2007), "Finding Dionysus," in D. Ogden (ed.), *A Companion to Greek Religion*, 327–41, Malden, MA: Blackwell.

Collard, C., ed. (1991), *Euripides: Hecuba*, Warminster: Aris & Phillips.

Collard, C., and M. Cropp, eds. and trans. (2008), *Euripides: Fragments: Antiope-Meleager*, Loeb Classical Library, Cambridge, MA: Harvard University Press.

Connor, W. R. (1968), *Theopompus and Fifth-Century Athens*, Washington, DC: Center for Hellenic Studies.

Connor, W. R. (1971), *The New Politicians of Fifth-Century Athens*, Princeton: Princeton University Press.

Cooper, J. M., ed., intro., and notes (1997), *Plato: Complete Works*, Indianapolis: Hackett.

Crane, G. (1998), *Thucydides and the Ancient Simplicity: The Limits of Political Realism*, Berkeley: University of California Press.

Cropp, M. J. (1988), *Euripides: Electra*, Warminster: Aris & Phillips.

Cropp, M., and G. Fick (1985), *Resolutions and Chronology in Euripides: The Fragmentary Tragedies*, ICS Bulletin Supplement 43, London: Institute of Classical Studies.

Csapo, E. (1999–2000), "Later Euripidean Music," in M. J. Cropp, K. H. Lee, and D. Sansone (eds.), *Euripides and Tragic Theatre in the Late Fifth Century* (*ICS* 24–5), 399–426, Champaign: University of Illinois Press.

Dakyns, H. G. (1892), *The Works of Xenophon, Vol. II: Hellenica Books III–VII, Agesilaus, The Polities, and Revenues*, London: Macmillan.

Dalmeyda, G., ed. (1960), *Andocide: Discours*, Paris: Les Belles Lettres.

Davidson, J. (1997), *Courtesans and Fishcakes: The Consuming Passions of Classical Athens*, New York: St. Martin's.

Davies, J. K. (1971), *Athenian Propertied Families 600–300 B.C*, Oxford: Clarendon Press.

Davies, J. K. (1975), Review of W. R. Connor, *The New Politicians of Fifth-Century Athens*, Princeton, Princeton University Press, 1971, *Gnomon*, 47: 374–78.

Davies, J. K. (1981), *Wealth and the Power of Wealth in Classical Athens*, New York: Arno.

Debnar, P. (2005), "Fifth-Century Athenian History and Tragedy," in J. Gregory (ed.), *A Companion to Greek Tragedy*, 3–22, Malden, MA: Blackwell.

Denniston, J. D., ed. (1939), *Euripides: Electra*, Oxford: Clarendon Press.

Dentith, S. (2000), *Parody*, New York: Routledge.

Diggle, J., ed. (1981), *Euripides: Fabulae*. Vol. 2: *Supplices, Electra, Hercules, Troades, Iphigenia in Tauris, Ion*, Oxford: Clarendon Press.

Diggle, J., ed. (1984), *Euripides: Fabulae*. Vol. 1: *Cyclops, Alcestis, Medea, Heraclidae, Hippolytus, Andromache, Hecuba*, Oxford: Clarendon Press.

Diggle, J., ed. (1994), *Euripides: Fabulae*. Vol. 3: *Helena, Phoenissae, Orestes, Bacchae, Iphigenia Aulidensis, Rhesus*, Oxford: Clarendon Press.

Dillery, J. (1995), *Xenophon and the History of His Times*, New York: Routledge.

Dodds, E. R., ed., intro., and comm. (1959), *Plato: Gorgias*, Oxford: Clarendon Press.

Dodds, E. R., ed., intro., and comm. (1960), *Euripides: Bacchae*, 2nd ed., Oxford: Clarendon Press.

Donlan, W. (1970), "Changes and Shifts in the Meaning of Demos in the Literature of the Archaic Period," *PP*, 25: 381–95.

Dover, K. J., ed., intro., and comm. (1968), *Aristophanes: Clouds*, Oxford: Clarendon Press.

Dover, K. J. (1972), *Aristophanic Comedy*, Berkeley: University of California Press.

Dover, K. J. ed., intro., and comm. (1993), *Aristophanes: Frogs*, Oxford: Clarendon Press.

Dover, K. J., ed., intro., and comm. (1997), *Aristophanes: Frogs: Student Edition*, Oxford: Clarendon Press.

Dover, K. J. (2016 [1978, 1989]), *Greek Homosexuality*, 3rd ed., London: Bloomsbury.

Drews, R. (1974), "Sargon, Cyrus, and Mesopotamian Folk History," *Journal of Near Eastern Studies*, 33: 387–93.

Due, B. (1989), *The Cyropaedia: Xenophon's Aims and Methods*, Aarhus: Aarhus University Press.

Dunbar, N., ed., intro., and comm. (1995), *Aristophanes: Birds*, Oxford: Clarendon Press.

Ebener, D. (1966), "Zum Schluß des *Orestes*," *Eirene*, 5: 43–9.

Edmonds, J. M., ed. and trans. (1957), *The Fragments of Attic Comedy after Meineke, Bergk, and Kock*, 5 vols., Leiden: Brill.

Edmunds, L. (1987), *Cleon, Knights and Aristophanes' Politics*, Lanham, MD: University Press of America.

Erbse, H. (1966), "Xenophons *Anabasis*," *Gymnasium*, 73: 485–505.

Erikson, E. (2008), "'Hillary is My Friend': MySpace and Political Fandom," *Rocky Mountain Communication Review*, 4.2: 3–16.

Ferguson, J. (1987), *Euripides Medea and Electra: A Companion to the Penguin Translation of Philip Vellacott*, Bristol: Bristol Classical Press.

Ferraio, S. B. (2017), "Historical Agency and Self-Awareness in Xenophon's *Hellenica* and *Anabasis*," in M. A. Flower (ed.), *The Cambridge Companion to Xenophon*, 57–83, Cambridge: Cambridge University Press.

Festinger, L., S. Schachter, and K. Back (1950), "The Spatial Ecology of Group Formation," in L. Festinger, S. Schachter, and K. Back (eds.), *Social Pressures in Informal Groups: A Study of Human Factors in Housing*, 141–61, Palo Alto: Stanford University Press.

Finley, M. I. (2004 [1962] [1985]), "Athenian Demagogues," in P. J. Rhodes (ed.), *Athenian Democracy*, 163–84, New York: Oxford University Press.

Finley, M. I. (1983), *Politics in the Ancient World*, Cambridge: Cambridge University Press.

Fisher, N. R. E. (1976), "Introduction," in N. R. E. Fisher (ed.), *Social Values in Classical Athens*, 1–45, London: Dent.

Fisher, N. R. E. (2000), "Symposiasts, Fish-Eaters and Flatterers: Social Mobility and Moral Concerns in Old Comedy," in D. Harvey and J. Wilkins (eds.), *The Rivals of Aristophanes: Studies in Athenian Old Comedy*, 355–96, London: Duckworth.

Fisher, N. R. E. (2008), "The Bad Boyfriend, the Flatterer and the Sycophant: Related Forms of the '*Kakos*' in Democratic Athens," in I. Sluiter and R. M. Rosen (eds.), *KAKOS: Badness and Anti-Value in Classical Antiquity*, 185–232, Leiden: Brill.

Flower, M. A. (2012), *Xenophon's Anabasis, or The Expedition of Cyrus*, New York: Oxford University Press.

Flower, M. A. (2016), "Piety in Xenophon's Theory of Leadership," in R. F. Buxton (ed.), *Aspects of Leadership in Xenophon*, *Histos* Supplement 5, 85–119, Newcastle upon Tyne: Histos.

Flower, M. A. (2017), "Introduction," in M. A. Flower (ed.), *The Cambridge Companion to Xenophon*, 1–12, Cambridge: Cambridge University Press.

Flynn, F. J., R. E. Reagans, and L. Guillory (2010), "Do You Two Know Each Other? Transitivity, Homophily, and the Need for (Network) Closure," *Journal of Personality and Social Psychology*, 99: 855–69.

Foley, H. P. (1985), *Ritual Irony: Poetry and Sacrifice in Euripides*, Ithaca, NY: Cornell University Press.

Fornara, C. W. (1971), *The Athenian Board of Generals from 501 to 404*, Wiesbaden: Franz Steiner.

Fornara, C. W. (1973), "Cleon's Attack Against the Cavalry," *CQ*, 23: 24.

Fornara, C. W., ed. (1983), *Archaic Times to the End of the Peloponnesian War*, 2nd ed., Cambridge: Cambridge University Press.

Frazier, F. (2003), "Quelques remarques autour des antonymes de demos chez Thucydide," *Ktèma*, 28: 59–69.

Frisch, H. (1976), *The Constitution of the Athenians*, New York: Arno.

Fuchs, C. (2019), "Boris Johnson Takes His Demagoguery to the Social Media Sphere," *Truthout*, 31 August. Available online: https://truthout.org/articles/boris-johnson-takes-his-brexit-demagoguery-to-the-social-media-sphere/.

Funke, H. (1964), "Aristoteles zu Euripides' *Iphigeneia in Aulis*," *Hermes*, 92: 284–99.

Gera, D. L. (1993), *Xenophon's Cyropaedia: Style, Genre, and Literary Technique*, Oxford: Clarendon Press.

Goff, B. (2004), *Citizen Bacchae: Women's Ritual Practice in Ancient Greece*, Berkeley: University of California Press.

Gomme, A. W. (1956), *A Historical Commentary on Thucydides, Vol. II: Books II–III*, Oxford: Clarendon Press.

Gomme, A. W. (1974), *A Historical Commentary on Thucydides, Vol. III: Books IV–V.24*, Oxford: Clarendon Press.

Gomme, A. W., A. Andrewes, and K. J. Dover (1970), *A Historical Commentary on Thucydides, Vol. IV: Books V.25-VII*, Oxford: Clarendon Press.

Gomme, A. W., A. Andrewes, and K. J. Dover (1981), *A Historical Commentary on Thucydides, Vol. V: Book VIII*, Oxford: Clarendon Press.

Gould, J. (2001), "Mothers' Day: A Note on Euripides' *Bacchae*," in J. Gould, *Myth, Ritual, Memory, and Exchange: Essays in Greek Literature and Culture*, 235–43, Oxford: Oxford University Press.

Gray, V. J. (1989), *The Character of Xenophon's Hellenica*, London: Duckworth.

Gray, V. J., intro., ed., and comm. (2007), *Xenophon on Government*, Cambridge: Cambridge University Press.

Gray, V. J. (2010), "Introduction," in V. J. Gray (ed.), *Oxford Readings in Classical Studies: Xenophon*, 1–28. Oxford: Oxford University Press.

Gray, V. J. (2011), *Xenophon's Mirror of Princes*, Oxford: Oxford University Press.

Green, P. M. (1995), "Text and Context in the Matter of Xenophon's Exile," in I. Worthington (ed.), *Ventures into Greek History*, 215–27, Oxford: Clarendon Press.

Gregory, J., ed. (1999), *Euripides: Hecuba. Introduction, Text, and Commentary*, Atlanta: Scholars.

Griffith, M. (2013), *Aristophanes' Frogs*, Oxford Approaches to Classical Literature, New York: Oxford University Press.

Grote, G. (1888 [1846–56]), *A History of Greece; from the Earliest Period to the Close of the Generation Contemporary with Alexander the Great*, 10 vols., London: John Murray.

Gruber, G. (2001), "Kleon's Silence in Thucydides," CAMWS Annual Meeting, Provo, UT.

Gurt, S. A. (2005), *Iphigenias at Aulis: Textual Multiplicity, Radical Philology*, Ithaca, NY: Cornell University Press.

Halliwell, S. (2020), "Politics in the Street: Some Citizen Encounters in Aristophanes," in R. M. Rosen and H. P. Foley (eds.), *Aristophanes and Politics: New Studies*, 113–36, Leiden: Brill.

Halperin, D. M. (1990), "Why Is Diotima a Woman? Platonic Eros and the Figuration of Gender," in D. M. Halperin, J. J. Winkler, and F. Zeitlin (eds.), *Before Sexuality: The Construction of Erotic Experience in the Ancient Greek World*, 257–308, Princeton: Princeton University Press.

Hamilton, D. L. (2007), "Understanding the Complexities of Group Perception: Broadening the Domain," *European Journal of Social Psychology*, 37: 1077–101.

Hamilton, R. (1974), "*Bacchae* 47–52. Dionysus' Plan," *TAPA*, 54: 139–49.

Hansen, M. H. (1983), "The Athenian Politicians 403–322 B.C.," *GRBS*, 24: 33–55.

Hansen, M. H. (1991), *The Athenian Democracy in the Age of Demosthenes: Structure, Principles, and Ideology*, trans. J. A. Crook, Cambridge, MA: Blackwell.

Haslam, N., B. Bastian, P. Bain, and Y. Kashima (2006), "Psychological Essentialism, Implicit Theories, and Intergroup Relations," *Group Processes and Intergroup Relations*, 9: 63–76.

Henderson, J. (1990), "The *Dēmos* and Comic Competition," in J. J. Winkler and F. I. Zeitlin (eds.), *Nothing to Do with Dionysus?*, 271–313, Princeton: Princeton University Press.

Henderson, J. (1991), *The Maculate Muse: Obscene Language in Attic Comedy*, 2nd ed., New York: Oxford University Press.

Henderson, J., ed. and trans. (1998), *Aristophanes: Acharnians; Knights*, Loeb Classical Library, Cambridge, MA: Harvard University Press.

Henderson, J., trans., intro., and notes (2008), *Aristophanes Frogs*, Newburyport, MA: Focus.

Henderson, J. (2019), "Demagogues," in A. H. Sommerstein (ed.), *The Encyclopedia of Greek Comedy*, Vol. I, 244–6, Hoboken, NJ: Wiley-Blackwell.

Henderson, J. (2020), "Patterns of Avoidance and Indirection in Athenian Political Satire," in R. M. Rosen and H. P. Foley (eds.), *Aristophanes and Politics: New Studies*, 45–59, Leiden: Brill.

Henderson, J., ed., intro., and comm. (forthcoming), *Aristophanes: Knights*, Oxford: Oxford University Press.

Henrichs, A. (1984), "Loss of Self, Suffering, Violence: The Modern View of Dionysus from Nietzsche to Girard," *HSPh*, 88: 205–40.

Henrichs, A. (1993), "'He Has a God in Him': Human and Divine in the Modern Perception of Dionysus," in T. H. Carpenter and C. A. Faraone (eds.), *Masks of Dionysus*, 13–43, Ithaca, NY: Cornell University Press.

Hershkowitz, A. (2018), "Rise of the Demagogues: Political Leadership in Imperial Athens after the Reforms of Ephialtes," diss., Rutgers University, NJ.

Higgins, W. E. (1977), *Xenophon the Athenian: The Problem of the Individual and the Society of the Polis*, Albany: State University of Albany Press.

Hignett, C. (1950), *A History of the Athenian Constitution to the End of the Fifth Century B.C.*, Oxford: Clarendon Press.

Hirsch, S. W. (1985), *The Friendship of the Barbarians: Xenophon and the Persian Empire*, Hanover, NH: University Press of New England.

Hobden, F. (2020), *Xenophon: Ancients in Action*, London: Bloomsbury.

Hodgart, M. (1969), *Satire*, New York: McGraw-Hill.

Holland, P. W., and S. Leinhardt (1971), "Transitivity in Structural Models of Small Groups," *Comparative Group Studies*, 2: 107–24.

Hoeller, S. (2008), "Palin — A Demagogue in a Skirt," *Huffington Post*, 9 November. Available online: https://www.huffpost.com/entry/sarah-palin---a-demagogue_b_133114.

Holmes, D. (2011), "Re-eroticizing the Hoopoe: Tereus in Aristophanes' *Birds*," *SyllClass*, 22: 1–20.

Homans, G. C. (1950), *The Human Group*, New York: Harcourt, Brace, and Company.

Hornblower, S. (1991), *A Commentary on Thucydides, Vol. I: Books I–III*, Oxford: Clarendon Press.

Hornblower, S. (1996), *A Commentary on Thucydides, Vol. II: Books IV–V.24*, Oxford: Clarendon Press.

Hornblower, S. (2000), "The *Old Oligarch* (Pseudo-Xenophon's *Athenaion Politeia*) and Thucydides. A Fourth-Century Date for the *Old Oligarch*?," in P. Flensted Jensen, T. H. Nielsen, and L. Rubinstein (eds.), *Polis and Politics: Studies in Ancient Greek History*, 363–84, Copenhagen: Museum Tusculanum.

Hornblower, S. (2008), *A Commentary on Thucydides, Vol. III: Books 5.25–8.109*, Oxford: Clarendon Press.

Horowitz, C. F. (2015), *Sharpton: A Demagogue's Rise*, Falls Church, VA: National Legal and Policy Center.

How, W. W., and J. Wells (1912), *A Commentary on Herodotus*, 2 vols., Oxford: Clarendon Press.

Howland, J. (2000), "Xenophon's Philosophic Odyssey: On the *Anabasis* and Plato's *Republic*," *American Political Science Review*, 94: 875–89.

Hubbard, T. K. (1991), *The Mask of Comedy: Aristophanes and the Intertextual Parabasis*, Ithaca, NY: Cornell University Press.

Hubbard, T. K. (1998), "Popular Perceptions of Elite Homosexuality," *Arion* 3rd series, 6: 48–78.

Huitink, L., and T. Rood (2016), "Subordinate Officers in Xenophon's Anabasis," in R. F. Buxton (ed.), *Aspects of Leadership in Xenophon*, 199–242, *Histos* Supplement 5, Newcastle upon Tyne: Histos.

Humphreys, J. J. (2002), "The *Anabasis* and Lessons in Leadership: Xenophon as a Prototypical Transformational Leader," *Journal of Research Management*, 2: 136–46.

Humphreys, S. C. (1983), *The Family, Women and Death: Comparative Studies*, London: Routledge & Kegan Paul.

Hunter, V. (1988), "Thucydides and the Sociology of the Crowd," *CJ*, 84: 17–30.

Hutter, H. (1978), *Politics as Friendship: The Origins of Classical Notions of Politics in the Theory and Practice of Friendship*, Waterloo, ON: Wilfred Laurier University Press.

Hyland, D. A. (1968), "Ἔρως, Ἐπιθυμία, and Φιλία in Plato," *Phronesis*, 13: 32–46.

Imperio, O. (2020), "Aristophanes' Political Comedies and (Bad?) Imitations," in R. M. Rosen and H. P. Foley (eds.), *Aristophanes and Politics: New Studies*, 90–112, Leiden: Brill.

Johnson, J. F. (2016), *Acts of Compassion in Greek Tragic Drama*, Norman, OK: University of Oklahoma Press.

Johnson, R. (2022), "How Democrats Can Win in White Working-Class Districts," *Washington Monthly*, January/February/March. Available online: https://washingtonmonthly.com/2022/01/17/how-democrats-can-win-in-white-working-class-districts/.

Jones, E. E. (1964), *Ingratiation: A Social Psychological Analysis*, New York: Appleton-Century-Crofts.

Jones, N. F. (1999), *The Associations of Classical Athens: The Response to Democracy*, New York: Oxford University Press.

Kalinka, E. (1913), *Die PseudoXenophontische Ἀθηναίων Πολιτεία*, Leipzig: Teubner.

Kallet-Marx, L. (1994), "Money Talks: Rhetor, Demos, and the Resources of the Athenian Empire," in R. Osborne and S. Hornblower (eds.), *Ritual, Finance, Politics: Athenian Democratic Accounts Presented to David Lewis*, 227–51, Oxford: Clarendon Press.

Kilduff, M., and W. Tsai (2003), *Social Networks and Organizations*, London: Sage.

Keim, B. D. (2016), "Novel Leaders for Novel Armies: Xenophon's *Anabasis*," in R. F. Buxton (ed.), *Aspects of Leadership in Xenophon*, 121–62, *Histos* Supplement 5, Newcastle upon Tyne: Histos.

Kierstead, J. (2014), "Grote's Athens: The Character of Democracy," in K. N. Demetriou (ed.), *Brill's Companion to George Grote and the Classical Tradition*, 161–210, Leiden: Brill.

Knowles, E. D., and L. R. Tropp (2018), "The Racial and Economic Context of Trump Support: Evidence for Threat, Identity, and Contact Effects in the 2016 Presidential Election," *Social Psychological and Personality Science*, 9.3: 275–84.

Knox, B. M. W. (1972), "Euripides' *Iphigenia in Aulide* 1–163 (in That Order)," *YCS*, 22: 239–61.

Konstan, D. (1985), "*Philia* in Euripides' *Electra*," *Philologus*, 129: 176–85.

Konstan, D. (1993), "Friends and Lovers in Ancient Greece," *SyllClass*, 4: 1–12.

Konstan, D. (1996), "Greek Friendship," *AJP*, 117: 71–94.

Konstan, D. (1997), *Friendship in the Classical World*, Cambridge: Cambridge University Press.

Konstan, D. (1998), "Reciprocity and Friendship," in C. Gill, N. Postlethwaite, and R. Seaford (eds.), *Reciprocity in Ancient Greece*, 279–301, Oxford: Clarendon Press.

Konstan, D. (2006), *The Emotions of the Ancient Greeks: Studies in Aristotle and Classical Literature*, Toronto: University of Toronto Press.

Konstan, D. (2018), *In the Orbit of Love*, Oxford: Oxford University Press.

Kovacs, D. (1987), *The Heroic Muse*, Baltimore: Johns Hopkins University Press.

Kovacs, D., ed. and trans. (1994–2002), *Euripides*, 6 vols., Loeb Classical Library, Cambridge, MA: Harvard University Press.

Kovacs, D. (2003), "Toward a Reconstruction of *Iphigenia Aulidensis*," *JHS*, 123: 77–103.

Lafargue, P. (2013), *Cléon: Le Guerrier d'Athéna*, Paris: Ausonius.

Landfester, M. (1967), *Die Ritter des Aristophanes*, Amsterdam: B. R. Grüner.

Lane Fox, R. (1994), "Aeschines and Athenian Democracy," in R. Osborne and S. Hornblower (eds.), *Ritual, Finance, Politics: Athenian Democratic Accounts Presented to David Lewis*, 135–55. Oxford: Clarendon Press.

Lane Fox, R. (2004), "Introduction," in R. Lane Fox (ed.), *The Long March: Xenophon and the Ten Thousand*, 1–46, New Haven: Yale University Press.

Lawrence, S. E. (1988), "*Iphigenia at Aulis*: Characterization and Psychology in Euripides," *Ramus* 17: 91–109.

Lee, J. W. I. (2017), "Xenophon and His Times," in M. A. Flower (ed.), *The Cambridge Companion to Xenophon*, 15–36, Cambridge: Cambridge University Press.

Lefkowitz, M. (1981), *The Lives of the Greek Poets*, Baltimore: Johns Hopkins University Press.

Lendle, O. (1995), *Kommentar zu Xenophons Anabasis (Bücher 1–7)*, Darmstadt: Wissenschaftliche Buchgesellschaft.

Ley, G. (1987), "The Date of the *Hecuba*," *Eranos* 85: 136–7.

Liddel, P. (2014), "The Comparative Approach in Grote's *History of Greece*," in K. N. Demetriou (ed.), *Brill's Companion to George Grote and the Classical Tradition*, 211–54, Leiden: Brill.

Lind, H. (1985), "Neues aus Kydathen. Beobachtungen zum Hintergrund der Daitales und der Ritter des Aristophanes," *Museum Helveticum*, 42: 249–76.

Lind, H. (1990), *Der Gerber Kleon in den "Rittern" des Aristophanes: Studien zur Demagogenkomödie*, Frankfurt am Main: Peter Lang.

Littman, R. J. (1990), *Kinship and Politics in Athens 600–400 B.C.*, New York: Peter Lang.

Lossau, M. (1969), "ΔΗΜΑΓΩΓΟΣ. Fehlen und Gebrauch bei Aristophanes und Thukydides," in P. Steinmetz (ed.), *Politeia und Res Publica. Beiträge zum Verständnis von Politik, Recht und Staat in der Antike*, 83–8, Wiesbaden: Franz Steiner.

Louch, H. (2000), "Personal Network Integration: Transitivity and Homophily in Strong-Tie Relations," *Social Networks*, 22: 45–64.

Luccioni, J. (1947), *Les idées politiques et sociales de Xénophon*, Paris: Ophrys.

Ludwig, P. W. (2002), *Eros and Polis: Desire and Community in Greek Political Theory*, Cambridge: Cambridge University Press.

Lush, B. V. (2015), "Popular Authority in Euripides' *Iphigenia in Aulis*," *AJP*, 136: 207–42.

Ma, J. (2004), "You Can't Go Home Again: Displacement and Identity in Xenophon's *Anabasis*," in R. Lane Fox (ed.), *The Long March: Xenophon and the Ten Thousand*, 330–45, New Haven: Yale University Press.

MacCallum, M. (2018), "Thus Spake Mungo: ScoMo—the Authentic Demagogue," *Echo Net Daily*, 5 November. Available online: https://www.echo.net.au/2018/11/thus-spake-mungo-scomo-authentic-demagogue/.

MacDowell, D. M., ed. and comm (1971), *Aristophanes: Wasps*, Oxford: Clarendon Press.

Major, W. E. (2013), *The Court of Comedy: Aristophanes, Rhetoric, and Democracy in Fifth-Century Athens*, Columbus, OH: Ohio State University Press.

Manhart, K. (2000), "Balance Theories: Two Reconstructions and the Problem of Intended Applications," in W. Balzer, J. D. Sneed, and C. U. Moulines (eds.), *Structuralist Knowledge Representation: Paradigmatic Examples*, Poznan Studies in the Philosophy of the Sciences and the Humanities 75, 171–87, Atlanta: Rodopi.

Mann, C. (2007), *Die Demagogen und das Volk: Zur politischen Kommunikation im Athen des 5. Jahrhunderts v. Chr*, Berlin: Akademie Verlag.

March, J. R. (1987), *The Creative Poet: Studies on the Treatment of Myths in Greek Poetry*, London: University of London, Institute of Classical Studies.

March, J. R. (1989), "Euripides' *BAKCHAI*: A Reconsideration in the Light of Vase-painting," *BICS*, 36: 33–65.

Marchant, E. C., ed. (1910), *Cyropaedia, Xenophontis opera omnia*, Vol. 4. Oxford: Clarendon Press.

Marincola, J. (2017), "Xenophon's *Anabasis* and *Hellenica*," in M. A. Flower (ed.), *The Cambridge Companion to Xenophon*, 103–18, Cambridge: Cambridge University Press.

Markantonatos, A. (2011), "Wise Policy and Firm Resolve in Euripides' Iphigenia at Aulis," in A. Markantonatos and B. Zimmermann (eds.), *Crisis on Stage: Tragedy and Comedy in Late Fifth-Century Athens*, 189–218, Boston, MA: de Gruyter.

Markantonatos, A., and B. Zimmermann, eds. (2011), *Crisis on Stage: Tragedy and Comedy in Late Fifth-Century Athens*, Boston, MA: de Gruyter.

Markle, M. M. (1985), "Jury Pay and Assembly Pay at Athens," in P. A. Cartledge and F. D. Harvey (eds.), *Crux. Essays in Greek History Presented to G. E. M. De Ste Croix on his 75th Birthday*, 265–97, London: Duckworth.

Marr, J. L., and P. J. Rhodes, intro., trans., and comm. (2008), *The "Old Oligarch": The Constitution of the Athenians Attributed to Xenophon*, Oxford: Aris & Phillips.

Marsden, P. (1988), "Homogeneity in Confiding Relations," *Social Networks*, 9: 100–25.

Marshall, C. W. (2003), "The Consequences of Dating the *Cyclops*," in M. Joyal (ed.), *In Altum: Seventy Five Years of Classical Studies in Newfoundland*, 225–41, St. John's: Memorial University of Newfoundland.

Mastronarde, D. J. (1979), *Contact and Discontinuity: Some Conventions of Speech and Action on the Greek Tragic Stage*, Berkeley: University of California Press.

Mastronarde, D. J. (2010), *The Art of Euripides: Dramatic Technique and Social Context*, Cambridge: Cambridge University Press.

Mattingly, H. B. (1997), "The Date and Purpose of the Pseudo-Xenophon *Constitution of Athens*," *CQ*, 47: 352–7.

McDonald, M. (1989), "Vengeance is Mine, ll. 877–881. *Philia* Gone Awry in the Chorus of Euripides' *Bacchae*," *Proceedings of the IIIrd and IVth International Meetings of Ancient Greek Drama, Delphi 24–28 June 1987 and 7–12 July 1988*, 41–50, Athens: European Cultural Center of Delphi.

McGlew, J. F. (2002), *Citizens on Stage: Comedy and Political Culture in the Athenian Democracy*, Ann Arbor: University of Michigan Press.

McPherson, M., L. Smith-Lovin, and J. M. Cook (2001), "Birds of a Feather: Homophily in Social Networks," *Annual Review of Sociology*, 27: 415–44.

Mellert-Hoffmann, G. (1969), *Untersuchungen zur "Iphigenie in Aulis" des Euripides*, Heidelberg: Winter.

Mercieca, J. (2020), *Demagogue for President: The Rhetorical Genius of Donald Trump*, College Station, TX: Texas A&M University Press.

Meritt, B. D., and A. B. West (1925), "The Reconstruction of I. G. I², 193, 194, and 201," *TAPA*, 56: 252–67.

Mesk, J. (1922–3), "Die Tendenz der Xenophontischen Anabasis," *WS*, 43: 136–46.

Michelakis, P. (2002), *Achilles in Greek Tragedy*, Cambridge: Cambridge University Press.

Michelakis, P. (2006), *Euripides: Iphigenia at Aulis*, Duckworth Companions to Greek and Roman Tragedy, London: Duckworth.

Michelini, A. N. (1999–2000), "The Expansion of Myth in Late Euripides: *Iphigeneia at Aulis*," in M. J. Cropp, K. H. Lee, and D. Sansone (eds.), *Euripides and Tragic Theatre in the Late Fifth Century (ICS* 24–5), 41–57, Champaign: University of Illinois Press.

Millender, E. (2012), "Spartan 'Friendship' and Xenophon's Crafting of the *Anabasis*," in F. Hobden and C. Tuplin (eds.), *Xenophon: Ethical Principles and Historical Enquiry*, 377–425, Leiden: Brill.

Millett, P. (1989), "Patronage and Its Avoidance in Classical Athens," in A. Wallace-Hadrill (ed.), *Patronage in Ancient Society*, 15–47, New York: Routledge.

Millett, P. (1991), *Lending and Borrowing in Ancient Athens*, Cambridge: Cambridge University Press.

Mills, S. (2006), *Euripides: Bacchae*, Duckworth Companions to Greek and Roman Tragedy, London: Duckworth.

Mischenko, D., and D. V. Day (2015), "Identity and Identification at Work," *Organizational Psychology Review*, 6: 215–47.

Mitchell, B. (1991), "Kleon's Amphipolitan Campaign: Aims and Results," *Historia*, 40.2: 170–92.

Mitchell, L. G. (1997), *Greeks Bearing Gifts: The Public Use of Private Relationships in the Greek World, 435–323 BC*, Cambridge: Cambridge University Press.

Mitchell, L. G., and P. J. Rhodes (1996), "Friends and Enemies in Athenian Politics," *G&R*, 43: 11–30.

Mitchell-Boyask, R. (2006), *Euripides: Hecuba. Introduction, Translation, and Commentary*, Newburyport, MA: Focus.

Moggi, M. (2005), "Demos in Erodoto e Tucidide," in G. Urso (ed.), *Popolo e Potere nel mondo antico*, 11–24, Pisa: Fondazione Niccolò Canussio.

Monoson, S. S. (2000), *Plato's Democratic Entanglements: Athenian Politics and the Practice of Philosophy*, Princeton: Princeton University Press.

Montiglio, S. (2011), *From Villain to Hero: Odysseus in Ancient Thought*, Ann Arbor: University of Michigan Press.

Moore, J. M. (1975), *Aristotle and Xenophon on Democracy and Oligarchy*, Berkeley: University of California Press.

Morgan, J. D. (1986), "Μαρικξᾶς," *CQ*, 36: 529–31.

Morwood, J. (2009), "Euripides and the Demagogues," *CQ*, 59: 353–63.

Moskowitz, G. B. (2004), *Social Cognition*, New York: Guilford.

Mossman, J. (1995), *Wild Justice: A Study of Euripides' Hecuba*, Oxford: Clarendon Press.

Munn, M. (2000), *The School of History: Athens in the Age of Socrates*, Berkeley: University of California Press.

Nadon, C. (2001), *Xenophon's Prince: Republic and Empire in the Cyropaedia*, Berkeley: University of California Press.

Neil, R. A., ed. (1901), *The Knights of Aristophanes*, Cambridge: Cambridge University Press.

Nussbaum, G. B. (1967), *The Ten Thousand: A Study in Social Organization and Action in Xenophon's Anabasis*, Leiden: Brill.

O'Flannery, J. (2003), "Xenophon's (The Education of Cyrus) and Ideal Leadership Lessons for Modern Public Administration," *Public Administration Quarterly*, 27: 41–64.

Ober, J. (1989), *Mass and Elite in Democratic Athens*, Princeton: Princeton University Press.

Ober, J. (1998), *Political Dissent in Democratic Athens*, Princeton: Princeton University Press.

Olson, S. D., ed., intro., and comm. (1998), *Aristophanes: Peace*, New York: Oxford University Press.

Olson, S. D. (2002), *Aristophanes: Acharnians*, New York: Oxford University Press.

Olson, S. D. (2017), "On the Date of Eupolis' *Demes* and the Political Events of 412 BC," *Polis*, 34: 422–31.

Oranje, H. (1984), *Euripides' Bacchae: The Play and its Audience*, Leiden: Brill.

Osborne, R., intro., trans., and comm. (2004), *The Old Oligarch: Pseudo-Xenophon's Constitution of the Athenians*, 2nd ed., London: London Association of Classical Teachers.

Osborne, R. (2020), "Politics and Laughter: The Case of Aristophanes' *Knights*," in R. M. Rosen and H. P. Foley (eds.), *Aristophanes and Politics: New Studies*, 24–44, Leiden: Brill.

Ostwald, M. (1986), *From Popular Sovereignty to the Sovereignty of Law: Law, Society, and Politics in Fifth-Century Athens*, Berkeley: University of California Press.

Page, D. (1934), *Actors' Interpolations in Greek Tragedy*, Oxford: Clarendon Press.

Pecorella Longo, C. (1971), *"Eterie' e gruppi politici nell' Atene del IV sec. a.C.* Florence: L. S. Olschki.

Pelling, C., ed. (1997), *Greek Tragedy and the Historian*, Oxford: Clarendon Press.

Pelling, C. (1997), "Conclusion," in C. Pelling (ed.), *Greek Tragedy and the Historian*, 213–35, Oxford: Clarendon Press.

Pelling, C., ed. (2000), *Literary Texts and the Greek Historian*, New York: Routledge.

Penner, T., and C. Rowe (2005), *Plato's Lysis*, Cambridge: Cambridge University Press.

Phiddian, R. (1995), *Swift's Parody*, Cambridge: Cambridge University Press.

Philippart, H. (1930), "Iconographie des 'Bacchantes' d'Euripide," *RBPh*, 9: 4–72.

Platnauer, M., ed., intro., and comm. (1964), *Aristophanes Peace*, Oxford: Clarendon Press.

Pownall, F. (2016), "Tyrants as Impious Leaders in Xenophon's *Hellenica*," in R. F. Buxton (ed.), *Aspects of Leadership in Xenophon*, 51–83, *Histos* Supplement 5, Newcastle upon Tyne: Histos.

Preciado, P., et al. (2012), "Does Proximity Matter? Distance Dependence of Adolescent Friendships," *Social Networks*, 34: 18–31.

Price, A. W. (1997 [1989]), *Love and Friendship in Plato and Aristotle*, new ed., Oxford: Clarendon Press.

Price, J. (2001), *Thucydides and Internal War*, Cambridge: Cambridge University Press.

Rabe, H., ed. (1971), *Scholia in Lucianum*, Stuttgart: Teubner.

Rahn, P. J. (1981), "The Date of Xenophon's Exile," in G. S. Shrimpton and D. J. McCargor (eds.), *Classical Contributions: Studies in Honor of Malcolm Francis McGregor*, 103–19, Locust Valley, NY: J. J. Augustin.

Reinders, P. (2001), *Demos Pyknites: Untersuchungen zur Darstellung des Demos in der Alten Komödie*, Stuttgart: J. B. Metzler.

Reisert, J. (2009), "Xenophon on Gentlemanliness and Friendship," in S. R. Krause and M. A. McGrail (eds.), *The Arts of Rule: Essays in Honor of Harvey C. Mansfield*, 23–41, Lanham, MD: Lexington Books.

Rhodes, P. J. (1981), *A Commentary on the Aristotelian Athenaion Politeia*, Oxford: Clarendon Press.

Rhodes, P. J. (1986), "Political Activity in Classical Athens," *JHS*, 106: 132–44.

Rhodes, P. J. (1994), "The Ostracism of Hyperbolus," in R. Osborne and S. Hornblower (eds.), *Ritual, Finance, Politics. Athenian Democratic Accounts Presented to David Lewis*, 85–98, Oxford: Clarendon Press.

Rhodes, P. J. (1995), "The 'Acephalous' *Polis*?," *Historia*, 44: 153–67.

Rhodes, P. J. (2006), *A History of the Classical Greek World: 478–323 BC*, Malden, MA: Blackwell.

Rhodes, P. J. (2016), "Demagogues and *Demos* in Athens," *Polis*, 33: 243–64.

Ribbeck, O. (1883), *Kolax: Eine ethologische Studie*, Leipzig: Teubner.

Ringer, M. (2016), *Euripides and the Boundaries of the Human*, Lanham, MD: Lexington.

Roberts, J. T. (1982), "Athens' So-Called Unofficial Politicians," *Hermes*, 110: 354–62.

Robson, J. (2013a), "The Language(s) of Love in Aristophanes," in E. Sanders, C. Thumiger, C. Carey, and N. J. Lowe (eds.), Erôs *in Ancient Greece*, 251–66, Oxford: Oxford University Press.

Robson, J. (2013b), *Sex and Sexuality in Classical Athens*, Edinburgh: Edinburgh University Press.

Roche, P., trans. and intro. (2005), *Aristophanes: The Complete Plays*, New York: New American Library.

Roisman, H. M., and C. A. E. Luschnig, ed., intro., and comm. (2011), *Euripides' Electra: A Commentary*, Norman, OK: University of Oklahoma Press.

Roncali, R., and C. Zagaria (1980), "πλῆθος," *Quaderni di Storia*, 12: 213–21.

Rosen, R. M. (2010), "Aristophanes," in G. Dobrov (ed.), *Brill's Companion to the Study of Greek Comedy*, 227–78, Leiden: Brill.

Rosen, R. M. (2020), "Prologomena: Accessing and Understanding Aristophanic Politics," in R. M. Rosen and H. P. Foley (eds.), *Aristophanes and Politics: New Studies*, 9–23, Leiden: Brill.

Rosenbloom, D. (2002), "From *Ponêros* to *Pharmakos*: Theater, Social Drama, and Revolution in Athens, 428–404 BCE," *CA*, 21: 283–346.

Rosenbloom, D. (2004). "*Ponêroi* vs. *Chrêstoi*: The Ostracism of Hyperbolos and the Struggle for Hegemony in Athens after the Death of Perikles, Part I," *TAPA*, 134: 55–105.

Rosenbloom, D. (2011), "Democracy and Its Discontents in Late Fifth-Century Drama," in A. Markantonatos and B. Zimmermann, *Crisis on Stage: Tragedy and Comedy in Late Fifth-Century Athens*, 405–41, Boston, MA: de Gruyter.

Rosenbloom, D. (2014), "The Politics of Comic Athens," in M. Fontaine and A. C. Scafurio (eds.), *The Oxford Handbook of Greek and Roman Comedy*, 297–320, Oxford: Oxford University Press.

Rothbart, M., and M. Taylor (1992), "Category Labels and Social Reality: Do We View Social Categories as Natural Kinds?" in G. R. Semin and K. Fiedler (eds.), *Language, Interaction, and Social Cognition*, 11–36, London: Sage.

Rowe, C. J., ed., trans., and comm. (1986), *Plato: Phaedrus*, Warminster: Aris & Phillips.

Rubin, L. (1989), "Love and Politics in Xenophon's *Cyropaedia*," *Interpretation*, 16: 391–413.

Ruderman, R. (1992), "The Rule of a Philosopher-King: Xenophon's *Anabasis*," in L. G. Rubin (ed.), *Politikos II: Selected Papers of the North American Chapter of the Society for Greek Thought*, 127–43, Pittsburgh: Duquesne University Press.

Ruzé, F. (1984), "*Plethos*, aux origines de la majorité politique," in le Centre G. Glotz (ed.), *Aux Origines de l'Hellénisme: La Crète et la Grèce. Hommage à Henri van Effenterre*, 247–63, Paris: Publications de la Sorbonne.

Ryzman, M. (1989), "The Reversal of Agamemnon and Menelaus in Euripides' *Iphigenia in Aulis*," *Emerita*, 57: 111–18.

Saïd, S. (2013), "Thucydides and the Masses," in A. Tsamakis and M. Tamiolaki (eds.), *Thucydides Between History and Literature*, 199–224, Berlin: de Gruyter.

Saldutti, V. (2014), *Cleone: Un Politico Ateniese*, Bari: Edipuglia.

Samons II, L. J. (2016), *Pericles and the Conquest of History: A Political Biography*, Cambridge: Cambridge University Press.

Sandridge, N. B. (2012), *Loving Humanity, Learning, and Being Honored: The Foundations of Leadership in Xenophon's Education of Cyrus*, Cambridge, MA: Harvard University Press.

Sancisi-Weerdenburg, H. (2010), "The Death of Cyrus: Xenophon's *Cyropaedia* as a Source for Iranian History," in V. J. Gray (ed.), *Oxford Readings in Classical Studies: Xenophon*, 439–53, Oxford: Oxford University Press.

Sartori, F. (1957), *Le eterie nella vita politica ateniese del VI e V secolo a.C*, Rome: L'Erma di Bretschneider.

Schein, S. (1975), "Mythical Illusion and Historical Reality in Euripides' *Orestes*," *WS*, 88 (n.s. 9): 49–66.

Scholtz, A. (2004), "Demophilic Courtship in Aristophanes' *Knights*," *TAPA*, 134: 263–93.

Scholtz, A. (2007), "Concordia Discors: Eros and Dialogue in Classical Athenian Literature," *Center for Hellenic Studies Series* 24, Cambridge, MA: Harvard University Press.

Schutte, J. G., and J. M. Light. (1978), "The Relative Importance of Proximity and Status for Friendship Choices in Social Hierarchies," *Social Psychology*, 41: 260–4.

Schwartz, D. (2007), "Friendship as a Reason for Equality," *Critical Review of International Social and Political Philosophy*, 10: 167–80.

Scullion, S. (1999–2000), "Tradition and Innovation in Euripidean Aitiology," in M. J. Cropp, K. H. Lee, and D. Sansone (eds.), *Euripides and Tragic Theatre in the Late Fifth Century (ICS 24–5)*, 217–33, Champaign: University of Illinois Press.

Scullion, S. (2002), "'Nothing to Do with Dionysus': Tragedy Misconceived as Ritual," *CQ*, 52: 102–37.

Scullion, S. (2003), "Euripides and Macedon, or the Silence of the *Frogs*," *CQ*, 53: 389–400.

Seaford, R. A. (1982), "The Date of Euripides' *Cyclops*," *JHS*, 102: 161–72.

Seaford, R. A., ed., intro., and comm. (1984), *Euripides: Cyclops*, Oxford: Clarendon Press.

Seaford, R. A., ed., intro., trans., and comm. (1996), *Euripides: Bacchae*, Warminster: Aris & Phillips.

Seaford, R. A. (2006), *Dionysus*, New York: Routledge.

Seager, R. (1963), "Herodotus and *Ath. Pol.* on the Date of Cleisthenes' Reforms," *AJP*, 84: 287–9.

Sealey, R. (1956), "The Entry of Pericles into History," *Hermes*, 84: 234–47.

Sealey, R. (1973), "The Origins of *Demokratia*," *CSCA*, 6: 253–95.

Segal C. (1978), "The Menace of Dionysus. Sex Roles and Reversals in Euripides' *Bacchae*," *Arethusa*, 11: 185–202.

Sidwell, K. (2009), *Aristophanes the Democrat: The Politics of Satirical Comedy during the Peloponnesian War*, Cambridge: Cambridge University Press.

Siegel, H. (1980), "Self-delusion and the Volte-face of Iphigenia in Euripides' *Iphigenia at Aulis*," *Hermes*, 108: 300–21.

Siegel, H. (1981), "Agamemnon in Euripides' 'Iphigenia at Aulis,'" *Hermes*, 109: 257–65.

Simmons, R. H. (2006), "Reflections of a Crisis of Athenian Leadership in Euripides' Last Plays," diss., University of Iowa.

Simmons, R. H. (2018), "'Men, Friends', The Sociological Mechanics of Xenophontic Leaders Winning Subordinates as Friends," in S. Bell and L. Holland (eds.), *At the*

Crossroads of Greco-Roman History, Culture and Religion: Papers in Memory of Carin M. C. Green, 31–44, Oxford: Archaeopress.

Smith, J., and J. F. Zipp (1983), "The Party Official Next Door: Some Consequences of Friendship for Political Involvement," *The Journal of Politics*, 45: 958–78.

Sommerstein, A. H., ed., intro., trans., and comm. (1980), *Aristophanes: Acharnians*, Warminster: Aris & Phillips.

Sommerstein, A. H., ed., intro., trans., and comm. (1981), *Aristophanes: Knights*, Warminster: Aris & Phillips.

Sommerstein, A. H., ed., intro., trans., and comm. (1982), *Aristophanes: Clouds*, Warminster: Aris & Phillips.

Sommerstein, A. H., ed., intro., trans., and comm. (1996), *Aristophanes: Frogs*, Warminster: Aris & Phillips.

Sommerstein, A. H., (2000), "Platon, Eupolis, and the 'Demagogue-Comedy,'" in D. Harvey and J. Wilkins (eds.), *The Rivals of Aristophanes*, 439–52, London: Duckworth.

Spence, I. G. (1995), "Thucydides, Woodhead, and Cleon," *Mnemosyne* 4th series, 48.4: 411–37.

Stadter, P. A. (1991), "Fictional Narrative in the *Cyropaedeia*," *AJP*, 112: 461–91.

Stanford, W. B., ed., intro., and comm. (1968), *Aristophanes: The Frogs*, 2nd ed., London: Macmillan.

Stockton, D. (1990), *The Classical Athenian Democracy*, New York: Oxford University Press.

Stockert, W. (1992), *Euripides, Iphigenie in Aulis*, 2 vols., Vienna: Österreichische Akademie der Wissenschaften.

Stoneman, R. (1992), "Introduction," in *Xenophon: The Education of Cyrus*, trans. H. G. Dakyns, London: J. M. Dent and Sons.

Storey, I. C. (2003), *Eupolis: Poet of Old Comedy*, Oxford: Oxford University Press.

Storey, I. C., ed. and trans. (2011), *Fragments of Old Comedy, Volume II: Diopeithes to Pherecrates*,. Loeb Classical Library, Cambridge, MA: Harvard University Press.

Strauss, B. S. (1987), *Athens after the Peloponnesian War*, Ithaca, NY: Cornell University Press.

Strauss, L. (1975), "Xenophon's *Anabasis*," *Interpretation*, 4: 117–47.

Stronk, J. P. (1995), *The Ten Thousand in Thrace: An Archaeological and Historical Commentary on Xenophon's Anabasis, Books VI.iii-vi – VII*, Leiden: Brill.

Sutton, D. F. (1980), *The Greek Satyr Play*, Meisenheim am Glan: Hain.

Tajfel, H., and J. C. Turner (1986), "The Social Identity Theory of Intergroup Behavior," in S. Worchel and W. G. Austin (eds.), *Psychology of Intergroup Relations*, 7–24, Chicago: Nelson-Hall.

Tamiolaki, M. (2016), "Athenian Leaders in Xenophon's *Memorabilia*," in R. F. Buxton (ed.), *Aspects of Leadership in Xenophon*, 1–49, *Histos* Supplement 5, Newcastle upon Tyne: Histos.

Tatum, J. (1989), *Xenophon's Imperial Fiction: On The Education of Cyrus*, Princeton: Princeton University Press.

Thalheim, T. (1901), *Lysias: Orationes*, Leipzig: Teubner.

Tharoor, I. (2018), "Trump Finds a 'Like-Minded Demagogue' in Bolsonaro," *The Washington Post*, 4 November. Available online: www.washingtonpost.com/world/2018/11/05/trump-finds-like-minded-demagogue-bolsonaro.

Thompson, W. E. (1981), "Athenian Leadership: Expertise or Charisma?" in G. S. Shrimpton and D. J. McCargar (eds.), *Classical Contributions: Studies in Honor of Malcolm Francis McGregor*, 153–59, Locust Valley, NY: J. J. Augustin.

Tierney, M. (1946), *Euripides: Hecuba*, Dublin: Browne and Nolan.

Tuplin, C. J. (1987), "Xenophon's Exile Again," in M. Whitby, P. R. Hardie, and M. Whitby (eds.), *Homo Viator: Classical Essays for John Bramble*, 59–68, Bristol: Bristol Classical Press.

Tuplin, C. J. (2017), "Xenophon and Athens," in M. A. Flower (ed.), *The Cambridge Companion to Xenophon*, 338–59, Cambridge: Cambridge University Press.

Tylawsky, E. I. (2002), *Saturio's Inheritance: The Greek Ancestry of the Roman Comic Parasite*, New York: Peter Lang.

Tye, L. (2020), *Demagogue: The Life and Long Shadow of Senator Joseph McCarthy*, Boston, MA: Houghton Mifflin Harcourt.

Van Berkel, T. A. (2020), *The Economics of Friendship: Conceptions of Reciprocity in Classical Greece*, Leiden: Brill.

Van der Valk, M. (1967), "Observations in Connection with Aristophanes," in R. E. H. Westendorp Boerma (ed.), *ΚΩΜΩΙΔΟΤΡΑΓΗΜΑΤΑ: Studia Aristophanea, viri Aristophanei, W.J.W. Koster in honorem*, 125–45, Amsterdam: Hakkert.

Van Veelen, K. R., K. Eisenbeiss, and S. Otten (2016), "Newcomers to Social Categories: Longitudinal Predictors and Consequences of Ingroup Identification," *Personality and Social Psychology Bulletin*, 42: 811–25.

Versnel, H. S. (1998), *Inconsistencies in Greek and Roman Religion*, Vol. 1: Ter Unus. 2nd ed., Leiden: Brill.

Wade-Gery, H. T. (1958), *Essays in Greek History*, Oxford: Blackwell.

Wankel, H., intro., ed., and comm. (1976), *Demosthenes, Rede für Ktesiphon über den Kranz*, 2 vols., Heidelberg: Winter.

Waqas Shabir (2017), "Is It Right to Brand Imran Kahn a Demagogue?," *The Nation* (Lahore, Pakistan), May 10. Available online: https://nation.com.pk/10-May-2017/is-it-right-to-brand-imran-khan-a-demagogue.

Wassermann, F. M. (1949), "Agamemnon in the *Iphigeia in Aulis*," *TAPA*, 80: 174–86.

Waterfield, R., intro. and trans. (2005), *Xenophon: The Expedition of Cyrus*, New York: Oxford University Press.

Waterfield, R. (2006), *Xenophon's Retreat: Greece, Persia, and the End of the Golden Age*, Cambridge, MA: Harvard University Press.

Webster, T. B. L. (1967), *The Tragedies of Euripides*, London: Methuen.

West, M. L. (1981), "Tragica V," *BICS*, 28: 61–78.

Westlake, H. D. (1968), *Individuals in Thucydides*, Cambridge: Cambridge University Press.

Whedbee, K. E. (2004), "Reclaiming Rhetorical Democracy: George Grote's Defense of Cleon and the Athenian Demagogues," *Rhetoric Society Quarterly*, 34.4: 71–95.

Willink, C. W. (1986), *Euripides: Orestes*, Oxford: Clarendon Press.

Winnington-Ingram, R. P. (1948), *Euripides and Dionysus: An Interpretation of the Bacchae*, Cambridge: Cambridge University Press.

Wohl, V. (2002), *Love among the Ruins: The Erotics of Democracy in Classical Athens*, Princeton: Princeton University Press.

Wood, N. (1964), "Xenophon's Theory of Leadership," *ClMed*, 25: 33–66.

Woodhead, A. G. (1960), "Thucydides' Portrait of Cleon," *Mnemosyne* 4th series, 13.4: 289–317.

Yates, V. (2005), "*Anterastai*: Competition in Eros and Politics in Classical Athens," *Arethusa*, 38: 33–47.

Yunis, H. (1988), "A New Creed: Fundamental Religious Beliefs in the Athenian Polis and Euripidean Drama," *Hypomnemata* 91, Gottingen: Vandenhoeck & Ruprecht.

Yunis, H. (1996), "Taming Democracy," Ithaca, NY: Cornell University Press.

Zeitlin, F. (1990), "Thebes: Theater of Self and Society in Athenian Drama," in J. J. Winkler and F. Zeitlin (eds.), *Nothing to Do with Dionysus? Athenian Drama in its Social Context*, 130–67, Princeton: Princeton University Press.

Zeitlin, F. I. (1991), "Euripides' *Hekabe* and the Somatics of Dionysiac Drama," *Ramus*, 20: 33–94.

Zuntz, G. (1955), "The Political Plays of Euripides," Manchester: Manchester University Press.

Index

Printed in the USA
CPSIA information can be obtained
at www.ICGtesting.com
LVHW080224120124
768829LV00004B/50

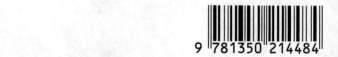